I think I'll slow down for this one . . .

And so I did, and put more time into those that had never let me down.

BLACK WOMEN ALWAYS

CONVERSATIONS ON LIFE, CULTURE & CREATIVITY

Kevin Morosky

PAVILION

CONTENTS

CONTENTS

FOR THOSE IN THE BACK

There are two main festivals in Cannes; the Cannes Film Festival and the Cannes Lions, the latter being centred around creativity and advertising. My first time attending the Cannes Lions was in 2019. I already knew about the festival; in fact, at one time all myself and Tom wanted to do was win a Lion. As time went on, we began to believe in ourselves. The more we believed in ourselves, the less that need to win felt important.

The Lions festival has a main venue, followed up by the usual fringe activities you'd find at most other events of this kind. You can expect to find the likes of Google, Pinterest, Meta and co all having their own branded 'beaches' as part of this activity. Other brands and agencies take over apartments, bars and villas along the seafront. Some even have yachts to party on. In short, a lot of money is spent flexing for B2B (Business to Business) purposes; lavish shows of generosity for the sake of new business opportunities.

There is free food and drink on tap, merch, gift bags and live music. I'm here now, writing this in 2023 (more on that later), and this time around got to see my good Judy, Jessie Ware, followed up by the Foo Fighters (Dave Grohl will always be peng). I admit that just to say – I understand I am a small part of the problem.

There's free-flowing WiFi, charging points and photo ops. All of this comes with the scramble to get on the relevant guestlists or curry favour for access – creating a nauseating, thick atmosphere of classism. Especially toward Black and Brown folk. In my experience, the staff that work these events, down to the organisers themselves, were not – and are still not – accustomed to Black and Brown creative executives. Meanwhile, underneath this 24-hour display of wanton capitalism, racist ignorance and outdated traditions, is a very serious homeless and drug problem within the town.

So picture this: all the bells and whistles on display at a no-expense-spared luxury experience, available at the cordoned-off beach paid for by your advertising business of choice.

8

Directly opposite, you'll find a store for one of the many luxury brands we all know, windows showing off the latest season's goods. In the space between these two poles of conscious consumerism – between the designer bags and the unpedicured feet of hungry ad-folk trying to climb the greasy career ladder – are the town's homeless folk. Overwhelmingly, they're Black or Brown. This is what struck me when I first got here, back in 2019.

That year was the inaugural year for a specific kind of beach; one set up to encourage more diversity in the creative industries. One aiming to bring all parts of the Black diaspora together to connect and inspire one another. It was cute. Ironically, it was the very last beach along the fringe's strip (go figure). During my time at this beach, I met some of the most incredible Black women who, unlike anyone else I had encountered, also felt uneasy being in this space when they knew there were people who needed help just a few feet away.

Every day at that year's festival, I met more and more Black women – all of whom encouraged me to continue what I was doing. They connected me to others they thought I needed to meet, and allowed me to swallow my feelings for a second so I could figure out the best way to help with what I was seeing.

On my last day, I went to the beach and took a photo. That picture is the one on this book's front cover. I took it believing I'd return a year later and really start making a splash within the industry's tired ways. Alas, as I'm sure you're aware, the following year was 2020 . . .

This book sits under a very passionate, poignant title – one that I chose with intent. It's a big title that will last lifetimes and be referenced in many public spaces. But, more importantly to me at least, it will also foster private conversations like the ones I had with the Black women who found me in Cannes.

As an artist, as a creative – and most importantly as a Black person – I must mean what I say. Even without the context above, this image still tells the same story: that Black women, even when they're vastly in the minority, will always find time to uplift and encourage and sometimes, like the women in the picture, have fun doing it.

If you don't take that from this image, then it suggests that you didn't do all the reading you said you did back in the 'Black Square Summer' of 2020. You're still aligned to problematic, racist patterns of thought and palatability.

Above all, this book was always going to be a love letter to Black women. I was only ever talking to them anyway. By all means, if you're not of that audience but have a genuine desire to bear witness to the conversation and empathise with others, then please do come along. Otherwise, believe me when I say that I don't care if you don't understand.

9

0

INTRODUCTION

I'm at Bowling Green park in lower Manhattan, fresh off the ferry from visiting the spot where Patricia Okoumou bravely decided to climb as high as she could. I find the subway platform Google Maps leads me to, for the No.4 heading uptown, towards the Bronx. My plan is to then catch the No.6 to Bleecker Street and walk to Greene Street, where a man with an eyepatch is selling old film scripts. Given that during this visit, I'm in the middle of writing four films and a TV show with my creative partner Tom, getting ahold of produced scripts to dissect is an absolute must.

I get to the correct platform with ease, wearing that sense of pride tourists have when they don't fuck up. Smug, like some fake New Yorker, taking in my surroundings. Standing near the platform's entrance, I watch as people come in and out of the station, all the while wondering if they, actual New Yorkers, can also feel how heavy the air is with ghosts from this place's past, echoes calling out from violently stolen lands.

Sounds dramatic? I assure you, all children of all diasporas do this. Looking for the history behind things is as natural as breathing to us. No matter what city or country I find myself in, the same question always repeats itself in my mind: *How much violence did it take for this to get here?*

As I stand and ponder this, I hear a woman singing. I know she's Black before I even look up; her voice has that tonal quality I've only ever heard Black women carry. It's a tone that sounds like home – church on Sundays and the kind of laughter you'll only hear when Black people are around other Black people.

Our eyes meet. She gives me a smile that makes me feel safe. I smile back, thankful, still watching as she passes me by. It suddenly feels like her safety is now my responsibility. I mean, don't get me wrong. I'm not going to follow her all the way to her destination – or even across the platform – like some weirdo man. Gross. But I do decide to keep an eye out for any dangers on the platform or train until we part ways.

At the emergency exit is a young Black man, waiting for something. I know he is, because I recognise his stance. I use it myself when I'm hopeful of something happening: a slight rise in the chest, weight shifting from one leg to another as the left heel inches up off the ground. I'm not accustomed to subway etiquette, so I don't get what he's waiting for.

Walking past the emergency exit herself, the Black woman who smiled at me spots this young man and, without hesitation, circles back round to push the gate open. An alarm sounds but no one does anything. The young man walks through. She gives him the same smile she gave me, and in return he repeats the one I gave her.

'Thank you.'

I'm annoyed I didn't realise what he was waiting for. I would've liked to help him. Nonetheless, he gives me the nod that all Black men give each other.

This nod is warmer, no doubt because of the woman's recent action. I'd bet he feels like his day has just begun to look up.

Now, you could be reading this thinking, 'Well, anyone could have done this, been this helpful.' And that's true. But that would be you attempting to twist this narrative to centre yourself – to insert a hero that looks like you into a true story where you didn't exist. All I'm saying is that, like the young man above, whenever I've been in need, Black women have always saved me.

Black women have always considered me, believed in me, backed me. Checked on me, and checked me. (I deserved it every time.) Defended me, even when my actions put them in arms. Voluntarily depleted themselves. That is to say, our cups runneth over because theirs are empty.

Black women have always shared. Respected me. Given, not lent, the last of monies, luck, and space, just so I could arrive at interviews, meetings, opportunities – and even first dates – unbothered, prepared, and able to concentrate on the task at hand without distraction. The same comfort gifted by the young Black woman above, to both that young man and myself.

Black women have fed not only my belly, but also my soul. They've loved me, even when I didn't love myself. Recognised me, in all my disguises. Reminded me of who I am whenever I became too comfortable – lost even – in those disguises. Pushed aside their own importance, just to centre me.

Planted laughter and joy within me. Listened to me. Applauded and cheered me. Gassed and hyped me. Prayed for me. Blessed me. Accepted me. Fixed me. Made space for me. Given up space for me. Validated me. Black women have always inspired me.

To talk about my creative work and practice – the journey I've had through both advertising and life – without mentioning the very architects behind my achievements, would be the closest thing to blasphemy a part-time pantheist like myself could do.

So, I mean it when I say: Black women have always been gods to me. And because of this, I have always been a child of a better god (to paraphrase playwright Mark Medoff).

There is a particular aim for this book; it wasn't only written to disrupt bookshelves full of very pale, stale, male advertising and creative manuals.

And it wasn't only written to show so-called 'smart mouths' and 'class clowns' Tyrone and Sharna that, despite what their teachers might say, their view of the world is not only valid – but vital. I've written this book specifically to centre Black women at the apex of both my own success and within the wider popular culture that I love so much.

I believe that creativity – whether that's in advertising or otherwise – should at its core be holistic, forgiving, welcoming, and reflective of society at its best. That is, admittedly, a difficult task when the majority of the creative industries invest in and worship capitalism.

This is a book that looks at creativity through two lenses. The first of these is my own lived experience, and how the fundamental shaping of me informs my creative choices. I know all the rules expected of a creativity in the service of capitalism, and I understand how to play the game and win. But this book isn't intended to inspire you along those lines. I couldn't care less about this book keeping company with all of those other advertising tomes that merely maintain the status quo.

I recently saw a TikTok where the creator's words really stuck with me. She said that whenever she feels unhinged, she remembers that Western psychology is entirely based on whether or not she acts like a white man. I feel the same can be said about the 'expected' narrative in all creative practices. The way I create and engage with the creativity of others doesn't fit into this supposed norm. I don't create to simply create, I do it to share a starting point for others – something they can then build on that lets them feel seen, heard, and remembered. Again, all the things that Black women have always provided for me.

The second lens is one of Womanism. First coined by Alice Walker, 'Womanism' is a more intentional approach to feminism; one that accounts for the day-to-day experiences of Black women, in light of how mainstream feminism largely ignores the intersectionality of privilege.

What follows in this book are essays capturing my thoughts on life and creativity – each followed by honest, emotional, and at times very funny conversations with some of the Black women who have not only helped me, but actively made sure I got to where I needed to.

There is some great advice in this book but that isn't why it's so special – at least, not to me. The content, whilst important, is a catalyst for a much more important effect. By the end of this book, I hope you'll be inspired to identify the qualities of your own authentic creative practice, free of the expectations placed on you by status-quo thinking.

Most importantly of all, this book is about really admiring and revelling in the magic **Black women always bring to the table**.

Thank you, to each and every one of you.

GOD'S RHYTHM

God's rhythm housed in patterned Mosh, Patrick Cox's and exposed ankles
Chops and gold rings, gold clowns on gold chains and gold bangles

Versace Blue Jeans floats atop of cocoa butter
Make magic with no effort from passed down trauma and clutter

Milk tokens gave birth to banquets
Phone cards and JR Hartley before bandwidths

Nestled in front of the universe and tender headed
Blessings bestowed upon me by Black women, my leverage

Gold tooth caps with Nike emblems, A-line skirts, lipstick plum
No future, but a shot at legacy eggs us on to be young dads and mums

Underestimated soft tones, I let them name call, they thought that shit hurt
Gangsters move in silence and some of us also lift shirts
In reality, my limp wrist produced great right hooks
My love language? Something of a mix of Ramsey and Fen and bell hooks

While you were having lunches with Mel and Sue
We were selling food while selling food
£3.20 per hour for the perfect cover
The narrative alleviated the stress for our mothers

I know my worth
The industry is – light work

Explain Crypto to someone accustomed to notes in socks
Or the irony of representation found on a dark and lovely perm box

I can, you can't.

Inherently intersectional, that's why culture sits at our core.
Black creatives are advertising's favourite whores.

1

THE PAST

I promise that I won't start every one of these essays with a scientific theory, or – as in this specific case – my thoughts on the phenomenological concept of experience.

But this first conversation isn't just a deep dive into the shared past I have with my mother, it's also a real-time documentation of us reconciling with it in the present moment.

There's a theory that everything we experience is actually happening all at once. This has always made sense to me. I don't think anything in my life has been a coincidence; everything has added up, moment by moment.

This idea offers a perspective on time where there is no 'that', 'this', or 'and then' – no past, present, and future as we traditionally perceive it. The theory instead suggests that we're actually experiencing all of time at once. The linear flow of 'time' is just how we process that information.

Think about those occasions when you've had a strong attraction to a colour or scent that seemingly brought you back in time, or visited a place that felt a little too familiar... even though you're sure you've never been there before. Or, more powerfully, when you meet someone for the first time yet feel like you've already known them for your whole life. It's because you have.

What we perceive our present-self feeling in those moments is what our future-self already knows, and so the experiences of encountering and remembering occupy the same space, at the same time.

When you start viewing time like that, the feeling of déjà vu starts to make a little more sense.

If this is the case, then the opposite must also be true: when we are placed in situations that do not serve or seem to facilitate what we have already experienced, the disconnect can leave us in an addled state, lost and off-track.

When I was at school, I hated it. Every fibre of my body wanted to shut down while I was there. Looking back, I understand that this reaction was brought on by me being told I would amount to nothing – despite the fact that now, as I sit here writing this, I have a full fridge, no drama, no bills to worry about, and a career building towards success. Future-me knows that those harsh words simply weren't – aren't – true.

But that younger, past-me was left feeling confused – alone and forced out of sync with my future-self by these mixed messages.

So for a period of time, I did nothing but believe the teachers and keep my head down. Then one day, in the place I hated the most, I witnessed something that put me back on track.

It all started with two Black girls.

I had seen them around school and, because they shared the same skin tone as my mother, I automatically thought of them as living, breathing safe spaces. Their dark skin was creamed to within an inch of its life, hair pristine, with every manner of hair bobble set in place. These bobbles caused a chorus every time they moved, so you'd normally hear the girls before you saw them.

They were cool.

I'd never looked at any of the older boys and thought they were cool. I think I could always tell those boys were lost like me, and if you were as confused as I was, how could you be cool? With the greatest humility, I now know how I actually was and am cool. By now I think we all know that brands and platforms use popular culture as tracing paper, and the thing they are tracing is Black culture – more time Black, queer subcultures.

These two girls were effortlessly cool. I never doubted it, and I don't think any of the other boys growing up did, either. In fact, they idolised Black girls so much that it at times wandered and galloped into pure jealousy.

They seemed to make magic without even trying. I saw them as invincible, devoid of flaws. There is a danger and pressure in such idolisation. There is a suffocating weight that Black boys, men – and indeed, everyone else – place specifically on Black women.

If there was a way to find and apologise to all of the Black girls and women that I held (no matter how respectfully) to obsessively high standards – thereby intruding on their space to just be – I would.

In the meantime, I hope this book finds you.

As I was saying though, it was these two girls that kickstarted a shift in how I moved through the world, and it happened in school assembly. I remember that hall well; it never held its own scent, instead carrying the lingering smell of hot lunches, the PE lesson that just finished, or the repulsive result of the floors being mopped with stale water instead of bleach.

It always amused me how a space could boast so much opulence and still smell so frowzy.

As soon as I sat on that cold, hard parquet floor, I was ready to be bored.

On this particular day, I looked around and spotted my favourites; they were sat a row or two behind me, so enthralled in their gossip that they missed the meek smile I threw their way.

Meanwhile, Mr Burns – who actually looked like the cartoon character he shared a name with – walked in as he always did, wordlessly moving to the front of the hall before standing still and waiting for silence. The other kids always seemed daunted by this, but my father – for everything else he lacked – had already taught me about world history, so every time he did this, I couldn't help but think he was trying to mimic Hitler's rally tactics.

And, like clockwork, that hush once again descended on the hall as three-hundred or more students fell silent. All except my two heroes, who were so busy chatting they didn't notice the sudden drop in volume, until it was too late.

Mr Burns singled them out with a loud, thundering shout: 'JUST SHUT UP!' My favourites immediately stopped talking. They looked at each other. And then Black girl number one did something I'd never seen before.

She rolled her eyes, slowly turned her head from her friend to the headteacher, and very calmly said, 'No.' Her friend burst into laughter and she did too, in this otherwise silent hall.

Something changed in me. Up until that moment, the idea of saying 'no' simply because it's what I wanted to do had never occurred to me. I mean, I wasn't, and have never been a victim of peer pressure. But to tell a teacher 'no'? In school? Never.

I had never considered civil disobedience up until that point. I had never thought about how what I wanted to do could credibly exist as an alternative to what I was expected to do. It had never occurred to me to follow my heart on all things. Seeing this instantly gave birth to the feeling of being comfortable in my skin.

I became excited about the future of not only myself, but all things. A wide Grinch-shaped smile sprawled across my face; I had witnessed something that reminded me of myself. The rebelliousness of this act, despite its newness to me, immediately felt like a perfect fit. I was excited to say 'no' – to debate and argue.

Unsurprisingly, Mr Burns lost it and called them up to the front of the hall, I imagine to try and embarrass them back into subservience. Big mistake. Once she got there, this girl made it abundantly clear that she wouldn't stand near him. Instead she pointed out that his breath stank, and that she didn't want to be spat on by one of his stray sprays of saliva.

It was mayhem after this moment; a powerful source of gossip for the rest of the year. Even then, these two didn't seem to care. They, again, showed an awareness of something I had never considered: they weren't going to be at this school forever. They would soon leave for secondary school and never look back.

Before this, I think I'd only ever thought of endings in the context of having to finish or leave behind something I loved. Ending as a loss, rather than a gain.

THE PAST

This was a new way to look at time, and it changed me for the rest of my life. From that point on I started thinking about what I did and didn't want to do. Where it was that I felt happy and didn't.

Most of all, knowing that saying no to my teacher and them losing their shit was my new favourite thing to do.

Now to be clear, my mother never raised no fool; I knew I would still have to 'learn my book', but at least it would be on my terms. This is what your work should be too: indelibly you, through and through.

Do you have a vision? An idea that calls out to you in the most familiar way? Go for it, because whether you – like myself – believe it's your future-self guiding you, or else you just sense it as a good feeling, nothing can interrupt the magic of feeling aligned within yourself. That sense of being exactly where you need to be.

Because what I have learned about the past is ... you never look back with regret if you have consistently chosen yourself.

"I THINK ABOUT THAT HARD."

MUM AND TAYLA

The kindest human and the biggest pain in Kevin's backside, respectively

ON THE PAST

[Tayla helps Mum get set up for our video call]

> **Tayla** Okay, Mum, I can get you some light . . . You see that? You see that? Niiiiice.

Mum Are you getting grey hairs?

Kevin I'm not getting grey hairs.

> He is getting grey hairs.

I guess Tayla's in this conversation now.

> Oh, sorry. Oh, let me get out of it.

[Kevin kisses his teeth]

> Why are you like this?

Mum, I just wanted to talk to you about what I was like as a child. Creatively. I remember one time you were really upset and crying . . . I'd had a parent–teacher night, and you were saying that the teachers at school didn't get me. They didn't want to get me. There was one teacher who you cussed out. She'd cried because you said she was too inexperienced for the job. I remember you made this point more so around her 'only knowing what she knew'. I didn't get it at the time, but looking back I realise you were referring to her privilege. I remember you defending me.

> Which school was it?

South Norwood.

> Young teacher?

Yeah, I would say she was a lesbian just based on her hair.

> What is wrong with you?

I can say that because I'm a gay.

> True.

You were really upset because they were talking to you about my rate of learning, saying it was slow. I also remember another teacher being like, 'Oh, no, he's really good. He takes his time with the details. He treats everything like art.'

> Whenever there was an open evening or a moment they could grab me in the playground as I dropped you and your brother off, they would want a quick word.

What would they say?

That you were a little bit behind. But the thing was, they'd give me the work to take home with you – to almost prove it – and you were able to do it with me; you had no problems with the work. So I didn't understand. You'd do it in no time, like it was a waste of your time. Honestly, if I had my way, you'd have never gone back to school.

Was I terrible?

No! Not at all. I didn't like what they were saying about you, or, to be more clear, I didn't like the lies they were telling about you. I would give you the work to do – work that I thought was a little bit too much for a child, actually – and you would do it no problem. Easy peasy. There was something else going on, and they just didn't want to take the time ... they didn't care about finding out what ...

Look, if you are explaining a problem to someone and they don't understand what it is you are trying to tell them, what should you do? Be impatient or find a different approach? They never wanted to find out what was wrong. Just to point it out.

Was there ever a conversation about dyslexia?

No, definitely not. Because when you got diagnosed as an adult, I thought to myself, 'But how wasn't that picked up?' I also felt guilty; why didn't I pick it up? But, again, back then we didn't really know about such things. There were just a few kids that had that and got help.

When it came to me, I was just the class clown. And yes, for the readers, those kids were white. The only teacher who really tried to work with me was Miss Munson.

Who?

You don't remember her?

Looked like an owl. *[Tayla laughs]*

She'd do lessons with me separately and also didn't understand what was going on in the classroom, because I was excellent at everything when I worked with her. I guess I just didn't have the language at the time to be like, 'Oh, the problem is that we live in a white supremacist society and the educational system is a mess. It's biased.'

I'm either under attack, or the teacher just ignores my questions, you know? So I just refused to do any of the work, because what's the point? And my thinking was, I might as well ignore them. More times I secretly did the work. I just didn't write it down. I wanted to ignore them the same way they ignored me.

Yeah, they were just on you and I honestly just wanted them to just leave you alone. I didn't realise what you were doing.

Kevin Yeah. I actually really hated it. I really hated it. I didn't enjoy it at all. And I feel like I just . . . I just never had a peaceful time. I was never able to really enjoy the subjects. And maybe that's why I enjoyed art so much? Because it's a solo mission. In art, people can't question how you got to your final execution.

        Mum Yeah. Yeah.

It wasn't the greatest experience in primary school. And then in the first secondary school, everybody was just a demon. *[Everyone laughs]*

        That's why I sent you both to the other school, because that secondary school was . . .

Although you didn't calculate how long we'd be travelling for to get there and back. *[Mum laughs for an extended amount of time]*

        I know, I know. Years later, when I would have to travel them ways, and I saw the actual distance . . .

        Tayla Nah, liberty.

        I thought to myself, 'Oh my gosh, I'm so sorry, darling. I'm so sorry.' It was, you know, a good school. I didn't want you to keep going to that other school. I just never realised how far it was; when we'd go for parents' evening it was in the car, so not as bad because you drive the way you wanna drive. Or at least your dad did. But on the bus? Lord, I'm so sorry. *[Mum laughs to herself]*

I get that, but we would leave at six in the morning to get to school for nine! Please, I beg, why did you think we were leaving so early?
[Tayla and Mum laugh]

Tayla, after you've been on the bus for about an hour and a half, there was this one road that was at least three times as long as Davidson Road.

        Sorry, what?

Yeah, it was long. Then like another twenty minutes on the bus. That's just the bus journey, then you have to walk to the school. There's three ways: the white path, which was like a mile-long woodland alleyway and racist by name . . . *[Tayla and Mum laugh]*
. . . through a field, which still had a ten-minute walk after, or just directly down the street, which was about thirty minutes. All the while we were going there, there was a man that was like a flasher, so we had to walk in groups as a rule.

        Is this why Byron used to come home with his pants ripped up? *[Everyone laughs]*

24

Do you remember your first day? You rang to say the bus had broken down
– that you were waiting on the next bus. And I said, 'Where Byron?' Do you
remember where he was?

In the tree. *[Everyone laughs]*
        That school was a real culture shock. The kids there were mostly
rich, the houses were already million pounds back then. You know like how
now everything is already million or more, but back then those houses
were already bussing. Like, some had pools, some had horses ... like proper
mookooland.
        The kids there just wanted to learn, but I arrived with the energy
from the previous school. Meaning I was just ready to fight, very much
looking for who was the biggest and baddest, so I can knock him out and let
it be known not to play with me.
        Them kids were not on it like that. They were like, 'Are you all right?
What is a gang?'

                    'What is a gang?' I'm dead.

They enjoyed school and were still curious, but they weren't about that life.
There were one or two kids in there that were a bit wild, but other than that it
was completely different. It really was the Fresh Prince of Bel-Air, you know.

                            What school did you go to before the
                            mookooland one?

Ashburton.

                            I think it got worse after you left. Why didn't
                            you move me to that other school?

        Ashburton improved.

                            Brudda, no it didn't. It was like Waterloo
                            Road, what do you mean? We had bars on the
                            windows.

Because of the previous tenants, meaning us. Nah, it was better when it was
your time, trust me. There was this one boy who got rushed and put in a coma
for a while when I was there.

                            Oh.

They'd tear gas the bus. Actually, they'd just run up in the school and gas the
classrooms for fun. Teachers would get robbed. Knife fights had just about
started then, but really it was Lucozade bottles. In fact, we're the reason
they're now plastic. *[Everyone laughs]*

        We shouldn't be laughing.

Kevin I'm just talking about the violence of my generation. Like, it's my generation's fault that only two school children are allowed in the corner shop at once. I remember that maths teacher who was fully in a relationship with this one girl. People constantly started fires – a very 'Mad Max'-themed school.

> **Tayla** Okay, so you were all just mad?

Who is all, please? *[Everyone laughs]*
    But even then, at this new school, I still didn't get on with all of my teachers. There was still that sense of them treating me in a different, funny way. And in hindsight, I know that all of my teachers in primary school were racist, and most of them were in secondary school, too. Ms Harvey from Ashburton was a real one, though; she really took an interest in my writing and was like, 'You're good at arguing. You're really good with words.' She took the time to talk to me about music – specifically hip hop – and I told her about Biggie and she showed me similar patterns in the way Shakespeare wrote.
    She encouraged me to find the ways in which it all made sense to me. She didn't push me to do group activities either. She saw I liked to do stuff on my ones, and so when leaving that school she was the only person I missed. I don't think I even told anyone I was leaving, I just bounced.

> **Mum** When you and Byron would go outside to play, Byron would be outside until the street lights came on. You might hang out and play out for an hour, but then you were in. Drawing and thinking and reading, or watching 'The Goonies' again and again.

You mean I didn't like anyone from early? *[Everyone laughs]*

> Yeah. You know, you'd come in early from playing and find something to do, even if it was just helping me if I was cooking, or watching something. You'd ask if you could help or join, and we'd finish it together. Not Byron. *[Everyone laughs]*
>   That one? Every minute I'm getting complaints about Byron's doing this and Byron's doing that. And it's like, the kid's playing – go away.

Maybe, though … *[Tayla laughs]*
    Maybe you should have got him? *[Everyone laughs]*
    Do you remember a time when the art stopped?

> I don't know if it's when you got that first job at the burger place. You hadn't left school yet, but you slowed right down. Because before you knew it, you became a manager. Wait, had you left school?

No. Grace helped me forge my birth certificate; I was definitely not meant to be working.

> Oh, yes, I remember. You were meant to be older. So naughty.

> Wait, what?

Yeah but we had bills, and I needed money too. I think for the first time I actually wanted to hang out with people. I had friends that I liked being around. But mostly we had bills, and by that time Tayla's dad—

He's your dad too?

He had become a myth, so I had to do something.

I know.

Where my birthday falls, if I was born two or three days later, I could have been placed in the year below.

Yes.

Did you ever feel like maybe that was the reason I struggled? Because I should have been in a younger year?

No. Like I said, you refused to do work at school, but when we did the work, you were ahead of your age. I would test this by making you do the work for the year above, and the year above that, without you knowing – and you do it no problem. Easy. You have always known what you were doing, always had a plan. You were doing this and doing that. And I didn't have to worry, because I knew you knew what you were doing. You just had to do things your way.

I didn't know that. I never knew you thought like that.

No, no, no, no, no. I was very proud of you.

I hated school, as I've said. And oddly enough, if I hadn't been hard-headed enough to push through, but instead really did refuse to do the work and take on what they thought of me, I wouldn't be here now. Yeah, those teachers were not nice to me at school. I still have to block it out. I don't know if you remember, but that teacher robbed me of those stones? Not stones. Fossils. From when I went to church with Grandma and Grandad, and I found fossils.

No?

I took them to school for show and tell. And then that stupid bitch of a teacher was like, 'Oh, I just need to show my friend.' And then she never came back to school. And in my head I was like, 'You are rich now. You've taken that.' They were like pristine fossils. And if I ever . . .
      You know what? When I have enough money and enough time to relax, I will invest into finding her and dealing with her BS.

Oh my God, you never told me this.

I didn't want to upset you, but yeah. Hated all the schools. The second secondary school was okay, and I made some friends there. In some ways, I was lucky, because more time kids have to deal with bullies their age, but for me it was mainly the teachers. When it did come to other students, I would just fight back. Be violent. I had a temper, but more as a form of protection rather than because of it being who I was.

I remember in school there was this new kid who was older, and he was on his last warning. Him coming to that school was a last chance. One day, the buses aren't running. So we have to walk.

Tayla Not the far away school?

Kevin No, Ashburton.

Oh, I was gonna say.

So this white kid starts on the new kid, pushing him and calling him a 'black bastard'. This and that. Now, the white kid had friends with him, but when he started throwing out stuff like that, his friends were like, 'Nah, you're on your own.' They kind of walked on and left him running his gums. He was too gassed to realise, and just keeps throwing words at the new kid. This new kid has had enough – he punches the white kid, knocking out his front teeth and sending blood everywhere.

It's only myself, my friends, and some other elders that see this – we were in Year 7 at this point. I remember seeing the panic set in on this new kid's face, as he remembered he wasn't allowed to be in any more trouble.

Later that day, my friends and I were called to the headmaster's office and asked what we saw. We all say nothing – new kid doesn't get expelled. But the next day, some of the Peckham 28 were at the back gate, robbing anyone they felt like robbing. They start approaching us. I know I'm gonna lose – maybe get stabbed, or if I'm lucky, bottled – but I get ready to fight for my bits all the same.

Long story short, the new kid steps in. Turns out he's also a part of the 28s, and he says, 'Those are my little friends, leave them.' He'd known we didn't snitch. I say all of that to say that during school I really didn't spend much time having fun or getting a first-hand experience of just being a youth. It was more that I was spending time trying to understand why people do the things they do – and with things like that happening regularly, I got good at it.

Mum And with work? Why did you love those friends more? Or even make friends?

A lot of the people who worked there were just trying to pay bills and get through uni. Because they were all older, I think I just kinda got them more; they didn't seem as slow as kids my age. And things happened that demanded adult attention: Bush had Shan, so we would all babysit while Bush did her shifts. Ashley was very clear on her goals – I never really met someone so focused before – and all the friends from that job were loyal. Like really down to ride for me, you know?

Yeah.

Looking back, did you think what I'm doing now is what I'd be doing now?

No idea. No. I just would look at you and say, 'Well, I think that you'll be okay. You know what you're doing and you will be okay.'

I didn't either. I didn't know anything about advertising or making films, even though I had always loved film and photography.

Do you remember your Ninja Turtle camera?

Yeah, ha. I loved that camera. I think the first time I even heard the term 'art director' was when I was going out with this guy Robbie, and he was studying to be one. But when he said those words, they sounded familiar. My future-self hollering back.

Like a future memory? Like it just fit? That was later on, right? You would've been twenty?

Twenty-two, twenty-three, yeah. They never talked to us about those sorts of careers at school; options that aligned with your creative intelligence or interests. I remember career day, and a man said, 'You could be a cleaner or a bouncer.'

What?

Yep.

Looking back, I do wish I could have done more. I brought in tutors, and you just didn't like them. Once you made up your mind on them, that was it. And I just refused to force you into anything, you know. But I do wish I did more.

Did Byron's dad say anything at that time?

He's your dad, too.

He didn't. He didn't. And he didn't show any interest to me; I dealt with it all by myself. No interest. All on my own. Now you're gonna make me start crying ... *[Mum starts crying]*

Why are you crying? From a space of regret?

I just wish I had done more. I couldn't bring the words to my mouth to say, 'This isn't working, so we need to go our separate ways.'
      So every weekend that God sent, I got up, got my kids ready, and we didn't come back until it was bedtime. We went out, we enjoyed ourselves. Ate out – we didn't eat in. It was like that for a while until he realised – or I saw that he realised – and he slowly backed off. It should have been me saying 'Get out!' but he finally took his things and left. Which was fine by me.
      Just as he did that, we finally got the house. And so it was just me and my kids in this big house, and I was happy as Larry.

Who's Larry?

No idea.

I think everything had to have happened as it did or we wouldn't be here right now, you know?

Mum Everything happens for a reason. And now look at us. Look at you all. And that fucker—

Tayla and Kevin Wow. *[Kevin and Tayla laugh]*

Tayla There's no need to cry. You did the best you could.

Kevin Hindsight can be a dangerous thing. You're looking back at this stuff and imagining that you had all the tools and options we do now, and you didn't. So I think we can look back on the past – or a better way of describing it is just remembering the past – and just let it be. Because the story is the story and a part of us currently.

I love you so much. I'm so proud of you. I think about you when you were at school. How far you've reached. I show you off. I show all of you off. When the friends get together, we talk about our kids. I can't wait. Yeah. I am proud. Look how far you've reached. And I think about that hard, but I always knew it somehow. More than just belief. I knew it.

FOLLOW

The past

Whether you believe time functions in the way I do or not is of no importance. It's about following the feeling. You are, in some regard, an aerial trying its best to intuitively pick up the right stations and channels. If it feels good – if the conversation and inspiration once you're in that space feel effortless – then that's where you're meant to be. There will always be a time to move on. It is what it is; all things must end. But the ending of a thing doesn't mean you were heading in the wrong direction, it just means there's something else now.

TODAY'S TAKEAWAY:

If it's gonna be what it's gonna be, what is the worrying for? That is easier said than done. My upbringing was impacted by racist motivations in society. My adult life is as well – and I'd be a liar if I said I easily focus on what should be happening (the correct signal) instead of being derailed by the nonsense. I'm human, as are you.

All I can say is, I take time once a week to think about where I want to be, ask myself if I am happy, and pinpoint wherever I'm not feeling happiness so I can make changes. Do it every week, or every day if you'd rather – but make time for that check-in.

THAT FEELING

2

RESILIENCE

Resilience is what you make it.

Yes, by definition it is 'the capacity to withstand or recover quickly from difficulty'. But how we practise it, and what we take from it is up to us.

Channelling anger is the stereotypical way and, look – I'll be the first to admit it – I'm guilty of using my temper to get back on my feet quickly, sometimes by saying the meanest things.

But I've found that there's a problem within that. When you move that quickly, you lose the chance to grab on to the one thing resilience is the perfect tutor for – wisdom.

The quicker the bounce or snap-back, the stronger we are perceived to be. But how does that test of elasticity fare in a society that thinks less of you? Or, to focus in a little more, how does it help in a working environment that, as a reflection of the society it serves, is almost designed to misunderstand you?

To me, that sounds like one never-ending merry-go-round of torture, and in the words of the lady that had bronchitis, 'Nobody has time for that.' What I would advise you to have time for is, ironically, getting back up at your own pace. Take time to set your own time; after all, it's about actually getting back up. When we put the focus on the speed of recovery, rather than the quality of it, we lose focus on advocating for ourselves.

I wanna let you in on a little secret. The resilience you show – which is a little bit like the act of forgiveness – isn't intended to soothe those around you. It's for you.

Resilience is a form of self-care – or at least, it can be. So take your time and gather what you need from the situation to come back bigger and stronger (if that's what makes you happy).

In the next conversation, you'll hear how my friend Kuchenga talks about resilience in a way unique to her. Her resilience is full of learning, acceptance, and dark-humoured joy. Through her honest handling of the facts, she has reached a place that allows her to look all difficulties in the eye and say, 'Yeah, I see your hate. And I meet you with even more love.'

"I WENT TO THE RIGHT SCHOOLS, AND I SUCKED THE RIGHT COCKS."

A CONVERSATION WITH

KUCHENGA

Author and journalist

ON RESILIENCE

Kevin Look at this hair.

> **Kuchenga** I know. Where am I going? *[Kuchenga laughs]*

It looks beautiful.

> Thank you!

Why shouldn't we look beautiful in our own homes? In fact, I want to talk a little today about the idea of carrying our best selves with us, wherever we go. Because when we are in creative agencies, or in fact anywhere that's specifically designed for the white middle class – spaces where, in respect of gender, sex, race, etc., we are the ultimate minority – in those spaces, the task of creating authentic work is a myth. You know, it's just not real.

So, in those situations, I find that we have to do this magical thing: show the utmost resilience to those problematic ways of thinking, while still trying to create work from a very happy place. Still trying to tap into that warm, inspired part of you where all of the great ideas come from. And, specifically in your case, where all of those amazing words reveal themselves. You describe and pull things together in such a magical way.

> Thank you.

But at the same time, you've got to practise resilience, right? That means a certain thing to me and how I personally navigate the world, but I'm wondering if there are other spaces of resilience that people wouldn't necessarily associate with you, or about you? With your lived experience as a Black woman, as a Black trans woman, there must be things that are normally spoken about you (or over you) by people who've never even lived those experiences.

And I ask this because I worry about us getting into a dangerous future where people think that, just because they've read a couple of books they can interpret the lived experiences of others, rather than circling back and thinking that what it actually means is that they should make more room for other voices.

With that in mind, what are the things that affect you? How do you look at resilience, and how do you use it to get what you need? I think resilience can be used as a defence for sure, but I also believe it can function as a propellant to get you where you need to be.

> Right? Well, to start with, I'm half Zimbabwean and half Jamaican. My dad's from Zimbabwe. My mum's from Jamaica. They view themselves as pan-Africanist. My dad loves to tell their 'origin story' at Christmas after a few drinks. They met in Brixton in the early '80s, and they worked on the Scrap Sus Campaign; my mum was doing the administration, while my dad – who did maths at Oxford Brookes and trained as a teacher – was coming in to do the statistics. You know, statistics looking at the numbers of young Black people who were arrested by the Met police on suspicion of being about to commit a crime. Very 'Minority Report'. Basically, the Met police at the time were just looking at young Black kids like, *[Kuchenga puts on a mock-authoritarian voice]* ''Ello, 'ello, 'ello – off to the market, you say? Off to smoke some of that ganja?'

Kevin That wacky baccy?

> **Kuchenga** That wacky, wacky baccy. How am I cracking jokes about Black British trauma?

Because if we don't laugh about it, we'll cry. And oddly enough, that in itself is a form of resilience, right? But anyway, go on.

> So yeah, as much as my dad used to joke about the passion of that time, I really did grow up wearing the mantle of that activism. Like, I really was aware that I was born into a pan-Africanist home and that my parents had certain expectations. My mum was good friends with Olive Morris, and yeah, we had a picture of her in China, wearing revolutionary clothes. We had a massive library; my parents had very colonial educations, but they were also trying to decolonise on the fly, you know?
>
> So there were the Ngũgĩ wa Thiong'os, there were the Chinua Achebes – my dad read broadly but my mum, specifically, was very contemporary. So we had a lot of Black feminist books, reading groups, book clubs – everything. Her literary tastes were so expansive. So me and my sister just followed them – their friends would always remark that we were such big readers, but you just follow your parents, init?
>
> And so I was reading far too much, far too young. I was reading *Waiting to Exhale* at nine, thinking I was a big woman, taking in all the man problems and everything. But yeah, basically, my concept of resilience was forged at a very young age; it was distinctly pan-African, you know? My concept of Blackness was diasporic. We were just really conscious that there was a huge difference in our experiences, but that people growing up here also still shared something with the Black resistance movements in Brazil, Kenya, Atlanta, Paris, wherever, you know? We were the diaspora.
>
> And for me, I knew that I was trans from a very young age: three, four-ish. Looking back through therapy I remember fighting for the girls' clothes at nursery. And it became necessary to suppress it in a violent way from around the age of seven until, eventually, I became estranged from my family at seventeen. I spiralled because of the acute pain of being rejected by them, but I still carried that sense of wanting to make them proud even in absentia.
>
> When I went to university I joined the African Caribbean and Asian Society immediately, I was an Ethnic Minorities Officer…very much involved in the, you know, discourse around intersectionality. So in that sense, my involvement in resistance movements was quite traditional; very much twentieth century, African Independence, the Black Panthers, third-wave feminism, the LGBT rights movements, and so on. And then after I went to rehab at twenty-eight and admitted to myself that I was a writer – once I got done with my Open University creative writing course – there was this need for me to write as a form of resilience. I became involved with the likes of Bent Bars – writing to trans women in prison – and then later Black Lives Matter UK. And there was all the social media stuff to be done, but I was also doing data entry and admin.
>
> You know, I've been thinking about the fact that, because I'm writing books now, I definitely need to have a dedication to my mum. I was thinking of calling her the Administrator of the Pan-African Revolution.

I've never had stage fright; it's something that I really noticed when I was in a talent show in year eight, where I stood up, singing and dancing. And the teachers always remarked on my confidence. On reflection, perhaps that's diminishing or patronising, but at the time, I just felt exceptional. And I didn't mind that at all.

And you still are.

Well, thank you! But yeah, I think because I had this confident, braggadocious energy, there was this expectation that I'd be a spokesperson, on stage, all that. And that's not really where I found my groove. I like doing the grunt work. I think it's dangerous in some respects because a lot of the labour I've put in has been invisible. In my day-to-day life or around cis-het men or whatever, this behind-the-scenes work is just not really commented on. But even though I've written a few articles here and there, I feel that my labour has really gone into the quiet organisation – the collating of emails, the Excel spreadsheets, and the contacting. I see that as really noble, and that's because that's what my mum did all those years ago.

My dad would love to get on his Dr Umar and come out with his grand proclamations. But I think growing up in our home, and having Mum's not-too-subtle Black feminist critique of why we ended up where we are, meant that I didn't want to be the spokesperson of anything. I didn't want to be Angela Davis or Marcus Garvey. I'd rather just be part of the team, quietly plodding away and doing the work. Hoping that one day there's a payoff that I might get to see, yeah, but the doing of the work itself is cleansing; it's healing as much as it is humanistic. It makes me feel part of stuff.

And you wanting to do the grunt work isn't because you view it as a safe space?

No, no.

I think we're similar in that way. Like when you said that because of you being able to go on stage and entertain people, there was that assumption that you actually wanted to be front and centre – that sounds very familiar. Like I one-hundred per cent don't mind being in a room full of people that I love and busting jokes, because that is an act of service. I enjoy servicing people, helping them heal with conversation and time. And I'm super empathetic; I would say that I have high emotional intelligence. So I'm able to observe and then pick out the things that aren't quite right and, like, lean into them to help. Would you say you're an introvert?

[Kuchenga thinks] Yeah, no. I don't think I've ever been allowed to be an introvert. I have a younger sister who definitely is, and we're chalk and cheese, so I know what it's like to love an introvert and cater to introversion. But I'm definitely an extrovert. Yet extrovert burnout is a huge thing; when I listen to these stories of artists and creatives working for the big one, you know? Someone like Alexander McQueen; just pushing, pushing, pushing – all the blood, sweat, and tears. Then there's the show, and then in the aftermath, that desolation and depletion. 'I'm empty, what's next?' Wow.

37

Kevin I think that works both ways, because if you take Amy Winehouse – she was introverted – I know for a fact that she loved giving her art over and entertaining people, knowing that people find solace in that art. But when you're so good at it, and then everybody leeches on it in such a way because they just want more and more without considering what your reserves are – or if indeed you have any more to give – it becomes dangerous. I think it can happen both ways.

Kuchenga Yeah, and I would also like to tag on something that I've noticed. I was watching the Dusty Springfield documentary on the BBC, and they were talking about how much of a perfectionist she was. And she had the beehive and the black eyeliner, too. And whilst I don't have any of those explicit visual shields – that separation between the performer and the person – I still definitely feel a bit of that Marilyn Monroe syndrome sometimes, even if my masking isn't immediately evident. I think because I'm a high femme person, and I'm aware that I'm hyper-sexualised, I think a lot of the time people just don't see beyond that. They think there's nothing but frivolity and fluff – even as a writer, with the code-switching and the middle-class voice, I'm still often assumed to be just frippery.

Do you feel like that's exaggerated by certain people because of you being trans? Because we know that Black women are already over-sexualised, etc., etc. Do you feel like you being trans multiplies that at all?

Yes. Yeah, of course.

And I hate even asking that, it feels weird to me in my heart of hearts. Because trans women are women, right? I say that with my whole chest, and I hate it seeming like I'm suggesting there's a difference between women who are trans and not trans.

I hear what you're saying, but I didn't think that at all.

Hold on one sec. *[Kuchenga grabs a book from her bookshelf]* As you were saying that, it made me think of this book, *The Sisters Are Alright: Changing the Broken Narrative of Black Women in America* by Tamara Winfrey-Harris. I read this in 2015, on the heels of also reading Janet Mock's *Redefining Realness*, which I took to rehab with me. And together, those two books really helped me parse out the interconnected nature of exactly what you're talking about. You know, the hyper-sexualisation as a Black femme, Black woman, Black transsexual woman. There was so much in Janet Mock's experiences that chimed with my own life, and it was the first time I'd read anything that I could identify with in that way. We lived very different lives, but I still felt like, 'Oh, this is me.' She's still a Black trans woman that I can relate to massively.

But then I read *The Sisters Are Alright*. And reading about the Jezebel, the Sapphire, and the Mammy – those stereotypes of Black women – I still needed that practice of Black feminist theory to understand what I was going through. I never felt that schism, that there was a difference between women and trans women. Because in the past, when I was reading Alice Walker or Toni Morrison, I was never reading with that distance.

I know that people other me, but no matter what they say, I can't feel that schism between the Black cis woman's experience and my own. It's literally just my life – I can't! There are differences – there's no point denying them – but both are directly related to my life. So it's really difficult to see the masculinisation of Black women in popular culture, and sit on the sidelines as a Black trans woman and think, 'Oh it's nothing to do with me.' If I hear transphobia coming from cis Black women, I'm like 'Okay, sis? Throw me under the bus for the day, and I'll see you under the same bus, tomorrow.' No matter how hateful it gets, I don't feel that distance. We are wearing the same chains, sis.

That's really beautiful, that idea that your resilience exists because you are rooted in the actual reality of your experience, across the board. Regardless of how others want to box or pigeonhole you.

Exactly. Like, no matter how much I get, no matter how hateful it can get, I can't stop loving them. It's not an option. It may be painful, but I'm always here.

Exactly, your experience is lived, not learned. You didn't read the books and think, I need to seek out that experience. You read it and thought, 'Sis, me too.' And so, it sounds like the best form of resilience for you – which I agree with – can be rooted in the facts of the situation at hand. Not this kind of fake, manufactured approach that decides what is what. And I'd see that all the time with white, pale, male stale people in advertising, just deciding what the culture is and how to talk to those who are immersed in the culture. And it's a parody, it's not real. What I am showing them is the facts, the reality, but these people have never been close enough to that reality to even recognise it.

It's like those early descriptions of animals when the likes of Christopher Columbus and his dirty mates saw giraffes and elephants for the first time, and came back with these terrifying descriptions of monstrous beasts. Meanwhile, the people who have lived on those lands forever and ever had real, lasting relationships with those animals. They lived in harmony with them, and they all kind of worked together. But, of course, that then goes into ideas like Tarzan.

While we're outlining the relationship between Blackness and whiteness in the creative space, and how *they* seek to objectify us, I want to mention an interview I watched with Richard Pryor, where he spoke about how jaded he'd become with these executives who wanted this simplified, cheap pastiche of Blackness, and the impact that had on him. Richard Pryor faced his demons and had to make some really difficult decisions. But what I find dispiriting is that the discourse hasn't really evolved that far. Like James Baldwin talking about, you know, 'People are always saying, we must wait, we must wait.' But that's all they've said, until it just becomes about wasting time. And they lie, and that's just so sad.

Going back to Columbus coming to the Americas. I recently read an excerpt of his diaries, and he spoke about coming into contact with indigenous people. And they came out in their canoes to his big ship, then climbed up on deck. They were so trusting and they were just really concerned about the protection of their headdresses, you know, because they've taken time to find these beautiful feathers and stuff. They lay the headdresses down carefully, curled up into the foetal position on the boat, and fell asleep. Because they hadn't realised these men had come to kill them. They had genocidal intentions. And Columbus can't believe that they're so trusting. 'Why are they trusting me? I'm gonna kill them.'

And I think that the reason we jump between all of this is because it takes all of our intellect to understand our existential position as Black people today. We have to go back and work it out to understand where we are now. Like it's wild that we can still be so feared. But now we're feared for our Black political consciousness. And I think that has been really important for me as a Black Briton, because of the conversations that we're having around Meghan and the Royal Family. The chickens really did come home to roost, and here we are; producing, creating. Resisting. And you can feel that anger.

Kevin 'The audacity.'

Kuchenga Exactly! 'The audacity.' That we can have Stormzys and our Bernadines, our Diane Abbots. Still enduring, remaining dignified. And then at the lowest level there are those saying, 'What's it gonna take? What's their ultimate aim?' And I'll always remember that my parents raised me to know that what we're actually facing is Enoch Powells. You see it in the glaring eyes when you're out. I feel it. It's a fear of us having power and what's going to be done with it. And there are links between people's fear of Blackness and their fear of women. You saw it with Princess Diana, like, 'Where does she get her power from? Where's she going to take it?' I really feel that on the day-to-day.

Princess Diana was the baddest one, no one will ever tell me different. The baddest of all. But I wanted to quickly go back to what we were saying about Columbus not believing that those people could be so trusting, or the police in the '80s with their thought crimes. And I think it all comes back down to reflection. Reflecting themselves on us: 'You must be as wild as I am. So therefore, of course I've got the right to paint with the same brush as what my heart is saying. You must be doing evil things, because I am doing evil things.' But one thing that Blackness has done, throughout time, is to resist going as low as the restraints that have been put upon us. And I think that's where some of that white fear comes from – the worry that one day we'll say, 'Enough is enough, we're done talking.' The fear that the damage will go beyond calling things out on social, that we'll galvanise and come back for everything. And the joke of the matter is that, take away all the trauma we've had to endure and reconcile with, and at the centre of Blackness you'll find the ultimate love. Forgiveness.

I think that there's an innate sense of knowing that if we were to retaliate to that Nth degree, so much would be lost. I think we value our humanity more than the riches that were taken. When I read Baldwin's *Giovanni's Room* I found it fascinating that an African American man from Harlem in the '50s knew white boys that well. Knew them! Better than they knew themselves. And I thought, 'Well, where did he get that from?' And I've written about this myself. I think there is something generative about pillow talk. I think that in the aftermath, when everyone is spent and splattered, and you're lying there, and they're vulnerable because they ain't got nowhere else to go – do you know what I mean?

They're at their most exposed.

Exactly. And I hear things that no one else knows about them. There is something fascinating for me, in my ... [sighs] ... otherness, to be lying next to these cisgender men, most of whom identify as straight heterosexuals, and for them to be pouring their hearts out about what their lives are like day-to-day. And here I am, at the bottom of whatever privilege pyramid anyone wants to draw up, and they're as close to the top as it's possible to get – irrespective of their ethnicity, by the way – and yet I'm the only one who they feel comfortable enough with to reveal the wholeness of themselves. And so I come to know them better than themselves.

And then when it came down to survival, so much of the conversation – growing up in our homes, with our families being part of the Windrush generation, what they faced with the National Front and Enoch Powell – so much of the conversation was about how you need to protect yourself, what to do. So we've always had to learn to know them better than they know themselves. Even in practical terms, growing up in the West I have this understanding of how to style European hair that was just received by reading *Cosmo*. We're just constantly learning about whiteness as a matter of survival, just because we're here. But on the reverse, we're just not known.

I don't think I feel as lost about it now, but I have found myself to be of a therapeutic use to these men, unfortunately. Because I've spent a lifetime understanding what their lives have been like, their hurt, their pain. And also, again, as a Black, transsexual woman, I feel it takes such courage. It takes such sacrifice in order to manifest yourself. And it is kind of wild, that we have to lose family, lose friends, lose jobs – lose a lot. And hopefully that's becoming less of a thing with the younger girlies, you know, they're being loved in ways that I could never have imagined. So I don't think it's necessarily going to be like a meta-narrative of Black trans women moving forward. But there's always going to be so much grief, and loss, and trauma. But having to stare down the barrel and say, 'You know what, I'm just gonna have to do it. I'm just gonna have to say goodbye. I'm just gonna have to lose you, in order to be me.' And yet, I'm lying next to a man who cannot even utter the words of what he desires. And that tension – that electricity – exists between us, because I have sacrificed everything to make myself who I am, but they are willing to sacrifice nothing in order to maintain the very crumbs of who they can be. It is kind of wild, but I do find it endlessly fascinating. And it does fuel my writing, to a huge extent.

Do you think those men have any understanding of what resilience is, and all the things that we've been talking about? Do you think they have their own version?

No, oh, no, no, definitely not. Because what have they got to resist? It's maintenance; they're just protecting their manhood, really. And yeah, there's so much that they can't admit because it will just immediately take away their respect, their dignity.

Also, by the way, I always use the word 'transsexual' to describe myself, because I'm trying to position myself historically, you know. I'm very happy with how the girlies are defining themselves these days. The reason I choose 'transsexual' is because I want to pay homage, to make sure that people know who I've been inspired by. The Tracey Africas, the Caroline Cosseys. There are transsexual women of previous decades who, I feel, I am the daughter of. I don't need the new respectability of a cleansed transgender experience. I like what I've done to my body, it's cool. It's adult.

Kevin So would you say you see yourself occupying a space in history as a bridge? Like, part of a connection between these two generations?

Kuchenga Oh yeah, very much so. I'm very happy to sit in that space because not enough of our history has been archived — I owe it to those women to continue to tell their stories. And by claiming the identity for myself, not only am I declaring my own pride, but it's also a proclamation of the work that I have to do. There's a need for me to archive our lives; I'm here for the girls, and I really want that to be known about me. I think every Black trans woman lives with a heightened sense of our own mortality. We get killed in too great a number for us not to think 'Okay, what's my purpose here? What's my legacy?'

Because, again, people don't see us as having any sort of intellectual regard ever. My last boyfriend commented on how intelligent I am, and how most girls really aren't like that, all they care about is handbags and I was like, 'What are you talking about?' But his access to us is only sexual, so he's coming with his certain precepts and he's only asking questions that confirm what he already thinks. And yeah, I've disrupted that, and in that moment it's impossible for him to not see me; we'd been talking about my own history, the fact that I'd just got a book deal.

There hasn't been a literary investigation into the interiority of Black trans women, about our minds — how we think. And so that's my role. I have to write stories that validate our lives, but also to let people know that we have a thinking mind. That's my gig.

And that story comes back to what we were talking about, about whether or not these men have that awareness or need for resilience in that way. And no, I don't think so. They don't have an ulterior sense of their own manhood and masculinity. They're not queer in that way. I mean, other people might see them as such, but I really don't see them as qualifying. They're not doing the reading. They're not collectivising. They're not doing any sort of political work. They don't have any sense of themselves as 'other' in that way; in spite of whatever sexual proclivities and choices that they make, they still shore up straight masculinity.

Speaking as a gay Black man, comparing my masculinity to a gay white man, then a white straight man . . . I will say the reason for that is that they've never had to work to claim that masculinity. They've never had to go find it, to actively own it.

One sec. *[Kuchenga grabs another book from her shelf]* So, I just purchased a Christmas present for a Black gay man in my life, who I love. This one is *In the Life: A Black Gay Anthology*, which I read at university. And why I think this is important is because it synthesised what Black queerness is for me. There is a distinct sense of the writers creating themselves in defiance, fighting their way back home through their Blackness and their queerness. And I think that something has been lost now, because we've oversimplified and cheapened queerness in the modern age.

Frankly, I posit that queerness requires political action. As a result, I don't feel that my conformity – and I say this as highly personal to me – but my conformity as a Black transsexual woman is not very queer. I know that my gender journey through life has been ridiculously queer, don't get me wrong. But I reify gender roles; I conform in certain ways, in a way that I feel is a deradicalization. I'm not calling myself out, or diminishing myself. I'm just trying to be honest. At the end of the day, I see myself just as a girl. It's not that special.

I've always thought that. Like, if trans women are women, then a trans woman attracted to men is just a boring straight woman like any other, right?

There we go! I'm so basic – after this call I'm jumping straight in to 'Emily in Paris'. I'm just trying to be real here. I would also say that we have lost a lot, because the centre of LGBTQ+ life has been commodified to such an extent that a lot of those radical elements have been removed. So I know, for example, if I were a Black trans woman in 1987? I know what I would have been compelled to be involved in. And so I would have felt more comfortable claiming queerness because of that. I feel that it's the political action that actually drives the work. And I know that there are broader definitions, and bell hooks has a fantastic definition of queerness that is a lot more inclusive. But, for me . . .

We spoke about my parents earlier, and even though they were pan-Africanist and revolutionary in the way they viewed themselves, my dad was a teacher and my mum worked in local government. We were low-middle class. And I've always been aware of the fact that I've been so aspirationally bourgeois. The life that I live today is too comfortable to claim all of the radical things that I've seemed to inherit just because of my subject position. I don't reject it, but I'm just saying, I'm a writer. Even the way I write is very Virginia Woolf, very *A Room of One's Own*. I am only here because of the schools that I chose to go to. If I didn't go to Camden School for Girls, if I didn't get into a relationship with a very rich white lawyer at the age of twenty-eight, I wouldn't have had the skills and resources to give my talent the space to create what I have done.

Don't get me wrong, to be a Black British writer now days is still hard – I'm still out here, chasing invoices and crying. It's rough. But there's a space that's been afforded to me that, I feel, only exists because of class privilege and cultural capital, frankly. I went to the right schools, and I sucked the right cocks.

TAKE

No one else's hurry

Take your time learning your lessons; the proof of your own resilience has no expiration date. Whenever you're in a moment of difficulty — especially within the workplace — you're allowed, and entitled, to ask for a space to consider your answer. And if that workplace doesn't allow you such time, then it's no longer a place of difficulty, but danger.

Leave.

YOUR

TODAY'S TAKEAWAY:

Understanding what makes you you means that no one else can tell you about yourself. Getting to grips with who you are as a creative, on even the most basic of levels, really enables you to answer any kind of question at any time from a space of integrity. That's not something that can be robbed from you, and knowing that will provide solid ground for your own sense of resilience.

Who are ya?

TIME

3

BOUNDARIES

BOUNDARIES

Boundaries that are set without a clear purpose – especially within a working environment – can in fact end up doing more damage than good to your long-term goals.

I've found that boundaries built on simple 'yes' or 'no' responses to the question(s) being asked aren't enough to help you get to where you need to be.

That's not to say the answers in and of themselves aren't valid, but they're reactive. They stop the immediate action that displeases you, or even causes you stress, right in its tracks, sure.

But what about after that?

If there is no greater goal than that, then great – throw out those 'yes'/'no' boundaries left, right, and centre. But if there's something more going on, whether that's the hope of a promotion or, more importantly, a better understanding of yourself, then really thinking about what purpose a boundary serves is key.

Boundaries without purpose can lack the range and space to evolve; if they can't relax or stiffen when needed, how will you – the one person they were created to protect, evolve, and, as we say, 'we move'? As an aside, there's a definite time and place for looking at boundaries specifically within the context of self-care, and whilst I'm not focusing on that particular context here, we do touch on it in the following conversation.

Right here, I'm just encouraging you to consider how flimsy any boundary can be without it having real thought behind it. A key question I ask myself is whether what I'm setting are boundaries or excuses; the latter literally excuses you from learning the lesson to be had, and the actual boundary you need to set.

But a true, well-considered boundary will take you anywhere you want to go. Having real intention behind it will help you stay on track. And I must stress here that I don't mean it will provide you with a straight road ahead. Nothing – least of all life – is linear. But boundaries can act as directions, if you let them.

An example? When Tom and I first started working together, I'll admit I knew we'd become best friends. He was the coolest person I had ever met, and super humble at the same time. A balance most would kill for. Making friends like that was important to me, to make connections and find my circle.

As you'll come to see, Julie is the one that taught me (accidentally, as it now turns out) about that particular boundary of looking at what you are building, and deciding when applications to join are officially closed. The intentional boundary I set with protecting my friendship with Tom was exactly that; our friendship could not and will never be impacted by any shiny things. I'd rather walk away from a million than not have that friendship.

How is this a boundary, rather than a rule?

When meeting people, if they do not pick up on how loyal I am to Tom, and how important loyalty is to me, then I do not need to work with them – let alone engage on a social level. It's doing the job of keeping away the people and work situations that do not serve me and what I believe in.

I'm not here trying to reveal a new meaning for boundaries, I'm just saying that boundaries are as complex and as intelligent as we are.

"WHAT THE FUCK IS THE POINT OF FLOWERS?"

A CONVERSATION WITH

JULIE ADENUGA

Broadcaster, presenter, and creator of Don't Trust the Internet

ON BOUNDARIES

Kevin I'm always aware that life can be taken away at any minute, so I just want to tell you again how much of an inspiration you are to me. And that is for all the things that you do, but also just by your existence. To see your smile, and even just to hear your voice, lights me up in such a way . . . it just puts a spring in my step to, like, keep going and do the next thing. I really want you to know, that's how I view and rate you. But anyway. The lesson that you taught me about boundaries comes from when we first met.

I was directing alongside a guy called Ben, something to do with a sunglasses brand. I don't even think it exists anymore.

Julie Oh my gosh . . . was it Hook LDN?

There you go. That was a really mad time for me, because although I loved working with Ben, the wider team almost didn't want me to go off and do this campaign by myself; they only felt comfortable if I did it with Ben. And now, in hindsight, if someone were to come up to me and say that they really loved what I did, but that they weren't entirely sure if I could manage it on their behalf, I'd just be like, 'Fuck your mum.' *[Both laugh]*

Why would I say yes to that? Either leave me to do my thing, or don't. But I still really like Ben, he's a really close friend to this day. So in that respect it was the right decision, getting to work with him. But I still could've told that brand to fuck their mum and I'd still have been friends with Ben and learned all the things.

But when you and I met, I felt we instantly got on, just on a level. I thought you were hilarious, even down to you – legendarily – having a Smart car so no one else could get in the car with you.

Then I remember, very clearly, you being like, 'Kevin, in the next two weeks we need to hang out. Things are about to change, and I'd really like to hang out before that happens.' And I wondered why you were so pressed, but it just didn't work out – we didn't get the time. And then the next thing I know, you're presenting on Apple Radio, and understandably your boundaries had to go up. Everyone was on you all of a sudden and you had to protect yourself. And I really thought, 'Wow, she's such a don! Like she really foresaw this whole thing and was like, "Hurry up! You've got two weeks of tryouts because after that point there's no time."'

I was never worried about it, because I really believe in fate, and that the people I'm meant to be around, I will be around. I knew you'd see that I was a real one, and vice versa. So I wasn't worried. And we got there in the end anyway, but once I clocked what had happened with all of that, I saw that you really pre-empted your boundaries, like thinking ahead to what they need to be. Before that, I'd always seen boundaries as this reactionary thing; not something you can set ahead of time. You showed me that you can pre-empt boundaries – you can really think about what the boundaries need to be.

So yeah, for me, that's what you told me about boundaries, or that's how I took it. You might tell me that wasn't what was going on at all! But I've really tried to instil that approach in myself since then.

That's so interesting that you say that Kevin, because I think I have terrible boundaries.

Kevin That's so mad. Really?

Julie Yeah. It's so funny that we're having this conversation. But that's how life works, isn't it? This past year, I've moved. I've been alone the whole year. No friends. I've seen my boyfriend a few times; he lives in another country. But while I've been in England I've just been alone, and it's because it felt like I had actually exhausted all of my energy, through a lack of boundaries.

I was just present for everything and everyone, even when people didn't ask me to be; I pre-empted when I thought they'd need me to be present. So even when they weren't around, I was still thinking about when they might need me, keeping an eye on what they're doing, you know. I was just listening intently to what it is they were saying, even if we were only together for three minutes and it was a passing statement ... My whole life just became that, and I hit breaking point. I had to just dip.

It's funny, I actually felt a bit like you. You know how you're just like, 'Later, everyone.' Like, 'I'm not playing, I'm not coming outside today. I'm inside, and that's what I'm doing.' I definitely adopted a lot of your energy for this move.

It's funny how life works, because maybe being on Beats 1 for five years meant that my boundaries were so set, that when that wrapped I just opened the floodgates up and let everyone in. Because I actually wasn't intentionally setting up boundaries when I was on Beats 1. I was just a bit scared, to be honest, a little bit nervous. I wasn't sure what was happening the whole time in the lead-up to it. And so if I made myself small and cut off any extra things, then I could really focus and manage whatever was about to happen. Whereas if I'm still trying to do a million tasks, I might drop the ball, and that was such a big stage in my career that I didn't want to do that.

And then I think people – like you did – maybe gauged that for themselves and also backed off a bit. Some people thought I didn't even live in England; they thought I'd moved to America. And I was like, 'No, I still live in the same place.' But that was how far people were away from me, I guess they were trying to be respectful of what that role meant. But it's only now, over the last three or four months, that I've started getting back into setting boundaries again. And I've missed it.

Do you feel like this new round of setting boundaries has let you find a balance between those two extremes?

I definitely haven't found a balance. Because I'm a 'why' person; I like to ask questions – too many questions – and then overthink. And I think this year I went to the extreme – I was literally ... When I say to you I was alone, I was alone. At home, not calling anyone, just off the radar, not replying to texts, nothing. Literally, the only person I was even able to hit back was my other half. And that's only because he lives in another country. You know if you say to your other half, like, 'Oh, yeah, I just need a couple of days,' or whatever? If you say that to someone in a long-distance relationship it's mad! They're like, 'What? What do you mean you need a couple of days? You're eight hours ahead of me.'

So bar him and my family – as in my actual blood relatives – I was out. I went so extreme in one direction that it's been hard to even just visualise what that balance is now. I can't even see what it looks like, because people have changed in my absence. Things have happened in people's lives. It's been a year, everybody's different. I don't know how long it's gonna take to find a balance again. But when I made the decision in the first place to go away for a bit, I accepted that this could be a possibility. So I'm cool with it. It's just been interesting.

This may seem like a really obvious question, but did you worry about how that might affect your career? Because within certain spaces it's all about keeping up with the Joneses.

Yeah, and that was one thing I wish I didn't feel. But I definitely thought that. I did. I took a job this year that I shouldn't have taken. But I took it because I was trying to prove a point that I'm still here. And I'm still doing these things, I'm still capable of this. And when I did it, I was a little bit . . . I wasn't disappointed in myself, that's a bit harsh. But I did think, 'Julie, you didn't need to do that. You could have stayed firm in what you were doing.'

But I feel that next year, I'm going to place more boundaries in my work, and less in my personal life. I think this year was more boundaries in person, less in work. So I'm gonna flip it in 2023.

I feel like there are a lot of people around me that are in this space. So, for instance, this year for me was spending a lot more time writing in the background, building up projects for next year that I'm proud of and want to grow. And because of that, I've said no to many a job – or done jobs and then I'm like, 'You know what? Don't credit me on this, I don't actually like you.'

[Julie laughs] There have been three or four things where I've fully said not to mention my name in any kind of tweet, as I do not like what this is. Just give me my money and I'm out.

Wait, did you know you didn't like it before you did it or was it part of the process?

It was through the process that I started catching on to their nonsense, because I'm really intentional, I really interrogate briefs. You know, 'Why are you doing this? Who's going to be in it? Are you going to give me free rein over the edit, the language of the thing? This is how I work. Have you seen my work? This is how I behave on Instagram.' I want people to know I have no behaviour so it's then up to them, because I don't want to be in a situation where I feel like I'm trying to hide my essence or go quiet on socials just in case they won't give me the thing. I am who I am. And they passed all those initial tests, and then as soon as I got on board they just started moving mad. But I was like, 'I've already explained that I'm mad; I'm madder than you, so why are you doing this?' So we got to the end and I was like, 'Oh, yeah, no, do not credit me in anything. I'm not interested.'

But all of that to say that, yeah, this year I've been much quieter. Because I'll usually be running up and down on the internet, making shorts – self-funding my own shorts – just so I can have a space to experiment in my art, right? And understand what it is that I'm doing next. And now all these big things are coming in, which should be major if everything goes to plan. But those things disappear all the time . . . it is what it is.

Julie Yeah, we keep moving.

Kevin Yeah. But this year, I really made a point of keeping myself quiet, and just really trying to work on these things to make them great. This book came along and I knew I'd have to sit quietly in the background to get it done – it takes time. But it's also given me a chance to see who's fickle and who's not. Because in 2021 I was doing a lot of, like, public-facing things – including 'Top 5', right? The way that certain people all of a sudden were on my dick because I was on 'Top 5'! In my head, I'm just having fun with you on stage, talking about an artist I love. Literally, my mate has asked me to come on her show, which I've watched from day dot anyway. It was just a privilege to be on that show. But yeah, all of a sudden people are like, 'Oh my God, we should hang out.' People I don't know. And I just thought, 'You lot are weirdos,' and I don't want any of that energy around me.

   I guess I share all of that to ask, is that some of the energy that you were trying to get away from when you did go into full on boundary-mode? Or have you always been trying to do that? Because you're an interesting one; you are who you are in your own right. Like it's beneficial to be spoken of in the same breath as you, to be seen in the same space as you; you're a superstar and no one can tell me any different or I'll punch them in their mouth.

   On another level, your brothers are who your brothers are as well. I've never told you this, but I've always considered that pressure for you, and so I've always tried to be very mindful of that in how I am with your time and space. Because you must have like, a million people asking you to be involved in a million things all the time. It must be jarring, and I refuse to be one of those ginnals.

   Do you know what, though? You'd be surprised how many people don't think that. And just you thinking that is enough, do you know what I mean? Because it will come through in everything that you're doing or saying to me, because you've had the thought. And I appreciate it, because you don't really realise what your life is until you compare it to someone else's. And I don't mean in terms of your success, or what you look like; I mean just basic things like how many unread text messages you have, or how many text conversations are on the go – in fact just your phone in general – within a certain time.

   I got a new number this year as part of my 'get out of here' phase, and I had a moment where I was sad because I've had my old number for so long. And so I was just looking through my messages, and I looked at how many conversations I'd had in just one year, and I realised that I speak to too many people, which I didn't think was a thing until I checked with others and asked, 'How many people do you keep in contact with?' And they said twenty or thirty. I realised it is virtually impossible to be speaking to three hundred people and be a normal human being. So to answer your earlier question, yeah, I'm always trying to get away from that. This year was no different. Interestingly enough, this year also included people that I would have called friends as well. It was about stepping away from everything and everyone.

   Right, random example, I think Rihanna is really cool. If she was my bredrin, I know I'd fuck with certain things that she does, and I always think to myself, 'If I met Rihanna, I imagine that we'd be cool. We'd be friends in a different lifetime. But not now. You're Rihanna.' And so I wonder how Rihanna makes friends. I wonder how Beyoncé makes friends. And then I realised they don't need to make any more friends – they've done it. There is a world where you've met all the people you need to meet. Everybody else? You don't need to meet them.

Oh, my God.

And I think I've met all the people I need to meet. I'm not saying that I'm going to walk around looking at the ground, you know, that I don't want to talk to anyone. But that thing of finding new spirits and bringing them into your energy; I don't want to do that anymore. Even being online now is jarring to me, because I'm not talking to anybody. Everybody that I want to talk to I have their phone number and I can ring them.

When I'm typing things online, or posting a picture online, I don't care for anybody's response. Someone tweeted the other day saying, 'The problem with Twitter is I tweet as if I'm talking to myself, but then strangers reply to me.' And I could never articulate it that way, but that's how I feel. I'm just putting something out, and then someone will reply directly to me as if I was talking to them. I wasn't talking to you. I had to step away, because you're just collecting this endless spread of conversations that just keep going. No one ever says 'bye' in a text message, so the conversation's never done, it's just endless. And then you're out and about and if you have a recognisable face people speak to you there. It's an overload, and I don't think we were made as human beings to be overloaded with that, it's too much. And so, going forwards, my boundaries mean more than ever.

Sometimes it's not even about my older brothers being famous, it's also because of my social circles, too. Sometimes it's that someone saw me leaving *Daily Paper* with a bag, and they wanna know if they can get something for free. And so my boundaries for 'extra-curricular' conversation – you know, the extra stuff outside of what you're supposed to know – I appreciate it every once in a while, but realistically, I've got my people. I know what I want. When I was a teenager and in my early twenties, I had that thing of always wanting to see and do more, but I don't have that now.

And I'm very okay with that.

You've really blown my mind with what you said about knowing you've effectively met everyone you need to meet. I've never considered that. So I run Pocc, which is a whole community in itself, right? That's more than one thousand people across the UK, America, the Netherlands. It's a community of Black and Brown creatives that's always popping off in one part of my phone. No one has ever given me this title publicly, but low-key I feel like I've always been the Olivia Pope of London. Like I run around saying, 'You should talk to this one here . . .' and 'You know what, you should hit up so-and-so . . .' There are people running around with whole big jobs – whether on TV, radio, or in the creative industries – just because I was like, 'These are the people for it.' And they have no idea that I'm the one that put the team together. And that's fine. I love that for me; I don't need any rewards for any of those things. But having that position within this culture, it's tiring. Because it means a lot of people have my number, and I think it's also why people get confused when they come to my Instagram page. Why are all these famous people following this guy? I've never heard of him.

Even that is too much light on me. I've always said this to you, I'm very much happy being a road yout. And what does that mean? I don't want anyone to really know my face, I want to kind of just be in the background. I will help and do anything that needs to be done to make sure the thing is done. So what you've said – that I've met all the people that I need to – that's really changed my life once again. I don't need all of that.

And I get that Twitter thing too; it's the same with my Instagram. Some people get that it's just a stream of consciousness, but then sometimes you get replies like, 'Where do you think I can buy...?' I don't know!

[Julie laughs] It's the equivalent of being sat on a bus, just in the corner, and then someone just suddenly pops up like, 'So what's this? What's that?' Why are you here? You're in my personal space. But I've never thought about it in such detail, and that's why I think you're the queen of boundaries.

Julie That's funny, maybe I am you know. And also, just to be clear, this is not a 'no new friends' mantra. It's that I don't have to go and seek these things out anymore. I can understand that if you're twenty-one and the internet exists, you're going to do everything. You're gonna have a TikTok account, Instagram, you're going to be on IGTV. And then when it flips to Reels, you do Reels. Now you're doing shorts because you just want to see everything. But it gets to a certain point where you've spread your net, and you've seen what's been caught, so you have to work out what to discard and what to take with you.

Don't get me wrong, there might be a person out there who's like, I don't know, my fucking soulmate friend, but I'm not seeking them anymore. I'm just being myself. And everything else happens naturally, so that person will happen naturally if they're meant to be. That's what it will be.

Because let's be honest, social media is just a place where people show off. There's never any moment in your life where something happens and you think, 'I want to show everybody else this,' without also having the thought, 'and people will think – insert ego boost here – when they see it.' You feel a little bit of excitement because it's just showing off. So if I really think about what my boundaries are about, it's my sanity. Like, to some people it may feel like it's about furthering my career or, I don't know, whatever. But in reality, it's just for my sanity, it's just for me to remember what matters and what doesn't matter. That's what my boundaries are for.

Kevin But if people were, in my humble opinion, really paying attention to who you are as a presenter, then they'd know that you don't go away and put on this façade – 'And now I'm Julie.' It's inherently based on who you are, your actual love of music. All of these things are you. Therefore, if you are not protecting who you are 24/7, there is no protection. There is no 'entertainment side'; you don't have to hype yourself up to get into that space. So when you're doing the things you do – holding debates, arguing about who's top five, all of these things – you can really see the essence of you. That's why it's such a joy to watch you in those spaces. You are naturally so hilarious, so smart and on point. It's all you. Because, no tea no shade, there are certain other people who really have to go home and study and practise to find some iota of personality to present wherever it is that they're presenting. You do that shit in your sleep, but that doesn't mean you don't also have to cultivate or nurture yourself. If it is your essence, how can anyone be surprised when you then have to go off and look after that essence for yourself?

Thank you, by the way. But the funny thing about what you're saying is, I feel like I've got to a stage in my life where I've completed the mission of showing myself and other people who I am. I'm not bored of myself, but I think I need to upgrade my software. I've shown everybody what life looks like when a Nigerian girl, who was born in England and grew up in Tottenham, wants to talk about music. Now I think, 'Okay, cool, I want to read and learn more, and I want to find new things in life for myself.' I want to see what life looks like when a forty-year-old Nigerian woman from Tottenham marries the Ghanaian American man and builds her career internationally. And then maybe I'll show everybody what that looks like. But I've got to do it for me first, just like I did in the first phase of my career. I'm excited about that. I think learning my boundaries, and learning what needs to stop so things can continue or things can start from scratch is probably going to pay off tenfold in this next stage. Because I think this is probably the most difficult bit, when everybody knows who you are and you have to take 'you' away from them, so you can grow and evolve.

You're pruning. Do you do any gardening?

Gardening? No. You know what I hate more than anything? When people buy me fucking flowers. Because I don't have the scissors to cut the stems. So when you get flowers, you've got to put the water in a vase. First of all, sometimes they don't come with a vase, so that's mad. Then you put the food in the water, then you cut whatever it is, like, five or four centimetres off the bottom. Kevin, sometimes they're not even flowers. It's like a piece of wood. I've gotta find a way to cut it, so I'm there with a knife trying to cut the stems off to put the fucking flowers in a vase and then they only live for like a week. What the fuck is the point of flowers? Fucking hate them. I hate them so much. I've tried to tell everybody that I know that I hate flowers, so I don't get them. And then I did a job the other day and this woman sent me flowers. Luckily, they were the most beautiful flowers I've ever seen in my life.

I'm always surrounded by plants.

But notice you're saying plants. You're saying plants, not flowers. Notice what you're saying. [Both laugh]

But this is the thing, right? You have to cut the flowers off a plant. So the main plant that they came from continues to grow. We're talking about what are you talking about. Sometimes there will be a part of a plant that isn't growing so well, but another part is growing an abundance of leaves. So I'll prune some of them off, and then the energy is diverted into that other bit to help it grow. And I feel like that's what you're talking about. You hate fucking flowers, yes, but that's essentially what you're doing right now.

Yes. Oh my gosh, that is what I'm doing.

I'm gonna send you the scissors. You need to cut the flowers.

Thank you. That's all I want, and then I'll have flowers all the time.

PRUNING

Cut,

cut,

cut

Prune: *to trim a plant by removing dead or leggy branches, encouraging growth in the right places (FYI Julie).*

In short, cut off the dead bits. Why would you put energy into dead spaces? It's a waste.

TODAY'S TAKEAWAY:

Diverting is cool

Try looking at boundaries as opportunities to divert energy to where you most need it to be.

Diverting energy towards yourself could be as simple as:

- Scheduling lunch breaks every day at the same time.
- Spending time with family and close friends.
- Seeking spaces that cleanse your palate
  (for me, this is any big body of water or greenery).

Whereas shifting energy away from yourself could mean:

- No work calls after 5 p.m.
- Donating any clothing that reminds you
  of stressful or bad times. **Get rid of them.**
- Unfollowing accounts on any social platform
  that low high-key annoy you.

56

4

PATIENCE

As I sit and write this, what I currently know about patience is that it's a bit like software. It needs upgrading regularly. In order to do its job, patience has to learn. It has a never-ending job of getting better. Because the truth is, whenever the world – in whatever way – gets more of whatever we find good, it also gets more of the bad, too. Cause and effect.

For a brief moment in 2020, a large number of people suddenly realised that not only do we live in a white supremacist patriarchy, but that the system likely oppresses them, too. And what happened? Some changes were made, sure. But did all the racism go away? Or did it just evolve again in order to continue surviving?

No matter the circumstance, when something gets stronger, its equal opposite will do its best to evolve and get back on top. Patience is the key to surviving these power struggles – giving yourself time to look at the situation, and then make a plan to follow, is vital. It will allow you to get back to safety, and put the needed boundaries in place (see Chapter 3).

As humans, we are supreme at the art of desensitisation. We're shocked for an hour – if we're lucky – and then we move on. The patience doesn't fall far from the tree. (More than aware that's not how the ting goes, but you get my point.)

Your patience will always hit a plateau, and when you reach it, you find yourself losing your shit while someone else is recording you losing your shit, all the while screaming 'Worldstar!' (Is Worldstar still a thing?). It's a long road to success of any kind, so stamina is key. Especially in work spaces where you are a minority.

Back to my point about 2020. Or more specifically, five years prior. George Floyd was forty-one, Fetty had everyone singing 'Baby won't you come my waaayyyyyy,' and I was working at a particular agency.

In fact, this was the same place I worked at with Nana (see Chapter 24). And, as you will later read, despite her being the head of one of the most important departments in that building, the misogynoir – unsurprisingly to us – was rampant. During that time, though, I was very outspoken, and could afford to be because Nana was my boss, and in that space we could have each other's backs whilst making space for ourselves.

There were, however, still times where I had to bite my tongue slightly, where I had to be patient, making a note of the disrespect and bullying and then waiting for the correct moment to expose it. Implementing changes that would save anyone else dealing with it.

To be clear, what I'm trying to convey here is that in those early years, I learned that my patience also needed resolve. A couple of years later, Nana had moved on and her absence meant that the level of patience I practised had to step up. Nana's replacement was clueless in all things, but especially his job.

Meanwhile, the shorthand I'd developed with Nana had now disappeared; I was teaching the basics of culture to someone who didn't even care about it, despite the fact that his job was being funded by the exploitation of that culture. At this point in time, women had barely started to be heard via the #MeToo movement of the same year (it's important to note that the term was coined by Tarana Burke, a Black woman, in 2006).

This moment in time – 2017 – is significant to the following story. 'You have this thing where you think people are after you, and they're not,' is something other senior staff members would often say to me as reassurance for misdeeds being done. They didn't believe I was dealing with racism – just office banter and jokes. Did people in the office believe that overt racism existed? For sure. But the other kind? The moments that do the real damage? Nah.

They didn't recognise the kind of insidious racism that leaves you off email chains or meeting invites on purpose, or calls you by the same name as the only other Black person in the building. The type that ignores your concerns, all the while comparing your hair to all sorts of fluffy animals and prickly fruit. That's just banter.

At this point, Tom and I worked under a very short man who was racially aggressive in all the ways one could imagine. I had no choice but to wait it out with my patience. With Nana gone and no senior Black or Brown people to talk to, I was very much on my own – bar Tom, who definitely used his voice and privilege to speak up. But it all landed on deaf ears.

I made sure every interaction that contained a trace of ugliness or aggression was documented with HR – just so there was a log of it all. And the more I chose not to respond to his bullying, the more aggressive he became, working ever harder to eke a response out of me.

After months of unsuccessfully getting a reaction out of us, he called a meeting with the ECD (Executive Creative Diretor). In fact, he tried to make it a surprise meeting, one that would catch us out by revealing all of the work we'd apparently not done. There were two issues in his plan: A) we had done all the work, and B) he was hated agency-wide, whereas we were actually liked. Some of our colleagues tipped us off to his plan. The ambush had been foiled without him even realising. Prepared, we headed into the meeting.

This meeting took place in one of those big, square meeting rooms made entirely of floor-to-ceiling windows and, by now, the 'showdown' gossip had made its way around the office. Everyone was making a very careful show of not looking at the room, while clearly looking at the room. Immediately, he begins by claiming we've been unresponsive, shunning our work, and letting others carry the can. We let him finish before quietly laying out page after A3 page on the floor – each one showing a different piece of work we'd apparently not done.

Because we'd been tipped off about the ambush, we'd taken the time to print everything out – all the pieces of work he'd consistently ignored whenever we'd try to show him.

I can't tell you how many pages were there – it got to a point where we ran out of floorspace – and at the sight of this, he lost it. Shouting at the top of his lungs, calling us liars, stamping his feet. An angry Tom Cruise yelling at Oprah. Again, just in case you'd forgotten, this meeting was in a glass box, and most of the agency had stopped pretending not to watch, and may as well have had popcorn in their hands. He'd been exposed.

Shortly afterwards, Tom and I found ourselves a new job, and I was able to push the button on all my notes with HR, kickstarting an investigation that allowed others to speak up. The result was a light tap on the wrist for our bully, followed by a promotion after we left.

I share all of that to say, my patience was the thing that got me through those times.

Do you think the patience I used back then would suffice in 2020? Or that the patience I'm using now is the same that I used three years ago? Not at all. Could he have gotten away with how he treated us nowadays? No.

I think there now exists a language that we could use successfully and be listened to. But, that also means he would have just found another way to target us, rather than do his actual job. Cause and effect.

And what was the reason for his hatred towards myself and Tom? For one, the fact that we refused to participate in his misogynistic jokes and banter. That's not to say that I'm blaming the #MeToo conversation at that time for his actions, but that this was a specific moment in time where the world was changing for the better, and men like him were running out of places where they could get away with saying the most disgusting, dehumanising things about women. Myself and Tom wanted nothing to do with those conversations, and so the bullying continued.

For every step forward, you are actively moving away from the space in which a platform, business, group, or individual would prefer things to stay. Shit, sometimes that person is you. After all, the good or bad of any change depends on perspective.

My suggestion is to constantly work on your patience as its own individual thing. As we discuss in the following conversation, there's a process within that; the better you understand what you need, the better you can defend, help, and reassure yourself when you need to.

"MY FACE SAYS THAT SO OFTEN."

DAME ELIZABETH NNEKA ANIONWU

Sickle cell and thalassemia nurse specialist, health care administrator, and lecturer

ON PATIENCE

[Kevin bursts into tears]

Kevin Sorry, but just seeing your face – I've seen your face before, obviously – but seeing it now, on this call . . . you look a lot like my grandmother. I lost her a few years ago.

> **Elizabeth** Oh, I'm sorry.

I'm just overwhelmed with emotion because—

> I can see it in your face, Kevin. Don't apologise, because emotions are there, aren't they? It's a healthy emotional reaction.

It's from a happy place as well, but it's like, 'Oh.' Even the way your hair is short, you two could literally have been twins. I just want to explain that in case I get a bit emotional.

> Thank you.

With that said, I'd love to talk a little bit more with you about patience.

> Of which I do not have a lot! *[Both laugh]*

I just know that, because of your story and all the amazing things you've done, that, as a Black woman, there is no way you won't have faced unnecessary roadblocks all along the way. How did you get through that, every single day? I feel that this is an important thing to discuss in light of that easy trope of, like, the 'Strong Black Woman' – which Black women are – but you're also human, and you also get tired. We have to say that out loud.
But just to go back a step – you said you don't have much patience. What star sign are you?

> I'm Cancerian.

Ah, yes. So your not having patience makes sense from a place of you just wanting to get to the root of the thing at hand. You're emotionally invested in it, and that emotion is your love language. So you pushing to get to the cause of the issue is an expression of engagement.

> Exactly, yes.

How have you managed that in working environments over the years – balancing that side of you to ensure that you hold back – or don't – when necessary?

> I love reading; I'm curious about how people live their lives, the way they went.
> But when I was doing my memoirs, I noticed that some autobiographies are quite self-centred, very 'me-me-me'. I didn't want my memories to be like that, and it got me thinking about how other people think of you versus the perception of yourself that you carry. And in order not to

make the same mistake with my books, I contacted people who've known me from all sorts of different aspects of my life – family, friends, and colleagues. More than thirty agreed to be interviewed by me and, basically, I was asking for their very honest perceptions of me. I wanted a more rounded view of myself, and I knew that maybe I wouldn't get the fully unvarnished truth, but because I knew these people well, I really did ask them to be as truthful as they could.

And interestingly enough, one of my cousin-in-law's comments was that I can be impatient; I don't realise that not everyone else is keeping up with the speed of my thoughts. Other people have said it too; they're trying to catch up with me and I'm totally unaware of it. So that made me realise that I have an impatient personality at times. I can be patient, particularly in a professional setting. In terms of my work in Sickle cell anaemia, you really have to listen to the patients and the relatives. You don't do the talking; you just listen. So in that setting, I'm told I am patient.

Even then, I'm patient with the patients. But with the professionals, not so much so! So I am aware, and it doesn't faze me, although I hope I haven't been unwittingly rude. Because sometimes you can be unaware of what effect your impatience is having on other people.

Yeah, I have a similar trait. Tom, my writing partner and one of the editors of this book, comes at it from a slightly different angle, so we make a good pairing. We both think at the same speed; sometimes I will speak out in the middle of my thought, expecting everybody to already be there and they're not. Whereas Tom will say, 'Oh you mean this.' And so sometimes you'll catch us talking and it just sounds like complete nonsense, but we're simply excited about the work.

In terms of when you do lose patience with colleagues in a work setting, though, how have you managed that – particularly in the early days, before you had the authority that you have now? Because you have a privilege now that wasn't there coming up, right? How was that?

Oh, I had difficulties. I frequently got slapped down – not physically – and I didn't have the insight then that I do now in terms of reflecting on those moments. And in general, I'm not a particularly reflective person, even now. To be honest, that's probably part of my impatience as well; I'm constantly trying to move forward – I'm a problem solver. When I want to get from A to Z, I don't want to be slowed down by D and H. And I became aware of that much earlier than I did my own impatience. It took me years, with the help of close friends pointing out the positives and the negatives, to get more of that insight in a trusting, amicable way.

But to be fair, it's also become apparent to me in other, less constructive ways. Either I've seen the nonverbal cues in others that suggest I need to put a brake on what I was up to, or someone has verbally pointed something out that actually, again, speaks to this impatience. I cannot stand committee meetings, for example, and my friends have pointed out how you can just see it on my face that I'm getting really annoyed about somebody droning on and on, or else that petty adherence to the agenda so that the meeting goes on forever without actually achieving anything. That's why I'm not on committees; I've only ever been on a few. I do realise that it's tough on some people.

Kevin In those moments where you have, as you said, been metaphorically slapped down, how did you pick yourself back up again and keep going? That also ties into resilience (see Chapter 2) to an extent, but I suppose I'm looking at it from the perspective of tolerating those moments in the service of a longer-term goal.

Elizabeth I've picked up the answer to that from having read President Obama's original autobiography, *Dreams from My Father*, where he talked about having a belly full of anger – I may be paraphrasing that – but that's what drives me: anger. When I first started explaining this, I saw frowns on people's faces. But anger can be positive as well as negative. And I've had to learn that I need to keep away from the negative aspects of anger, because that could eat into me and damage relationships with others, as well as not being good for my health. But the positive version of anger means using the energy that's created to drive you forward with others in order to get the problem sorted out. Hopefully.

Yes, I one-hundred per cent agree. Oddly enough, that's also a very 'me' answer. When people ask me a similar question it's like, 'No, I was angry about it. But then I had two choices. It's either I'm going to do something about the problem and show that I was right. Or I'm going to self-destruct, not show up, and mess up my own plans.' And so I choose the first one. And obviously within that, when I am proven right then, yes, there's an ounce of pettiness in that. You know, that 'haha' – that's the little reward. But overall I've put more goodness back into the world through the more positive choice.

I'm in a really weird space right now though, where a lot of my energy is coming from adrenaline, from putting myself into the sorts of situations that create adrenaline due to being worried. I'm trying to move into a space of harmony and peace, because the other way just isn't good for our health, like you said.

So I'm now doing lots of different things to try to build up my natural energy, rather than relying on that adrenaline. I didn't realise I was doing it at first, but that adrenaline often comes from a really negative space, because it implies entering some kind of survival mode. And I don't want that anymore.

But anger is an emotion, and it's how you choose to recognise and then handle that emotion, which we never really talk about. You know, I'll see things and there might be a split-second of envy, and there's a choice in that moment. How am I going to handle that? What do I need to do to get that thing I'm envious of? (As opposed to sitting in the emotion or pushing it away, or whatever.) It's about having a positive impact, because we're all connected in one way or another. And what I really love about talking with you is that it's so clear how you have absolutely no intentions of hurting anybody else.

Thank you. I don't, at all. It's about recognising that sometimes you are upsetting people, unintentionally. And come on, that's just being human.

I know what you're saying. If you were genuinely acting with the best of intentions, then it's not worth taking on that upset unnecessarily. It will work out. I suppose that leads into my next question, actually. What's it been like seeing that patience pay off?

Life has been good to me and, as I've gotten older, I've realised that it's a bit like waiting for a bus. You wait for ages, and then three come along at once. For example, I haven't been waiting for awards – I really haven't – but then suddenly it's become a real moment for them now. It makes me wonder if there's a little list! 'Right, let's put her there and she'll get this, and this . . .' It's been really overwhelming in some ways, so it's good to reflect on what came before.

I get that. I've had a funny year myself, suddenly receiving quite a few awards for the short films I've been making, and a lot of opportunities are coming up all at once. Which is wonderful, but there's part of you that thinks, 'I've been here doing this for the past seven years, why are you all suddenly here now?' So I wonder if you're right, and now it's my time to be put on that list, too. But in all seriousness, when you do look back does it all fall into place and make sense?

That's a difficult question, because I don't do a huge amount of reflection; it's more that things happen, and then I move on to the next one. And that's probably a protective mechanism. In fact, I self-published my memoirs; I didn't want to go through the whole process of submitting my manuscript to publishers. I looked into self-publishing, and I was in a good space financially to do it, so I thought, 'You know what? I'm just going to do it.'

But I wanted to make sure I did it as though I were an actual publisher, with all the independent reviews, etc. And it worked; it did very well. So well that a publisher then approached and said, 'Can we take this up and update it?' And so that's how that happened.

I just think it's really refreshing to hear that, because sometimes I do things and people will often go to tell you no, just because it's not how they would do it. I'm just not a fan of the red tape of it all – the six meetings about a meeting.

Yes, we're very similar. 'Just get on with it!' My face says that so often.

Same, it's so bad! *[Both laugh]*
To bring it back to practising patience though – what other strategies have you had to use, in terms of navigating the fact that a lot of the spaces we find ourselves in just weren't built for us? Because more often than not the people in power are just white, middle-class men, and on top of that, for a lot of them, the job's just the job. It kind of just stops there. But when you care to the extent that you do, and bring your whole self to the job, you automatically – in my humble opinion – become more qualified than those men. What other strategies do you use to deal with that?

I call it my virtual toolbox. A lot of it, to me, is common sense. But it's been pointed out to me that whilst that might be so for me, it's not necessarily common sense for everyone else. So I've realised I do have strategies. They don't always work, but I try them out.

For example, music. Music has had tremendous importance to me from childhood, so I'm very aware of what sorts of music can change my mood. Most genres I do thoroughly enjoy, but I know which specific types of music can pull me out of a darker mood, or else calm me down when I'm agitated. And then on top of that, it's all the stuff I suppose I've learned from my background as a nurse: nutrition, exercise, sleep, and extricating myself from negative forces. And I also apply this to spaces like Twitter, as well as in the real world. I try not to block people; I find that quite a hurtful thing to do.

So yes, I've built up this virtual toolbox over the years. But all of that starts with listening to my body, and realising that the sensations I'm feeling aren't healthy ones, so I need to do something about them.

Kevin I know I keep saying we're twins, but it's honestly true. I know exactly what you mean about the role of music in shifting your mood. I can spend up to half an hour trying to find exactly the right song to listen to when I'm writing. 'That's the right note. That's the right key.'

Funnily enough, I guess that's a miniature version of what we've talked about – being comfortable in sitting with the moment, until you find the thing that brings you forward in the best way possible.

ONE OTHER THING

That Beyoncé song

A final thought on patience: it is definitely a 'Me, Myself and I' kinda vibe. How patient you are with yourself directly informs how much patience you have for everything else.

TODAY'S TAKEAWAY:

The toolbox   I've found that the best way to work on my patience is via activities that really require patience being at the fore. Personally, baking has been the best one for me. From taking the time to get the ingredients just right, into the prep work, through to the slow closing of the oven door.

Here are other activities that may help you:

Gardening

Meditation

Computer games

Jigsaw puzzles

Woodwork

Fishing

Birdwatching

Découpage

Colouring books

ABOUT   PATIENCE

5

AUTONOMY

I think one of the biggest tragedies of life is the time spent fighting and arguing for autonomy.

Freedom over your own creativity can be an elusive thing; not just because of the obvious trappings of a capitalist society, but also because – to be brutally honest – our egos are fucking wild.

Our egos want to just show out, which stops us from looking for what art is needed. Art comments on what is happening and, in that moment, allows us to reflect on our collective experience. It brings people together.

But art created in an echo chamber, where you are the only resident, is akin to that one guy who most days sets up camp in Oxford Circus and shouts at passers-by. Telling them all – with quite fiery passion, ironically – why they are going to hell. Yes, you make art in solitude, and I'll be the first to admit how much I love that solitude. But your creation comes alive when it interacts with the world. You can still have your thoughts and feelings on it; you will always know what it means to you and where exactly that work came from. Yet it is the emotional reaction from the collective that allows the creator to see the work fully.

We are all connected, so conversation is the only way to share and experience each other's magic.

I'm not saying your art – your creativity – can't use its own voice; I'm saying your voice needs to actually be part of the conversation for its uniqueness to be heard.

With that being said, society, as it stands, isn't set up for the act of reciprocity. You can tell by the short lifecycles of social campaigns, our attention spans are embarrassing.

Clap for the NHS. Occupy Wall Street. Remember those?

We have to take into account how much ignorance, control, and capitalism tie into and support a white supremacist society that will do anything to survive.

White supremacy is a virus that mutates to keep functioning, and the optimum place for it to deal maximum damage and take over is via the aforementioned conversations about art.

Life, through a very simple lens, is an experience made of an infinite amount of smaller experiences. And for a large portion of that time, marginalised voices spend it fighting to be part of the conversation and eradicate that virus.

Marginalised voices predominantly carry words of inclusivity, love, and forgiveness.

But love is not profitable – conflict is.

So some marginalised voices sail in on breath that smells like the ball bags of the ones they want to impress … with just a hint of shit from where the owner of said ballsack hasn't wiped correctly. Harsh? No – I just want the explicitness of my words to match the level of Stockholm Syndrome some of my skinfolk are enthused to be experiencing.

Imagine being Black and homophobic? Imagine being a human and not being a Womanist? We have become comfortable with being told that a struggle is needed to warrant autonomy.

I disagree. There is a difference between working hard for your dreams and being inveigled into changing your dreams. It's manipulation of the highest form. No one should have to suffer to be who they are. I've heard people say that the true goal of a creative, or artist, is expression. But without true autonomy what have you actually expressed? An idea of someone else's idea … at best.

That's not true art.

Autonomy is all we are ever asking for. It's all we're seeking (or, in some instances, outright demanding). It is what enables us to truly communicate with one another.

As I sit and write this, my trans friends and family – in this country, the US, and the world at large – are under attack simply for trying to be who they actually are.

When you compare your fight for creative autonomy to our trans siblings' fight, I hope you realise how small your task actually is. In achieving your creative autonomy, I hope you decide not just to lend, but to actively give, your voice to theirs.

"I'M NEVER WAITING FOR SOMEONE TO TELL ME WHAT TO DO."

SHYGIRL

Multidisciplinary artist and co-founder of Nuxxe

ON AUTONOMY

Shygirl Had a fucking palaver today with my front door, so apologies about the noise in the background. My uncle has just come round to fix it.

Kevin I feel like every time we talk one of your uncles is about. Remember when we were shooting that thing and some man said 'Hi,' and I thought he was like trying it. And you were like, 'Nah, nah. It's my uncle'?

Yes, and guess what? It's the same uncle here now.

I really love that for us.

Bringing it all back. Yeah.

So, the future. Because you are the future. You effortlessly predict the future. You do this thing where you create magic and then, like clockwork, a month later, two months later, the industry is all over it. You're just always ahead of it. You pop up in so many conversations. I'm like, 'Yeah, that's the little homie. She's always been dope. Always been magic.' I'd love to know, do you view yourself as a curator of all things future? Or, I guess, to put it another way, how do you practise autonomy and consistently hold your own space, when you're always waiting for others to catch up?

It's funny talking about the future because I feel like I'm really trying hard to be present. I think being raised with one eye always looking to anticipate any dangers or problems, you tend to miss where you are right now. I think that's something really prevalent in the typical upbringing – immigrant parents, etc. – this idea of finding your place and proving yourself. Equally, I've been around so many people who have the privilege of enjoying their present. So, looking at the differences, I was like, no, actually, I think I deserve some of that too.

These last six months, I've been really focused on being present. Especially when I put out my album. I hadn't anticipated how it would feel making something and having it then make some kind of impact on my own life, not just on those who consumed it. I hadn't considered what that would mean for me in reality. I was always looking at the next step, and never really appreciating the step I just took before. I was so incredibly overwhelmed when I put out my album because, at that point, I kind of got what I had asked for – which was some critical acclaim. Some understanding. That was the biggest thing – having people understand what I had made, because so often people don't understand you. When I kind of acclimatised to that feeling I was like, now I've kind of made my bed I need to, like, lie in it. Make use of it. Feed myself a little bit more with the things that are provided.

I think that this is the biggest thing about perhaps being future-thinking, or forward-thinking – understanding yourself and human nature. I think that's probably my guiding signal – looking at humans from a voyeuristic perspective (which is kind of how we met, I guess) and semi-inserting myself just to better understand the subjects that I'm looking at. I'm still kind of doing that now.

I always still feel like I'm dipping in from looking in; looking inside to then be the thing being looked at. Then trying to understand what is human about me and about other people. Once you understand that a little bit, you can kind of anticipate what people are going to desire, or what you desire. I think I've realised that artistry, in a sense, is kind of an anthropological thing, about understanding relationships between different people and then looking at and comparing the relationships I want to cultivate in my own life. Asking, how can I add to other people's lives?

You can feel like you're losing yourself. I got to a point where I realised I've just been working so much, and then I asked myself if I'm even interesting anymore? My day-to-day is literally work; I'm clocking in and out, doing the thing. I don't want to talk about that all the time. Like, I just finished work and I don't want to talk about that, so then what else do I talk about? What do I give, you know? That really made me pause for a second because I was like, 'How am I doing all of these things and yet I feel like the most uninteresting conversation piece?'

I'm in a place where if I went on the internet today and said, 'I'm doing this with so-and-so,' the reaction would be, 'Oh my God, you've made it.'

Well, no, because things just disappear. All the time. Do not get me wrong, I am gassed, I'm not complaining. It's just that I know my work inside out now, and I understand how it could play out – good and bad. If the work comes out then you, the consumer, will get the surprise – that feeling of discovery – but I don't wanna talk about it anymore. It's boring for me now.

By the time it comes out, you're already done living it. I took two months out just to try and get away from all that; to try and make my life work for me. I just wanted to enjoy the fruits of my labour, whilst still labouring.

I've started to set aside time for reflection, like taking a year out just to be present. Looking back and asking, 'What did you do last year? What did it all mean? What are the best bits? What did you hate the most? What are the new rules? What are the intentional boundaries?'

That's how I practise being present. What you said about being present is really important. In order to predict the future – or as I like to think of it, align with your future – you do have to see what's going on now. Take in who the people are around you at this time. Look at your health right in this moment, the political climate . . . take in all the things and place your bets. And to come back to your point on human behaviour, even if you can't see a clear path ahead, you can still predict what's going to happen via what people are going to need and not need. Which I think leads to autonomy.

What's missing? Whatever you don't have, you're gonna need – and if I need it, then you'll need it. You know, like, I'm not the only one in anything that's going on with me. However unique the experience is, I'm really not the only one. As soon as I have shared an experience, someone else has been like, 'Yeah, me too.'

It's really funny because when we grow up people are like, 'Oh, you're special. You're unique; you see things in a magical way.' And they said that all with good intentions, but it just further alienates you. It doesn't make you feel good to know that you're the only one that thinks or feels that way – that isn't actually fun. I just want to know that someone else feels the way I do.

You're giving such strong Virgo vibes, but you're a whole Taurus.

Shygirl I'm always, always attracted to Virgo energy.

Kevin When it comes to both friendships and romantic relationships, Taurus gets on with Scorpio, Virgo, and Capricorn. I remember when we first met. You'd come to my night, Bounty, and you've always been so humble. Like, on another level of humbleness. You have such patience with the world.

> Thank you. Thank you. I do believe that whatever is for me will come to me. I don't need to grab and take from anyone else. Just travelling around, I've noticed differences in energies in different cities. In London, we kind of know that there are a few options out there. We take time looking for our personal opportunities. I don't need to push anyone else out the way. Actually, if someone wants to come in front of me and try to take something that was always for them, then cool. That wasn't for me, you know. I think there's a strong confidence in that. I have to tell myself that, otherwise I'm basically undermining myself.

I think fighting for an opportunity – not even fighting, scrambling? Nah. Not enough opportunity for all of us? Sorry, that seems really like low rent to me. *[Both laugh]*
>> That's not to say that privileges and structures don't exist that obstruct certain opportunities. But I can't not trust in the fact that what's for me will never walk by. I'm not warring over opportunity. I don't like it. So, please, have it. How can I help you get it? Take the seat, I'll get the next one, or else build one. It's nothing. I understand where I'm going.

> That's such a South vibe. Like, 'Okay, cool, you really want it? Cool, no problem. Have it.'

Even more so, South is like, 'Yo, like, if I really wanted to take it, I would. Double it, just for fun.' Like, it's not that deep. It's better we work together than the friction, because then I'm out of your way. *[Both laugh]*
>> It really is a South thing. *[Both laugh]* Do not ever tell anyone from South, 'No, you can't do that.'

> Literally. *[Both laugh]* 'I didn't want to do it before. But now? Now I'm going to do it.'

Like, 'Trust me, I can and will pause this whole career to learn this thing that you love inside out, just to show you why underestimating me was silly. Then go back to what I was doing like I never left, while treating your dream like an easy hobby.'

> That's the thing with music for me. The label asked me 'What do you want? What do you want it to do?'
>> I was like, 'Okay, I just want to make an album that's critically acclaimed.' Then I had to check myself afterwards. Because why was that my goal? Why do I need validation to prove that I can do this ting? You know, it's like coming from this sense of always being top of my class. Even if I didn't agree with the structure of something, I would prove that I could best it to then move off and do my own thing. I had to prove I can do it the way you

want me to do it. Everything after that is a choice. This is not an accident – everything is a decision. It's not because I can't do it any other way. Even if it stresses me out, or whatever, I'll still do it by force to prove that.

I think that's the thing that's missing with most people when they are doing their creative work in whatever field: they're aiming for number one, period.

Why don't you just aim to be the best that you can be? Because no one else can do that – no one else can be the best you can be. Therefore, you're inherently number one. What's more, those numbers become irrelevant – time becomes irrelevant – because you're just working on yourself being your highest self. Does that make sense?

Yeah, I think it's so easy to get caught up in social media, what your peers are doing. They – or your own insecurities – make it look easy, so you just end up going down a rabbit hole of comparison.

In moments when I think I need validation, I don't choose music as my vocation. Music is not the conduit to my emotional creativity right now. My vocation is me and my experience in life.

I think I've really acclimatised to that. I'm not looking for work to validate that; I'm really living life. I'm happy that I have that privilege, that I grew up in an environment where my parents just worked to provide this life for me. I'm taking full advantage of all of the opportunities they gave up to then give to me.

I could almost cry I relate so hard. I know exactly what you mean and where you're coming from. I find people get confused: 'I thought of you as a filmmaker? So why is it that you've written a poem?'

Because I consume lots of different things. It's like they're talking to me as if they don't know what the internet is, and how many things are going on on it. I can see all the things, and then what I give back is what's related to my soul, transformed into a piece of art.

I think Abbas Kiarostami said it in his film 'Close-Up': 'Art is the experience of what you've felt inside.'

It is not about the final product. It is about the discovery.

The goal is a short-lived moment. You made it, it's done, moving on. But the journey . . . when you're making the discovery, going through the process, making the mistakes . . .

Actually, there are no mistakes. Just the experimentation between starting and finishing. It's about getting lost in it all.

When I talk about art or creativity, I'm really intentional in sharing my thoughts on access – specifically around money – within the conversation at hand. You do need money to be able to do art because you do need the space and time to just do nothing.

You need other people's money.

Chillld. [Both laugh]

Shygirl That's why I made the decision to sign to a record label. I needed the investment, I needed to be able to do this, right now, the way I wanted to do it. No restraints. Then I can do the other things I want to do: write a book, write screenplays. I want to do all this other shit. I have not got ten years to be working on my first album, no. Someone else can pay for that. And buy into my dream real quick.

And it can be some white man money, please. *[Both laugh]*

Kevin It's not my portion to be out here being a bank. I'm just trying to be an artist. I've worked out my formula for that. I've done my part.

I don't want to be average; I want to be me. I need to be me. I've been working on the deluxe version of the album recently. I basically just stopped communicating with my label and started making shit by myself, then sending them the bill after the fact. Because I can do that now. I have a bit of money. I can just like, funnel it back into myself. Which is great for everyone because that's when I work best – when I'm just left alone. It's just always about following my instincts. There is this Del Boy element in how I get to the art.

I have no qualifications for any of the jobs I have. I love the Del Boy fake-it-till-you-make-it energy. I completely believe in that. What I don't rate is the people that do that, while having no intention of seeing it through. And by that, I mean improving the skill they started with. So that by the end of the project, no one would have ever known they were not 'qualified' in the first place. Have some pride in the scam, in the come-up.

Yeah. In my mind, I'm already good at it and will prove it to you. If I tell you a thing, that thing will be real.

This one job they asked about the Adobe After Effects software. I was like, 'I'm a bad man at After Effects,' when in fact I had no idea. As soon as I got that job, I watched every single YouTube video on After Effects and taught myself everything before the first day in the job.

Like, if you can't teach yourself then you're screwed in life because, honestly, I'm never waiting for someone to tell me what to do. I grew up in a house where if I asked my dad a question, my dad would tell me to go look it up and tell him when I had the answer.

Asking questions is okay, to be clear; I think what we are talking about is just pure laziness. Like when I ask questions you can tell I've already researched the subject to within an inch of its life.

I'm definitely disappointed by the creative industry, what the reality of it is. The fact that the people with the most power don't know what they're doing. I guess I did have an idea that when I got to this level, I would be with people who are intellectual, really interesting, you know? And there are those people out there, but they're few and far between. It's still such a pleasure when I find those people.

You're able to find those people by being present, by taking stock of what is actually happening, and what is actually needed. Being so confident in your ability it gives you space to feel relaxed in the creation of the thing, right? Which I think leads to that magical place called autonomy.

Yeah. This is it. I don't have anything to prove to anyone. I wanted the album to show this. Like, even my raps are comfortable. I'm not being too brash on anything. There was a lot of bravado before, but now the tonality is comfortable. Where I'm at is, if you have something to say to me, I know I can respond. I will respond in my tone and however I please.

And I think that was kind of what I needed out there. Because it's a strong thing to say you're comfortable; it's hard to get to that space. I have worked hard to be at this place. Which doesn't mean I'm not hungry. But I can still be comfortable at the same time. People have always said, 'Don't get too comfortable.' I don't actually agree with that. I think I can be a little bit comfortable and still work hard.

I agree. I think people get confused with the difference between what you're talking about and comfort zones.

Yes.

You can't evolve in comfort zones. It's about getting to a space where you are comfortable anywhere. When you reach that space, creation is the joy it's meant to be.

Yes, and that is a very South London thing. *[Both laugh]*

CATEGORY IS FACE

Listen to listen,

In your lifetime you will never, ever see your face. You only **not just react**
ever see your own face via reflection or visual tech.

None of us have ever seen our own face first-hand, and that's
the same with the work. We need each other to understand
ourselves. To understand the work we produce, via those
reactions.

Whether the work gets honest or disingenuous reviews is
irrelevant. Whether the work is loved or not is irrelevant.

What you are looking for in those moments – amongst
the most uncomfortable of criticism – is the answer to a
straightforward question: Do you still love your work?

It's here you'll hear your voice among all those others,
and it's here you'll find a space in which to figure out what
you want to do next.

It's here you'll find autonomy.

TODAY'S TAKEAWAY:

You're only trying to answer one question

After all is said and done, do you still love the work?

Yes?

Great – follow that feeling.

No?

Then the work has only just
begun, and that can actually
be more exciting than
getting tens across the
board straight (see what
I did there?) out the gate.

6

VIRGO

I once did this course on creativity and leadership – I've mentioned the particulars of it in Chapter 18 – and the whole experience was just baffling. However, I knew right from the start that, by the end, I would have gone through a life-changing experience.

And I did.

It also firmed me up, made me resilient to certain situations, problems, and conundrums in a way that was less about developing a thick skin, and more about being confident in my own wisdom.

Believing in the choices I made.

Looking at problems without the weight of time and all the extra pressures we unnecessarily place on ourselves. I remember, when the course ended, thinking, 'Is this what people feel like after a Virgo upgrades them?'

I wanted to create that experience within at least one of this book's chapters.

So you could read it and yes, be annoyed by the confidence and cockiness. But, at the same time, be able to admit that you're going to finish this chapter feeling inspired.

Feeling changed.

If nothing else, never did you think I was going to write a book and not take a moment to remind you that Virgos are better.

"I SEE OTHER PEOPLE DO WORK AND THINK, LIKE, 'DID YOU THINK THAT WAS OKAY?'"

A CONVERSATION WITH

GYNELLE LEON

Award-winning photographer, author, and founder of PRICK

ON BEING A VIRGO

Kevin I wanted to talk to you about growth. But I feel like I can't talk about that with you, without also talking about being a Virgo. I feel like we should.

   Gynelle I was like, 'I wonder what the book's about? Is it all about Virgos? Like, I wonder if it's just purely on Virgos.' *[Both laugh]*

There's definitely a range of topics, but I take that fact really seriously. So let's talk about creativity in Virgos. I don't know if I'm a perfectionist; I just want to make the best possible work. That sounds like the definition of a perfectionist.

   See, I was gonna say it's high standards. But I feel like what it is with us Virgos is that our standards are up here and potentially other people's are down there. So it makes ours seem unattainable, but we can do it. And that's what I think frustrates a lot of other people; it can be frustrating being around us, living with us, relationships. Cause we will want them to get to our level as well. But for them, they're like, 'No, I can't do that.' And that's what makes it seem like Virgos are constantly, like, nit-picking. We're not. I would say we just have an innate way of knowing what's best. It's wild when I see other people do work and think, like, 'Did you think that was okay?' Like, come on.
   People will ask for me to break down why it's not okay, but it's just a feeling, I can just see it's not connecting. But I see it from a place of wanting to help and get it better. It's just like, we want to do, as you said, the best possible work to our level of high standard, which seems to just naturally exceed most people's standards. So I think that's what the issue is.

I don't know where all these other signs would be without us. Because they're doing wild things. I will admit that I have spent a lot of my adult life teaching myself to understand that it's not okay to be frustrated if people cannot meet your standards, if they cannot do the thing you can do – and that not everybody thinks like you, or reacts like you, or views the situation like you. Because I used to go wild: 'Why would you do that?' And they're like, 'Why wouldn't I?' And it's back and forth.
   It's always going to be about compromise and finding that middle ground. But yes, there were moments of, 'I gotta put me first, Lucius.' Sorry.
   [Both laugh] There's always moments of trying to find that space where it makes sense for everybody.

   Yeah.

We are also known for being stubborn, apparently. But, again, I rebuke that. Because I feel like the only times I am steadfast in my answer is when the facts are not matching up. If what you're saying isn't making sense, I will not let that go. And I think a lot of time in business, there's a lot of gaslighting, to be like, 'Oh, you're inexperienced, you're not meant to be in this space, so how would you know? Oh, that's just business, do not burn that bridge, do not expose this.'
   And it is not working for me, this mould you would love for me to fit in even though you need me to provide this piece of culture because you are lacking in your business. It doesn't actually work for me. So we're going to have to change the thing.

When I was younger, I'd get really upset about people doing things to me, or reacting to me, in a way that I wouldn't do. And my mum would always say this one thing: 'Gynelle, not everybody's like you.'

I was very honest; I appreciate the truth. Even if it's maybe negative. And my mum used to say, 'Not everyone can handle the truth.' I always felt like I was trying to help people grow by telling them straight the truth, 'cause that's how I wanna hear it.

Every year, I would be sad if I couldn't look back on the year before and say, 'I've evolved in this way.' I'll do evening classes, I'll teach myself this, I'll put out a new product. Push myself in some way so I can look back and go, 'Yeah, that's what I did.'

And, for me, that's an essential part of going through this life. That's part of living as a human in this world, to continually grow, year on year. But I've learned that's not for everybody, even though I think it's wild.

How for five years would you want to be doing exactly the same thing? It would just make me feel stagnant. There'll be nothing to look forward to.

But then some people will say I'm too goal orientated. I've chosen to always be ambitious with myself. I'm not ambitious with anyone else, and I think that's why I enjoy being around Virgos. I've got so many Virgo friends, like so many people that just naturally do it too. 'Cause you understand that drive, that determination, where it's still healthy. I'm not driving myself into the ground – I actually get off on it.

There is that film, 'Legally Blonde'...

Yeah...

And he's like, 'You got into Harvard Law?' And she says, 'What? Like it's hard?' That's literally my energy. Do not tell me I can't do a thing. Just appreciate the thing and be like, 'This is great.' But even then I'd be like, 'It's only great? Nah, it needs more.'

It's a bit dangerous with that one, because people, if they know they can use it against you, will try and get you to do something wild.

When I was in school I wanted to do forensic science, and I remember my tutor saying 'Well, they only teach it at King's College, London. And I didn't get into it.' This is my biology teacher saying 'I didn't get into it.' So what did I do? I went and did the masters in forensic science.

Not just for that reason, but I mean, it was in my head the whole time. That's back when I thought I wanted to be a forensic scientist, but then I came out and was like... no.

Then you've got to start addressing, like, how much of what you're doing is just to prove that person wrong? And I can wholeheartedly say there are bare things that I've done – which have worked out to be good – where I've been like, 'Okay, you thought I'd fail. Let me show you up. Let me write two books. Let me show you what I can do.'

And I don't think there's anything wrong with being driven by that, just as long as it's something that you actually wanna do, or that you can take transferable skills from, I guess.

Kevin I wholeheartedly agree and I think, as you get older, you realise that your potential literally is limitless. Therefore, you, and only you alone, are allowed to put a limit on your potential. That has to be the rule. Nobody else is allowed in that room. That one might speak to Virgos, but really it's just a good rule of thumb for everybody.

Gynelle I always get that question in interviews, where people go like, 'Well, how did you have the self-belief to start up PRICK without knowing anything about plants?' And, you know, it's really hard to be able to communicate that I've always just known I can do anything that I want to do. People say, 'Even as a Black woman? In a very white industry?' That didn't even play in my mind.

From a young age I've always known, if there's something I want to do, I'll just do it. I'd work it out and just do it. And I'd love to be able to bottle that for people that just don't have it. Because it's so innate. That's something I've seen in quite a few Virgos, and something I'd love for others to feel.

I will take it further. Like, I wouldn't even do the thing you said I couldn't do, I will own the building. I will buy your company and take it into my company, then shut down the thing for fun. But as you said, that's a dangerous thing. Because that really lives in the space of, like, ego. And I'm not about ego, because I've definitely learned that my superpowers flourish when the intention is really clear, peaceful, and from a space of helping people. That place of being a cheerleader is, for me, really my sweet, happy spot. But that place cannot exist when my ego is inflated and I'm moving mad to prove a point. But it's very easy to avoid that: just don't tell Virgos no.

I get called a cheerleader all the time, but I'm like, appreciation is free. It costs me nothing to tell you how much I rate you, or to support you. Like, what do you need? I'm here. And that's why I love being around other Virgos, because I can get that from another Virgo. Sometimes you might tell someone your news, and it just falls flat and you're like, 'Oh God, I wish I never told you.' I find that with Virgos I always get the reaction where it's like, 'Yes, well done.' We're gonna rate you and we're going to support you.

What are some of your ways to deal with overthinking? I'm not even asking if you do, I just know that you do. *[Both laugh]*

Wow. I feel like there are so many coping strategies we come up with in life that we're not even aware of. With overthinking, therapy definitely helps. Because I think the worst part about the overthinking is that quality of thought. So if that quality of thought is a positive one – it's uplifting – it's fine. But very often it's one of self-doubt, especially as we're people that are constantly trying to achieve. 'Why haven't you done that yet? Maybe you should get on that now.'

It's being able to catch those thoughts before they turn into emotions, because emotions turn into action. Like the other day, I was online for like four hours until two in the morning, looking for a backup studio. Because my head said, 'What if you don't sell out your stock, what are you gonna do?' But instead of me acting on that thought I need to catch it, and balance it out. That's what I do with the NATs – the negative automatic thoughts. That's what they're called. Sorry, I'm bringing in CBT. Well, you know, I'm training as a therapist.

That's amazing.

Being able to catch the thought and recognising that you need to balance it out is really, really helpful with any negative thoughts. Before, it would be there and it wouldn't just be like a few hours, it might be a few days where that thought stays with me, and stays with me. 'Why did that person act like that? What were they trying to say? Why haven't they spoken to me? What was it?'

And that's the overthinking people talk about Virgos doing, where you've got the receipts. 'Cause when you have the receipts, you'll be like, 'Oh, no, actually, you said that last week, Thursday, on the lunch break. And I know where we were – I even know what you were wearing.' Like, that's banked.

So I think for me, with the overthinking, I question it. I try to challenge the thought, asking myself what I'm getting out of this line of thought? What's on the other side of it? I try to see it fairly from both sides. Is it actually helping my goal to dwell on this? I think a lot of the time you just overthink, overthink, overthink, and then it just starts being the way that you're thinking. But actually, it's just one voice. And we've got another voice in there that can balance it out or completely disregard it.

I will get myself in a tizzy while asleep, and it becomes almost like a repeated nightmare, over and over again, and I'll wake up. And then I'll go back to sleep. And it's the same pattern, over and over, until I realise I haven't actually had any sleep. Or the other thing will be, I'll wake up with this piercing thought, similar to what you said. And then I'll be researching, and before I know it, it's 3 a.m.

So one thing I do to help the before-bed overthinking, because I have the same, is I will write it down before bed. I literally have a pad next to my bed. And I tell myself I don't have to think about it now because it's on the paper; I don't have to hold on to it overnight so I can immediately put it into action in the morning. It's not even just me looking out for me. It's all the other people you care about, like, oh, yeah, I need to check on that person to see if they're doing okay. So I think all of that just causes the cogs to constantly be turning – but you need that downtime of sleep.

But sometimes you can't help it, I'll wake up and know exactly what I was thinking about, or if it's a good idea. And then I get excited. Like you said, then you start researching, and then before you know it, you've made candles, you've made stickers for the candles you don't have yet, and you've designed the box. Everything backwards.

Those candles, let me tell you. When I started, I had samples of stickers and papers coming in, and designs. Meanwhile, I was still figuring out my percentages and getting the science right. But then I'm very bad; I get bored very easily.

Same.

Kevin The closer I get to mastering the thing and it's no longer a challenge, then I don't care anymore. I'm very blessed to be able to say that it's not the same with people. But with projects, my personal projects as well, that is also the kicker. Never with anyone else's projects – because I'm like, that is your child and I'm feeling to make sure this is fine. But with my personal projects, the closer that I get to, yeah, the goal of perfection, then I'm like, 'Ah. Hmm.' There's also a bit of self-doubt. Tom and I had this conversation the other day where we were like, 'Well, if I've done it, it can't be that hard.' [Both laugh]

Gynelle You know I feel like that with – like – absolutely everything, and I have to play stuff down for people. When I wrote my first book, I literally wrote it in six weeks, and I had to stop telling people that because they'd look at me like, 'What.' I don't even know. I remember being like, 'You gave me a book deal – have you never read anything I've ever written?' Like you can just do anything you want. You know what I mean?

Yes. When I'm talking to kids or students, or whoever, I always let them know that absolutely nobody knows what they are doing. It's all make-believe.

You know what? That's exactly it. I ran a workshop and people were like, 'Oh, I don't know what I'm doing.' And I replied, 'Neither do I.' I think there's this facade the world gives you; this idea that people in success, people in places of power – they've got everything sorted. That's not true. We're all in the state of learning and growing. And every time you do something you don't know how to do, and then you nail it, you're like, 'Okay, that's another tick.' And then on to the next scary thing. But a lot of people feel that fear of the unknown, or feel like an outsider, and they let it stop them. But everybody learned to do the thing they did somehow. Just go online; it's all there ready for you.

I always tell people that I went to the University of YouTube – and I still do. I will spend an hour or two fully absorbing the thing and, all of a sudden, I'm looking at the people on the YouTube video, thinking 'No, it should be like this, because you would get more retention here,' or whatever. And again, the audacity – how can I critique the people I came to to teach me? But again, that's something you can recognise with age. Because boy, young Virgo versus mature Virgo . . .

Oh yeah. Young Virgo? Out of control, mate. I think having that much confidence as a young person without being able to like, regulate your ego? Pshh! Nah, mate. No filter. If I thought anything was stopping me from acting out what I'd thought of? Nah.

You know what, I'm going to embarrass Tom. When we met at the first agency that we worked in, I had taken the job as an in-house editor. It wasn't even as a creative, but I was just like, I need to get in this building. Once I'm in this building, it's a wrap because I'll do what I want. It is what it is. Tom had been hired as a copywriter upstairs, doing copy on like, I think it was manuals. Really boring stuff. It wasn't creative. It was like the booklet that came with the Samsung washing machine. Anyway, we met, realised everybody else was a dickhead, and became quick friends. So then we made our plan, right?

We're gonna be a team.

But I'm an editor. So like, we have to work out how we're gonna get me upstairs. Meanwhile, in all of this time, I would go into that workplace at 5 a.m., get all of my editing work done, and then I would know – because I was in the production department – what briefs were live. So then I would just walk up into meetings I wasn't meant to be in and be like, 'Hi, I got ideas.' They'd be like, 'What the fuck.' And then Tom would be in there just because he was a writer. They would just pull him in in case he had anything to say. And me? I wasn't meant to be in that room. But then my ideas were good and infused with culture. And because I live on the internet, I understand what's going on. None of those people in that room apart from Tom lived in the internet like that. It's very much a real thing in advertising, where half the time they talk about culture and all of these things, they know nothing about it. They don't live it. They don't breathe it. They saw a new hashtag and read a BuzzFeed article.

Anyway, I don't even know if Tom did this on purpose, he probably didn't, but he was like, 'Oh, it's gonna take you about six months to get upstairs. So we're gonna have to ... la la la ...'

I was like, 'Six months? I'll have my desk upstairs by the end of this month. In fact, I'm gonna have two desks because I want to keep my desk in the editing room. But I'll have one next to yours, too.' Two weeks later, I had a second desk, next to Tom upstairs. Don't you ever tell me no.

But that's also a really good segue into how we are different in several ways. We take different roles in sorting things out. So in terms of money and fees, I deal with that because I have no qualms about asking people for what we're actually worth. Whereas Tom is like, 'We'll do it for a packet of crisps and a sandwich.' You know what I mean?

Not to say he's not as wild as you or me; he's definitely a Virgo. He is zero, one, two, three – all the way up to a hundred; he'll let the anger build but when it's out, it's out. Don't get me wrong, if he sees an injustice being done, then he's on smoke immediately: 'Oh, you're transphobic? Let's go outside and fight.' Like, he's not about any of it. But if it's about him, he'll be like, 'Okay, they made a joke out of me.' But then, if I'm there, I'm like, 'Are you talking about him?'

I say all of that to say that I found someone who – like you said of the Virgos in your life – has a similar energy to me.

But how do you handle other star signs? Because I'm very quick to ask people what star sign they are when I'm in business with them. So I can understand how to communicate with them, what the tension or friction is going to be, if any. Do you find yourself doing the same type of thing?

I don't recall ever working with any other Virgos in business, sadly. I wish I could have. I think if I did have a partner in a business then it would be so good to work with another Virgo, 'cause you just get it. But yes, it is really important for me – I do always ask star signs. And now I've also started doing the personality test, Myers-Briggs. Because I think it's really insightful to see how we can work together and how we can complement each other. But one thing that I have thought of recently, only because I have a Libra son, is that it's not just our star sign that has an impact, but also the main person who raised you. Because even though Malachi is a Libra, he has very strong Virgo tendencies, since he's been around me so much. Even with people who have got Virgo partners, they will be better adjusted to working with a Virgo. So I've got people who have got Virgo mums, like my best friend, so she just gets it. Even though she won't match it, she'll just understand it, sort of thing. But yeah, I think finding out someone's star sign means you already know, off the bat, slight personality traits that they'll carry.

Kevin People act like that's a weird one to ask in business, but it's not. This is how I do business. I bring my whole self to the table. And that's important. If I know that you're a Pisces, I'm probably gonna get on with you to a certain extent, but I also know that you're stubborn. So the way I communicate with you, I'm going to put more leeway into it. If I know you are a Cancer, my dead tone of voice is not going to work in that situation. I'm gonna have to, like, put a smiley face at the end of the conversation.

Gynelle Yeah, it's the energy. I've had to do that, to sugarcoat. I'm aware of that. I've been described as loving, loyal, but not nice. And I think when you're honest, you can't also have nice in with that.

Yeah, because I can't deliver the full facts of the thing if I'm watering down. That's why sometimes, when we were in agencies, there was a difference in how our clients reacted to us than how they reacted to our colleagues. Clients loved us. Loved us. Generally, the employees work from a space of, 'Oh my God, everything's great, I love your product.' Whereas me and Tom were like, 'This is shit. Why did you make this?'
And the clients would be like, 'What did you say?'
'It's not a very good product. So let's talk about why you did it.'
And they were like, 'Oh, well, because we're trying to blah, blah.'
And like, within all of that explanation, there'd be the one key thing we needed to know to make it work. And then they're like, 'Oh my God, we love you guys. You tell the truth.'

That's the thing, because I think people come from the standpoint of wanting to tell people what they want to hear. And that's why even with me, I've had some friends maybe get a bit ... *[pulls face]*
I don't give unsolicited advice – that's something young Virgo used to do. Now, I will straight up be like, 'Would you like to hear my take on this?' And if it's yeah, then I'll just be like, 'Well, this is how it is. I don't like that, or I don't think that's done in the best possible way.' Or as you said, I'll be questioning things to get to the core of them. And I think people don't always like those questions. In business, I'll be straight up honest and be like, 'No, that's crap.' Like, I'm trying to save you here. Don't do that, whatever you do. And if you're gonna do that, I'm not gonna be a part of it.
In the past, no way did I feel able to do that. But I think it comes with confidence in yourself. Do you know what I mean? I don't mind if you're gonna walk away from this, but if you're employing me, I'm gonna be straight with you. So I think that if I'm not being honest, it eats me up. It's like the opposite of what I've realised some people are.
I've always felt more healthy knowing that I'm being the true, authentic version of myself. And that's where that overthinking can come from; sometimes it's ruminating on behaviours that resulted from not being your true self in that moment. So now people have judged you on being

someone that you're not. And then people go through life wondering why they didn't find success. But it's because what was meant for you didn't come to you, because you were projecting somebody else. You know what I mean? If you want the things that are meant for you, they will come to you if you are being yourself. So, I can totally understand why brands would be like, 'Ha, this is fresh and interesting. Someone being honest with us.' We're all on the same level here.

And that's another thing, when people say, 'That's out of my league.' It makes me want to throw up in my mouth. How could you say that about yourself?

I can't agree more with everything that you just said. I don't fear death. I don't fear any man or woman or person on this planet, I tell you that right now. Whether that's because I'm from South and I'm like, all of the things or whatever, I don't care. I really don't care. The only thing that I fear in this life is not being exactly where I'm meant to be. Even if that place is where I meet my death, as long as I decide for myself to go there, then I'm at peace with that. And the way I've tried to stay on that path is via being truthful at all times. I also am fine, as you said, with people not wanting to know me or thinking that I'm a dick.

I just can't quantify how much I hate not being honest and true, not only to myself, but to the people I really hold dear and love. It's my main gift and I'm always happy to share it. Looking back over the journey you've taken so far with PRICK and beyond, where have your superpowers really come into play, and really saved you?

I did a Black History Month talk at a PR firm and, at the end, they were like, 'Is there anything that you want to do?' And I told them that I want to do a podcast, there's this zine I've wanted to do for ages, I'd love to do a short series, like a TV series. And then lots of people were like, 'Wow, that talk has just made me feel like I've done nothing in my life.' And I don't want that to be your takeaway. It's that I feel like I've still got so much more to do. This is nothing compared to the grand scheme of what I want to do. I think I've had that experience so many times, where I tell them and then they go, 'Oh, gosh, whoa, like, you did that in five minutes? I couldn't do that in five months.' And they then reflect back on themselves. I love it when people use that reflection as inspiration, though, to push themselves. To be like, 'Rah, that's all it took? I can do that.'

If I go back to why I started PRICK, it was a time in my life where change was needed, basically. I was on this trajectory where I'd gone to school, I'd gone to uni, I thought I wanted to be a forensic scientist, and it turns out I didn't. So I stayed in banking until I could work out what I wanted to do. And I kind of just signed up to that society's idea of success, where it was like, 'Oh, get a job, get a house, get a relationship, get married, have a baby, boom.' And so I was kind of waiting for the relationship. I was like a serial dater. And they just kept failing, every time. And then the last one that failed, I was like, 'Bun this. I need to start again. Whatever I'm doing right now is not right. It's not for me.'

I didn't feel like I was living authentically. I was working in banking for those with high net worth, so it was millionaires. I'd get these really good relationships with lots of celebs and things like that. And they'd be like,

'Why are you here?' And that was a really weird thing to say, in front of my managers as well. They could see something in me; they were like, 'This isn't for you.' I didn't care about making rich people more money. Straight up. It was something to pay the bills. And so I had to kind of have that circuit breaker where I was just like, 'Hang on one second, I need to get out of here. But they keep paying me more while I'm being a dead fish.' Literally just going with the flow.

So I had to make an intentional break. I sold my house, I gave up my job, and I had to go away. And I think that going away realigned me with myself. The things I was doing before, I just didn't really care about. And I think that goes for quite a few people. And when I went away, I was able to be with my thoughts; I wasn't having to appease anyone.

So I went away and I came back, and I was like, 'I'm gonna open a cactus shop.' I'd always wanted to be a florist. I was always saying, 'When I'm forty I'm going to be a florist.' I don't know why, I just thought forty was this big-person number (it's not). And during that process, I found a florist to intern at. And while I was there, people kept coming in for houseplants, but that was when no houseplant-focused shops existed. And then I fell in love with cacti and succulents because they're so low maintenance and just really weird, unique, otherworldly plants.

When I found out about the range – how many thousands of cacti and succulents there are – and that there were these gatekeepers around, saying things like, 'Oh, no. General public? They can't look after them. It's just for us.' – I was like, 'Oh, no, no, no. I gotta change this. These things are amazing.' As soon as I came up with the cactus shop, I came up with a name. Growing up in Essex means bants and puns are part of our culture, so that's why I was like, 'It's got to be PRICK.' And people went, 'Ah, you can't do that.' So remember, don't tell a Virgo you can't do that.

And so when it comes to superpowers, I think it's that self-belief. There I was, coming up with an insane idea; there were no cactus shops that ever existed here. Actually, I found a woman that opened one in Ipswich in the 1970s. She wrote me a letter to tell me she was there, but in London, in this day and age, it never existed.

But that was the superpower: being confident in knowing that I can just do whatever I want. Like, I'm gonna call it PRICK. I'm gonna do it how I want it. I saw that horticulture, especially floristry, was all very whimsical. When we think of horticulture, we instantly think of roses. And, you know, this lovely lady in a flowing dress – where I'm wearing a tracksuit. I love T-shirts, I love streetwear. And I'm like, I'm gonna bring my vibe into this thing. So that's basically what PRICK was born from.

I feel like Virgos really have a lot of appreciation for ourselves and what we have to bring, which is something different. Instead of seeing our differences as 'other' and unattractive, I'm bringing something different to the table. And that's why PRICK is different to every other plant shop that's out there.

There are so many more shops like mine that have opened now, but none of them come with the same vibe. 'Cause that vibe comes from my lived experience. But, at the same time, it means that without me, it would fail. That's not a good business model. I couldn't just take myself out of PRICK – it wouldn't be the same thing. Yet that's what a good business is, where you can step aside and someone else could still run it with the same voice.

When I started PRICK, I actually said I'm going to do this for five years. And that's where that boredom thing comes in again. I acknowledged that whilst still setting a lengthy goal. I've never done a job for that long.

But with PRICK, I was constantly evolving so as not to get that boredom. Like, 'Okay, we're not just selling plants.' From the beginning I designed my own pots. I found someone to make my own pots. Then I commissioned different artists. I had exhibitions, stickers, prints, T-shirts, candles, key rings, and plant mats. All of it. People would ask, 'How did you know when to do the next thing?' But it's constant; I'm always working on something else – not to try and stay ahead but to keep myself evolving and engaged. So I think also, that's why it's quite good to talk about this right now; because I'm closing down the shop and going online.

Within that, I've had to really work on my idea of ending things versus failure. We've spoken about the superpowers, but it's also about shedding light on the other side, on the aspects that can sometimes not be helpful. I'm not good at giving up on things at all. I don't like letting go of things. I feel like I can let go of people if they're not serving me . . .

Kevin Why are we twins? *[Both laugh]*

Gynelle . . . but with this company, it felt like my child, and I just kept that. I think it's because it was born from me, I felt like I had that responsibility to keep it going and make it better. But at the same time, I was saying to my friend, it's a bit like playing God. If I made you, I can actually break you. I brought you into this world, company, I can take you out. And that's fine.

Sometimes things do need to come to an end. And that's for us to recognise and evolve around, even when some people want to keep us where we are. I could stay here, but I feel like I've done as much as I can, in this climate. My whole thing was to bring these wonderful plants to the world. Now there are a million plant shops, so many different plant shops, and I'm not able to get the really unusual ones that I used to. So I did it. It was a success, and now it will come to an end. But that doesn't mean it's a failure, just because it ended. So I think it's that relationship with endings and being able to accept that we do have superpowers, but there are times when we need to make space to use those powers in other ways. So I'm quite excited now to kind of be like, okay, cool, I've learned way more in the last seven years of running this company than I ever would have in another job, which means that I can now use that in a different way to be able to tell stories and work with different brands.

And also, just to touch on how you started that store, and go back to that part of your story, as soon as you broke away from the thing you realised you shouldn't be doing, you stepped into this space, and you met a man like Ike, got married, had a child. All of the things you'd been looking for before.

It just flowed. Like literally.

'Cause you were doing what you were meant to be doing.

I was where I was supposed to be.

I BET YOUR FAVE'S

A VIRGO

Let us help

We Virgos actually love to help – just let us make the thing better. We are here, by design, to see the things that others can't, and then improve on them. So make your life easier, and bring us in.

TODAY'S TAKEAWAY:

In all seriousness . . .

1. Virgos are better.

2. This chapter really speaks to temperament; how people function and view the world. Look, you may have read this conversation and said, 'These two need actual help.' But if that's all you thought, then you're missing the point of this chapter. At some time or other, you will come across people who will act in ways that make no sense to you. They'll view life, and creativity, in a way you just don't share at all. In those moments, it's not always about walking away. There is beauty and – most importantly – a lesson in finding a way to successfully communicate with those you may initially find intimidating.

3. Find the lesson, even in situations that annoy you.

4. Virgos are better.

7

IDENTITY

I have found that to be a Black creative is to be torn apart. You feel every inch of each rip as you try your best to cling to a middle ground, while – instead – you're being used in a game of tug-of-war between your Blackness and everything else.

All the while, your mind is laden with two questions:
1) If Black culture is the backbone of the mainstream, am I not already mainstream? and 2) Who said I wanted to be mainstream?

Even when the ripping has stopped, and you sit slumped in two meaty heaps on either side, the space that occupies where you used to stand, whole, is now prime real estate for critics who have never lived anywhere but in the lap of luxury and privilege. 'They're rough around the edges but they have potential,' is what we usually hear them say euphemistically.

For me, the real horror of all of this is when another Black person attempts to invalidate my Blackness by holding it against their definition of Blackness.

As if Blackness, and its experience, is a singular thing and not as expansive as the universe.

It can feel so heavy, the expectation to somehow have every single ancestor and generation that came before you displayed on your shoulders while, at the same time, having to walk the tightrope of avoiding recognition from the diversity-for-diversity's-sake crew.

Pressure, from the thing that was meant to alleviate pressure. Bullied, by the thing that you love the most.

Your art.

This conversation is really just confirmation, if indeed you needed it, that it's okay to walk away from conversations that are about you, rather than with or for you (see Chapter 5).

Yes, these kinds of conversations are always going to try to find you – that's just the set-up of the world – but that doesn't mean you are personally responsible for them.

Art, from birth, is political. But most of all, it is needy.

Because of this, I felt this book needed to have a space where two Black creatives just admit the weight and the stress of identity in their art, while simultaneously loving their Blackness.

"OH, MAYBE YOU SHOULD TRY STICKING TO ONE HAIRSTYLE SO PEOPLE RECOGNISE YOU."

A CONVERSATION WITH

BIANCA SAUNDERS

Award-winning fashion designer and creative director

ON IDENTITY

Kevin What's the process behind your work? How does your brand get from that initial idea through to being presented in a show – specifically something that you've created and then shepherded in the way that works best for you individually?

Bianca When I first started the brand, I wanted people to know the designs, rather than who I am. I wanted people to know that I'm a good designer, rather than think I'm just here to switch things up because of 'diversity' in the most cynical application of that word. Don't get me wrong, because I love being that person, but it took me a long time to learn that I should not get caught up in it all. Like, in terms of representation, I have the opportunity to act as a goalpost for the people who come after me. But I do sometimes wish I'd had that for myself, so I could just show up as myself and know that every single part of me was already accepted by the industry.

It's a double-edged sword I suppose, because I didn't want my identity to interfere with how my designs were received, but I also wanted them to be recognised as a product of me. I don't know. In some ways, it doesn't really make sense.

When I told this to people who were a little more outside the creative industry they were really shocked; they asked me why I wouldn't want to show myself. And my answer at the time was that I just wanted people to buy the work because it was good in and of itself. But I've realised that people do want to see more of me, because they enjoy the fact that I exist within this industry. I remember a tutor once said to me, 'Why can't you just make the work? Why does it have to be about your identity?' At the time I was just like, 'Whoa.' It made me cry. And it's only recently I've been able to think about it more and see it was because I was trying to find myself through my work.

I suppose what this actually comes down to is that I've realised, and come to love, the fact that there is no one way to tell a story. There are millions of ways to tell a story. One Black story isn't the same Black story as another; there are different forms of representation for everyone.

That was such a dangerous thing for your tutor to say to you, because why shouldn't your work be about you, in all the fullness of you? And I get why, when you hear things like that coming up in the industry, you might feel that you have to be careful about showing yourself. And while it might look like shame from the outside, it's actually about protection. You don't want to be made to feel that way. But that's really a 'them' problem, not a 'you' problem.

But yes, in terms of that realisation that your own, personal story of Blackness is as valid and equal as any other, I completely get that. Even in filmmaking, there can be this feeling of pressure. Like, in being a Black storyteller, you're speaking for everyone that shares a culture or lived experience with you. And as part of that, every time you take a step forward within that industry, you're taking a step forward for the community as a whole.

And that becomes a heavy burden, because you can get trapped in this idea that everything you do needs to not only be perfect in how it presents itself on behalf of the community, but also in how it speaks for the community, too. And that's a level of pressure that you just don't need during the act of creation. The act of pure creation should be about pure imagination – at that really early point in the process there doesn't need to be any sense of limitation – yet as Black and Brown creatives we still feel the need to restrict ourselves. And yeah, it's not even really about us restricting ourselves, but about how society forces us to conform in a particular way.

Yet, if you look at our white counterparts, it's just like, 'Yeah, I was having fun. I thought I'd do this, and have a go at that. I'm just being myself!'

I don't think we spend enough time talking about the level of discipline required to shed that burden, and the individual insecurities it creates within us, just so we can be free to find the ideas that speak to us. Because until you do that, anything you think is still being influenced by so many other, unnecessary restrictions that are actually about policing race, gender, and sexuality. Class, too. I certainly felt like I had to do things in a certain way, or else stay away from other things, because otherwise I wouldn't be seen as Black enough.

I definitely know what you mean. In the beginning, certainly a lot of my work was about my friends. I wanted to explore different aspects of their body language, and how that could then be interpreted in fashion. And I was doing that from a space of exploring their femininity via body language – gestures – rather than the stereotypical idea of, 'Oh, make it pink!' Exploring those subtleties really interested me.

But there came a point where I moved beyond that line of thinking, and into a space of creating garments that anyone could pick up and think, 'I can see a bit of myself in this.' I suppose that means I'm thinking more like a product designer: here is this object that you can take and then make your own. In that regard, I think my clothes occupy this space where they're both familiar and unfamiliar at the same time. So I definitely do see my work as an ongoing practice. Across the pieces – however different they may be – there are still shared conceptual threads linking them together.

Similar to what you're saying about filmmaking, I feel that there are a lot of non-Black designers in fashion who tell stories about themselves, their background and heritage, and in their case it's perceived as conceptual. There's this documentary by the designer Martin Margiela called 'In His Own Words', and it shows how, whilst people will see his work as being quite 'random', everything is to do with how he's grown up. You know, his twisted wigs are because his mum was a hairdresser, or like, how certain things were made because of what materials he could actually afford at the time. And I feel like that sort of freedom isn't allowed as much for someone like me.

But I decided that if he can do that, then why can't I? So my mum does all my hair for all my shows. I'm always changing my hair, all the time. That's just a part of my creativity, it lets me feel like a whole new person each time. To Black people, that's such a normal thing, but in the creative industry it's like, 'Oh, maybe you should try sticking to one hairstyle so people recognise you.' [Both laugh]

But you know what, it's actually nice not being recognised all the time. I can do the work and the name can be bigger than who I am.

I know what you're saying – my goal is always to make the best creative work. The work is the goal. What does excellence look like on this project, you know? And also making sure I'm not measuring myself with anyone else's ruler. What I mean by that is avoiding comparisons to films made by straight white filmmakers, because I'm never going to be making that stuff, anyway.

Instead, I set my own milestones – and sometimes they're so small other people might not even notice them. Stuff as specific as, 'Did that camera move work in the way I wanted it to? Did those actors vibe in that moment in the way I'd hoped?' Those are my wins, and it's not for anyone else to dictate that.

Bianca Yeah, I think I come from a similar place. People sometimes say that I'm really hard on myself, or I hold myself to too high a standard. But it's because in my head I'm setting the standard, and so it needs to be sky high. It's such a bad way of thinking, but I'd rather be criticised for something I've tried than for simply existing. Like, I don't want it to just be, 'Oh she's young and she's in the room.'

For me it's about those nerdy details, too, that you spot and think, 'For next season, that needs to be right.' If I had all the money in the world to do this brand again, of course it wouldn't be the same thing, because I could make things exactly how I'd imagined them first time around and then not be such a hard critic of myself when they don't work out how I'd planned. But at the same time, I don't regret the journey. It keeps you interesting, because you're able to return to things from before and make them right, with the knowledge you've gained since. Whereas sometimes, I feel that perfection – or just feeling that something is completely finished when you deliver it – means that there's no sense of continuity afterwards.

I enjoy the game of it; it's like running a race, because every six months I create a capsule collection and, at the same time, I'm looking at other designers to see who really stood out that season. Things like that. I'm not sure other designers think that way, and maybe that's my competitive side coming out a little bit.

Kevin No, I get what you're saying. I wanna look at the art others are creating and think, 'You, man, are living in 2030. And I need to catch up.' I think it's about creating an invitation to start new conversations. That's something I tried to do in my 2022 Black History Month films, by having each one relate to a different aspect of our bodies – and how we physically respond to this world we're in. The idea is that people can then stand on my shoulders and reach up for the next step in the conversation. But what I'm disheartened by, in my industry specifically, is how it can be a year on, and we're still having the exact same conversation.

I think the best we can hope for is to just be continually building on our own stuff, as you said.

Even the way I research is very much continuous; I'll be having a conversation with someone and it will trigger something that I was thinking elsewhere, so I'm suddenly like, 'Oh, I've really got it now.' And that can be going from something like, a person's T-shirt being twisted and I liked the way that looked underneath their jumper, through to that becoming something that informs the folds within the pieces of a collection. Or, another time, someone said in the middle of a conversation that men just want to feel hench – and that prompted me to focus on the shoulder line. How does that move? What does 'hench' even mean, specifically in terms of the sense of movement in shoulders? Things like that really fascinate me, and that's why I like talking to people all the time.

Sometimes, for me it can just be a single word – or the way someone phrased something. And I'll keep unpeeling that like an onion to get to the root of whatever made that word interesting for me in the first place. I might walk around with that word for a month, rewriting the thing in my head over and over (like Biggie). Only writing it down in full once I've got it. The idea of blowing up this one, single subject that seems so mundane on the surface is a really exciting starting point for me. Again, that starting point isn't necessarily something that anyone else will ever see.

But do you think about the context around your work, and how audiences might take that? Is that something you consider when you put on a show, or is it something you're not worried about? Are you happy for people to just absorb your work as it comes to them?

I think it's half and half. Like, last season I did something based on hard food. But it was more about the concept of it, rather than having bananas or a yam in their hand. I like literal, but at the same time, I don't. I wanted it to be more about the materiality, the process of taking something that's naturally really hard and making it soft. So the front of the jackets were double bonded and really stiff, whereas the backs were much more fluid, light fabrics, so there was a difference in movement between the front and the back.

The soundtrack was created by a woman we found on YouTube – it was her talking about making a recipe. And in the background we had certain ASMR-like sounds: chopping, cooking, things like that. So yes, it's sort of this halfway house of providing the context in a way that still feels at one with the pieces themselves.

I think that's one of the most exciting things about creativity – how we can each take concepts to very different places. What you said about the contrasting fabrics as a response to hard food – my mind was just blown. Whereas, off the top of my head, if I was going to look at hard food in film, I'd very much be thinking about it from a visual sense, looking at the different aspects of colour and texture – both in the fruit as they are, and during the process of cooking. And, like, now I'm thinking about the volatility of the oil as it spits and hisses in the pan, and how that could translate to the camera movements.

Everybody is able to conceptualise, but we're not taught that how we perceive these concepts is worthy of exploration. When we realise how even the smallest of things can trigger such an individual response though, you also realise that coming up with concepts isn't such a hard thing after all. The work, then, is holding on to that version of the idea you came up with for yourself, and building that into a finished piece of creative. But when you're able to trust your own approach, it really just becomes a case of following that through, best as you can.

BLACK WITH A CAPITAL B

YOUR BLACKNESS IS VALID

The world is a better place for the diversity in Blackness.

YOUR BLACKNESS IS VALID

YOUR BLACKNESS IS VALID

YOUR BLACKNESS IS VALID

YOUR BLACKNESS IS VALID

YOUR BLACKNESS IS VALID

YOUR BLACKNESS IS VALID

YOUR BLACKNESS IS VALID

TODAY'S TAKEAWAY:

YOUR BLACKNESS IS VALID

Just to say it again . . .

YOUR BLACKNESS IS VALID

YOUR BLACKNESS IS VALID

YOUR BLACKNESS IS VALID

Your Blackness is valid. Whatever it may be, it's valid.

8

FRONTING

In the Black community we often talk about, and take pride in, breaking generational curses. This subject matter usually pertains to wealth and education, indeed anything adjacent to affluence.

I myself prefer to dissect generational sin.

This is more about looking at the sins of people's ancestors, what led to their guilt or shame, and how they will now do almost anything not to atone for those indiscretions and refuse to work to improve society today. Basically, understanding what skeletons people are hiding – and why – makes it easier to expose them and then start the real conversations that are needed (rather than the same tired old ones that get rehashed once a year for Black History Month).

I prefer to look at my position within society from this standpoint because the weight of trauma seems unfair and unbalanced. Why is it my responsibility to work through all of that? This life is confusing enough with all the time spent trying to break rules and glass ceilings that shouldn't exist in the first place.

There are so many awards that look at the first Black this, or the first female that, when actually the conversation should be: why were your awards so racist and sexist in the first place?

That's why I'd rather shine a light on those who enacted the sins, and push for the living relatives of that generation to help atone for them – rather than expect myself and others to wade through hard emotions we vividly know and feel, despite never being present for the physical experience itself. It's not our job to fix the mistakes of others.

Inevitably though, I do still end up stumbling through generational curses, dusting them off to break them down. One of these curses – or perhaps more accurately, behaviours – that I've never subscribed to was faking how I feel.

As my grandmother always used to tell me: 'If you wanna cry, cry. Let it out. If you feel browned off, then feel browned off – don't it.'

I've held on to that advice for dear life ever since I first heard it, and it's probably one of the best generational blessings I've ever received. By 'generational blessing', I mean an inherited gift, passed down to encourage prosperity. Too often, advice from elders comes from a place of survival. Whilst well intentioned, this often results in putting up a front. What scares me the most about wearing such a mask is that my actual blessings and destiny won't recognise me.

As a celebrated athlete and Black woman, Perri is no stranger to the weight of expectation placed on us by those who demand we present ourselves in a certain way, at the cost of how we truly feel.

"THERE IS A BIG 'BUT' TO THE SMILE."

A CONVERSATION WITH

PERRI SHAKES-DRAYTON

Former Olympic-competing track and field athlete

ON FRONTING

Kevin I realised today that we first met in 2012, on a bus in Brighton.

Perri For the MINI Run in Brighton, yes!

I remember that day; they drove from Crystal Palace to Brighton. And there were one or two Black people, but there were bare white men with old Minis. And I was like, 'This is where Black people go missing.'

I didn't feel like I should be there, so I was quite stressed by the whole thing. But I got to Brighton, and it was a little bit of a mad ting, because I think there's a whole history going on between the current owners of MINI being German and the older fans who want MINI to be purely British. I don't know if you remember, but they were being a bit wild – like 'Why are you here?' – to this other car brand.

Yes, I remember. They wanted to fight BMW! 'It's not a British car; the engine is this-and-that.' All sorts.

Yes, and there was little old Black me in the middle of all this, not having a clue what all this is about. It's just stress. And then I knew I had to meet you, and whilst I wouldn't say I was worried, I was very aware of the fact that you were doing amazing things – you're an Olympian! – and I just didn't know if this day was going to keep getting wilder. Then I remember that as soon as I met you, you were just so lovely and normal. And then I think you looked at me and thought, 'You're normal too, let's just hang out for the day because this is a mad ting.'

Since then, whenever I think of you, I just remember how genuine and transparent you were – and still are. You wear your heart on your sleeve. Your smile is ridiculous because when people see it they can't help but smile, too. It's just infectious. I'm sure you must have been told all this before, but I want to talk a bit more about where you think that is from. What do you think about it? And how has it helped or hindered you in your career, given that we live in Babylon?

Good question. Yes, other people have described me in that way too, that they like being around my energy. No matter the accolades that I've had, or the people I've been with, people still say 'No you're cool, Perri. You're normal.' And I did used to call myself the athlete with the biggest smile, you know.

But!

There is a big 'but' to the smile. I feel like the smile is something I'm always associated with, but the reality is that I'm not always happy, I'm not always smiley. But, in every photo I was showing teeth, and so I just kept it up. But that's not always been reflective of my career; I've had highs and lows. Even in the lows, though, I've always found a positive; a reason to smile, shall we say. But I'd never really express how I may have actually been feeling; I felt like maybe people wouldn't want to know that. So I just kept thinking that I had to put a brave face on for everybody else.

I feel like that comes from my mum, maybe. She would never let me know that we were struggling and so, in my eyes, we never were. Because there was always food on the table, I had the nice shoes, the bag, the coat; we were fresh. It's not until you start mixing with other people – and I think for me that was at uni – that you start really hearing about other people's upbringings. For me though, my upbringing was fine; I had family around me, so I never felt like I was disadvantaged. And no matter how many jobs my mum worked, she was always able to smile and dance. The household was happy. I feel like I've adopted that.

I find that even when speaking to my mum about anything that I may be upset about, Mum doesn't want to hear about that. She doesn't want to hear me upset or unhappy. So, for me, it's always about finding that positive. When I say I've felt down or anything like that, I tend to write it in my diary, rather than actually express it to the public. When I had my really bad injury, the public wouldn't know how I felt. Only my diary.

And I think as I've got older now, occasionally I may share my story with somebody I'm a little bit more comfortable with. But when I'm going through it in the moment, I'll keep it to myself. I may say what's bothering me to someone, but then they might not give me the response that I was looking for. So I'm like, 'I'm not talking to you about it again.' It's one of them ones.

Do you feel that must be related to the way in which Black women are treated globally? I'm more than aware that, on the whole, Black women feel like there are no safe spaces available for them to just be human. And you're human, so there must be down days. But then it's also looking at that through the lens of you being an Olympian. And even I've been guilty of that, being like, 'Nah, that's my bredrin, the athlete. Like, we met and nearly died on a beach this one time. That will be my bredrin for life.' Because we really went through it!

But then because you're an Olympian, there's maybe this idea that you're like, a machine with all of this strength and control, so then of course there's no room for you to just be human. Was there a particular point when you reflected on that and how healthy it is for you to be viewed like that?

Okay, so the athlete in me would think that showing an injury, or expressing that you're going through something, would be seen as a weakness. When I watch sports now, and I see athletes talking about their mental state and stuff, I'm like, 'Oh, where was this when I was competing?'

Listen, I think there was one time they gave me a psychologist when I'd already gone through my injury. So it's like, right, you wait until the person's body breaks down, and then you come and help me. But that help and support should be there throughout – even post-career, too. There isn't any help or support for the athletes. Your career can feel like you're high, you're high, you're high. And then you've got this major transition where you might be a bit low, where you kind of start to think, 'Who am I?' You know?

I can't run anymore. So, you know, what else can I do? I feel like there is a lack of support; you act a certain way because you are an athlete, and yes, because you're a 'Strong Black Woman'. I feel like that's what we're associated with, you know – 'Gotta be strong, don't show your tears' and whatnot. If you're going through something, there are always worse situations, and people worse off. That's how I was brought up – to think 'It's not the end of the world.'

Yes. I think it's a generational thing, isn't it? Because if I think about my mum, it's a similar situation. And I think, in hindsight, I could say like, 'Oh, I think my mum was depressed at that point in time.' But in the moment itself, we didn't really have those words to hand. It wasn't a thing. And therapy? That was for really rich white people. The idea that we'd go to therapy? . . . No, go and learn your books. *[Both laugh]*

Perri No, no, no. 'Listen to me, I'm not chatting to no stranger.' That was my thing, right? That psychologist I mentioned earlier? I didn't trust the person! 'I'm not telling you my business, because in this institution of sport you'll chat.' So I'm just going to give you 'yes, no' – you don't know what I'm really going through, so I don't feel comfortable or safe sharing it with you.

Now, as a grown woman, this idea of therapy? Yeah, I've done it, and I feel comfortable talking about it. Why? Because I feel like more people are talking about it. And it's not seen as this sensitive topic. It's surprising how many people do go to therapy. It shouldn't have taken that long to get to this point of being able to talk about it, but again, I think it's a generational thing. For people my age, it's a norm.

Kevin Yeah, it has to be. There has to be an outlet for all of the unsaid things or pains. It's an interesting one; I'm pretty sure our upbringings were mostly the same, where you had that one auntie or uncle who needed real support for the mental health. But it was just explained as, 'they're a bit haunted,' you know. That's it. Shouldn't we find out why? But we never did. It was just accepted that that's it, that's Auntie.

Yeah, she's not all there, but we accept her for that. That's another thing you would get when it came to mental health. But then my mum worked as a mental health nurse. So when she studied that and became one, I feel like she was a lot more understanding. My mum would work among the community to the point it was getting too close to home – 'I know that person's mum.' But because it's confidential, my mum can't talk about it. And what's more, she wouldn't be able to anyway, because it would be seen as embarrassing.

Yes, exactly. I do have an aunt, my mum's sister. I remember, growing up, she would really mumble and talk to herself. But as a kid, I just thought it was fun. You know, I'd be at my grandparents' house with her and she'd play with me, but looking back, she needed more help than she was getting. But I'm not saying that trying to do my grandparents dirty; we have to look at it within the context of the society and country that we live in, you know, how mental illness – specifically when it comes to global majority people – is even treated. You only have to look at the statistics around Black women in medical care generally to see what damage is being done. You know, in childbirth, just the expectation that you can take a lot more pain. But who told them that?

Yeah, exactly. But again, it's that generalisation of us all that because we're Black women; we can take it. 'Your pain threshold's high, isn't it?' Is it really? Is it really?

Where are you today? Because you said you've done therapy and grown. Do you feel different now? Is there freedom in it?

Yes! Just like when I cut my hair, I feel liberated! Speaking to a professional, I realised my thoughts were normal. So that clarified a lot of things. I still don't talk to everybody about what I'm feeling. Even my husband doesn't get told everything. But having that professional allows me to ask questions in a way that feels separate.

Right, it gives you space to put it out there, and then come back to day-to-day life. What have been the side effects of feeling that freedom?

Yeah, definitely. I'll say, as an athlete, I was very selfish. But in becoming a wife and mother, I feel like that selfishness left. You know, my family always came first, to the point where I had to think, 'Perri, remember who you are.' And now I often tell myself that some of those attributes I had as an athlete I can bring into how I operate in society, you know? Like if I want to do something, I've got to be the one to go out there and do it.

When I started being an athlete, I wasn't the best. But I put the work in so that later, down the line, it paid off. And therapy reminded me of that, and of the importance to have time for yourself. And not caring too much about what other people think.

Exactly, as long as you're not hurting anyone else, what's the problem? And again, I think when we were growing up there was a real thing of treating others how you wished to be treated. That was instilled in us, right? But then there's also this aspect that, as Black, Brown, global majority people, we have the skill to code-switch. So, the two of us definitely did that on that bus in Brighton with the others, then went back to road when it was just us two talking.

But I think the part that's missing, is that whilst we're taught to code-switch for the benefit of others, we're not taught to do that in a way that serves our own energies and efforts. If we were to apply that care and consideration to our own way of being and the goals we strive for, we'd actually be moving through the world as a much more multifaceted person, because we'd be considering the angles a lot more for ourselves. Growing up though, we just didn't have time for that, to be honest. As Black and Brown people, we're not afforded the time to figure out those things because we're always on a survival tip.

Exactly that, man.

I CALL YOU 'PHA-REAL' CAUSE YOU THE TRUTH

Featuring Jay-Z

You have every right to
authentically express how you
feel. It's that simple.

No ifs, no buts, no maybes.

<u>**TODAY'S TAKEAWAY:**</u>

No big trick list here

Be honest about how you feel.
Let the good and bad emotions
flow through you.

Look for the generational
blessings as much as the curses.

9

INTUITION

INTUITION

It has always baffled me when people speak about culture as if it's a predictable system instead of the ever-evolving magic it is.

Culture is the space between us that transcends words while giving birth to them. It's an experience, a memory, a longing, and a loss. It's a connection, and by that very nature, it demands us to be present and available.

If you have not lived it, then you cannot possibly describe it or pin it down with a lazy definition. It is a feeling, a rhythm, a living thing that demands your full admiration and which cannot be dissected in the sterile, floor-to-ceiling glass rooms of short men. (I love short men – just not the ones who are misogynistic, egotistical culture vultures).

Culture is a heightened understanding and enjoyment of our current surroundings – it's a language you can only learn by feeling. What's remarkable about that language is that it enables you to talk to almost anyone, about anything.

In the world of advertising – where communication is wholly in service of capitalism – understanding that language is your golden ticket because advertisers see it as a way to sell anything to anyone. Think about the last item you bought for yourself. Not necessarily an essential, but something that made you pause and take the time to consider before purchasing. I guarantee that what swung it was the thought it would spark some kind of joy in you. Or else, it was already popular within your circle. The purchase didn't happen just because an advertiser said it should; it was because the product communicated with you on an emotional level.

Personally, I prefer a more wholesome approach. I make sure my work speaks to the people that need to be spoken to, in the hopes that when my sins are weighed up, it's clear to see that I tried my best to avoid greed. I want to always connect people with the things they need and not just fads and trends.

It's no wonder the aforementioned short men with no rhythm love to pretend to be fluent in their subject while acting as if you and I are not to be rewarded for our knowledge of it.

At the centre of any and all authentic work, you will find culture.

But why is it such an essential component? Fundamentally, it's because culture is the ever-growing diary of the human spirit.

That spirit, that culture – in my humble opinion – only answers to one thing. Intuition.

Intuition never leads you wrong; it only draws you towards the warm and safe. To exactly where you need to be. It is the expanse where the future, past and present meet. The flow from which the culture gets its rhythm.

It knows what you need.

Toni Morrison once spoke about believing in ghosts, and what our shared culture thinks of them. She said there was a need for ghosts or, more relevant to my thinking, a need for memory; a memory that can physically come and sit down next to us.

She said that this aspect of the culture stems from the belief that our ancestors are benevolent, guiding spirits waiting for our call.

This seems obvious to me once you look at it with regards to creative work. For me, creativity is meant to provide solutions, ways forward, and – as a bare minimum – true joy. So, it makes sense that any creative endeavour would attract the attention and support of our ancestors.

I follow my intuition in my work more than anything else. It is the only rule that I won't break when it comes to creating authentic work. I take the work I do seriously – and so should you. Because when you invoke creativity and the surrounding culture, you invoke your ancestors.

The trouble is, because we live in such a tumultuous world, we naturally find ourselves needing a little help 'fine-tuning the aerial,' as my good friend Kelechi Okafor puts it.

I'll be the first to admit that, at times, what I thought was intuition was actually a side effect of trauma. Whether that's the shared trauma of living in a white supremacist society, or the individual scars I carry, that voice wasn't intuition, it was Post-Traumatic Stress Disorder (PTSD) and working to untangle those feelings has made it easier to enjoy my creative work.

"OH, YOU THOUGHT I WAS FEELIN' U? IT'S JUST PTSD."

A CONVERSATION WITH

KELECHI OKAFOR

Actress, director, author, founder of Kelechnekoff Studio, and creator of Say Your Mind podcast

ON INTUITION

Kevin So, I've been thinking about the word 'intuition' a lot in preparation for this conversation. Sometimes 'intuition' is used to suggest that sense of survival in the moment (like a protective sixth sense) but, for me, it's also related to how we should talk about culture. A lot of the time, people look at culture as if it's just the current fad that's happening – but it's not, actually; it's the movement and feeling of the time, it's a spiritual experience, it's the way that we communicate with each other. What I want to talk about is real intuition in terms of being spiritually connected and doing things with divine timing.

     Kelechi Yeah, I mean, when I look at the definition that we have here, it says: 'the ability to understand something instinctively without the need for conscious reasoning.'
     I think that some of the definitions online can be wayward but what I like about this one is 'without the need for conscious reasoning,' because our conscious reasoning is impacted by so many external forces, right? Forces telling us that we don't know this, and we don't know that, and you're Black, and you're a woman, etc.
     All these things culminate together, impacting our conscious reasoning in so many ways. But then intuition, I feel, is like the frequency that we are inherently tuned into as part of the source of creation. We are naturally dialled into that frequency – and you can dial it up or dial it down depending on what you need in life. But we are inherently tuned into it. So when we call something a gut feeling, maybe, for some people, that is where they feel it. I just imagine us to be like human radios ... if it doesn't feel right, it's the equivalent of us struggling to tune into the station.
     When you vibe with someone, it's like you're literally on the same wavelength – like when you meet people where you don't even have to use words. Then you've got motherhood and the umbilical cord, and 'mother's intuition' – I think that's a perfect example, as well. When you give birth to a child, you are linked. They spent so long being created as part of you, formed from your cells. Everything. So, you can almost always dial into your children. Let's say something's happening to your child – you might not know consciously, but you just know.
     And even though we make fun of West African parents and Caribbean parents – where out of nowhere, they'll say to you, 'I had a dream about ...' and, as their children, we're like, 'Oh, here we go ... you and these dreams, girl. You're always dreaming.' But honestly, our parents can probably tune into us and the limitlessness of time as it pertains specifically to us as their children.
     I think, what the white supremacist heteropatriarchy has done is forced us to think only with the conscious mind, as opposed to the talent – the inherent nature – of tapping into this ability that we have, of being able to dive into the metaphysical suite of frequencies. That is intuition; it allows us to know things because we are part of a collective consciousness. And so, I think sometimes, when we're talking about intuition, we're also talking about the collective consciousness. You and I can dial into what everybody else knows because on a cellular level we're still connected to every other human being.
     If I need to know something, I need to just go into that space to get that information. And I can't tell you how I got that information but now I

have it, I can do this ting. So when you even talk about culture, sometimes it's like, 'How is it that Black Americans are doing what they are doing, and we're doing what we're doing over here?'

But you could put all of us in a room and we'd just get it. It's not just because of social media, because before social media came about, we were still doing that.

Kevin That's the interesting thing, and you just sparked something in my head – the reason that there is this literal fight against intuition (or the understanding of something instinctively, without that need for conscious reasoning), that resistance comes from capitalism not knowing how to make it profitable, so therefore, it must not be important.

Like when they say, 'Get rid of that. You're too emotional,' they're actually saying 'We can't commercialise these places you're tapping into so you need to live in these boxes instead – blonde Jesus, straight male – rather than, say, the multiple varieties of gods and genders that enrich this world. Forget them; this is where your spirituality lives now. You pray like this now; you think like this now.' Even these algorithms in Black social media spaces – again, it's about the profitability of the thing.

Kelechi Yes, but again, our collective creativity remains; we remain, regardless of all the trauma that we've experienced generationally, even intergenerationally. We still remain connected in a way that the white supremacist heteropatriarchy has unsuccessfully tried to sever. Therefore, even through the restrictions of Black Twitter, etc., we are still connected. And it's so strong that they're still able to come and siphon off what they can, and then make profits from it. And yet the people who are the originators of the ideas – the culture that these corporations and non-Black people are making a profit from – are not getting much.

Or none at all. That's what I found within the advertising industry as well … where it's like, 'I'm a literal wizard of my culture.' And so when I'm in a room, I'm trying to explain that this is not only how we should convey the story we're trying to tell, and be inclusive, but also how we should respect it and give credit to its creators. And I'm always baffled that I'm being questioned on my authority in this space, even though I'm literally a product of the culture. The same culture that pays your rent in this building and allows for you to have your mistress that your kids prefer. *[Both laugh]* I'm part of the culture that does all of these things that make the world go round.

When it comes to my creative work, I've always taken a very holistic approach: drawing from the source that I'm from, the collective culture of the Black diaspora. Using it to try and make really inclusive, safe, honest work that also opens doors and doesn't just glorify myself.

Which is why, half the time, people don't even know that I've done half the things I've done – it's never, ever, about the reward or popularity. It's literally trying to create access and trying to help my skinfolk realise how powerful and important they are, how central they are to certain cogs – if not all of them – that are turning for the benefit of others.

That's important and that's powerful. I do think that is why there's such a big attack on intuition or on us believing in ourselves; this idea that we carry intuition in our cells is treated as if it's impossible, but we've shown via epigenetics how different behaviours and environments – including those that induce trauma – can cause changes that affect the way our genes work. Yet, you still question the strength of our intuition?

I want to circle back to this conversation a little later, but first I was hoping to get your thoughts on tapping into the collective consciousness – how has that helped with your own creative practice?

I've learned over time that the more work I've done on healing my trauma, the more I've found myself to literally be that human radio. But then I only really allow myself to tune into the messages from the spirits – my guides and my ancestors – and avoid anything else because there are obviously darker frequencies. Sometimes you even feel caught in the darker frequencies because people are trying you and you're just like, 'Whoa, chile! If I dial down, it's over for the girls and thou shall not try me.' *[Both laugh]*

I love what you said about it not being about you and going, 'Well look how amazing I am and all the things that I've done, right?'

Because when I'm writing these stories for my book, I make a point of saying that I've never really believed myself to be a writer. It's only other people, later on, who pointed it out to me, saying, 'No, the way that you tweet is amazing.' But I don't see myself as a writer. I know that I'm a great actress, but I don't know myself to be a writer.

But then once I started writing, especially fiction, I didn't feel so much that I was writing, but rather that I was channelling something. Because I'm reading some of these stories back and I'm like, 'Where did that come from? How did that come about? How did I know that as part of the history of this story? Where did this world come from?' But then I decided to take a breath and really hone my spiritual practice. And so my ancestors that were incredibly talented in that way manifested like that: the ones that wrote, that spoke, that were orators – and they were incredible storytellers – I asked them to use me as the vessel to write what they need to write and, within that context, I then trust the process.

Maybe psychologists and psychotherapists will have a more 'rational' explanation for what I do when writing, that by doing this I'm shutting out my conscious mind so that the subconscious can just do its thing. However, what I would say is, I understand myself to be a physical vessel of spiritual histories – ancestral histories – and I just let that come out as it will.

And so I've really enjoyed the practice of writing, even to the extent that sometimes I'll go to write, and I'll get incredibly sleepy – I could have been perfectly fine right beforehand but the moment I go to write, I get incredibly sleepy. I become frustrated, and I'll be like, 'Why the hell am I sleeping? I've got things to do. I've got deadlines to meet.' But then when I started giving in to it, I realised that it was because I wasn't meant to be writing. And then when I didn't write, something would happen in the world, and I realised that I needed that thing. To be 'in' the story again, I needed to be able to take inspiration from that specific thing happening. And so more than ever, I'm learning to surrender.

Intuition is also about surrendering. To surrender to the unknown, to surrender to the fact that your conscious mind is not as amazing as you think it is. Because what you are capable of unconsciously – what you have available to you that you haven't even tapped into yet – is full of so much potential. But that need to surrender and be vulnerable is why we're deterred, I think, from accessing it.

If we were to go down that line, the power that we would know, that we have as individuals, and thus a collective – because we wouldn't be operating from a place of fear anymore – would be vast. And that would then mean that we wouldn't tolerate rubbish governance. We wouldn't tolerate all of the inequities and injustices that are happening in the world, because we'd better understand what power source we can tap into in order to override all of that. So the best thing for the status quo is to convince us that intuition is foolish.

'Astrology is foolish . . . Tarot is foolish . . . You're so silly . . . You're demonic.' All of the indigenous practices that actually helped us to train our intuition, and taught us the power we have, we were moved away from. And it's sad that even to this day, we've got people who say if you're into Tarot you must be a witch, or you must be this or that. Yet look how much peace I've managed to find in myself. And they are the ones still scattering themselves all over the place – discombobulating themselves – because they don't know peace, even though this dogma they've subscribed to was meant to provide it.

Kevin There is a real thing within creative industries and businesses where it's a tradition to be actively hostile. It's the norm to kill each other for this great work. I don't believe in that shit. What I do believe in is a holistic environment where everybody is heard, and that feeling is of the utmost importance when creating work. But that genuinely isn't allowed, because the structures within the creative industries – particularly the advertising industry – are predominantly built around worshipping very old middle-class white men and their egos.

And these are people who have absolutely no interest in whether you're getting enough sleep, whether you're happy with the work, or whether this work is feeding you and your soul. It's just about profit. I know for a fact that my ancestors don't care about money. And so I've always been at odds with these men because they operate from a space where that's all there is.

I operate from a space where my lights are on, my fridge is full and everyone around me is good. Community. Because, good or bad, our community was all we had growing up. Those were the only surroundings we knew, and when you're in tune with your community, you can better predict your shared future – I love that for us. The only problem is the bad parts. I mean, I'm always ready for war, but should I have to be? I've spent a lot of time questioning just how much of my trauma has bled into my intuition.

Kelechi I think when you have a certain kind of childhood, you know certain things. I would say specifically for us in South London you can almost smell . . .

You know how some people can smell the rain? I feel like I can smell when beef is about to erupt. I can now see how one action is going to lead to another, which will lead to armshouse. Just from growing up in an environment where if you chat shit, you get banged. Whether that's intuition or whether that's like a very well-trained skill of observation.

Because sometimes my intuition is like, 'I want to go, I want to go, I want to go,' and so, uh, you leave the place. And then you hear later that beef started, like someone got punched up, or whatever. This happened, then that happened. And you're like, 'Well, I'm glad I didn't stay for that.' Or you're invited somewhere and you feel like you don't want to go. You don't know why, because at first glance it looks like it's going to be a cool event. But then you see after the fact what went down and you're like, 'Ah, that's why I didn't go.'

That has been on my mind of late. And I've been untangling that and forgiving myself for it. Untangling my PTSD from my intuition.

I was watching 'Heartbreak High' – the reboot – and there's this character who has autism on the show and in real life. There's one episode where she's out on a date with her girlfriend. They go to the restaurant, and she just has a hard time within this space; the lights are too bright, everything is too loud or too close, and I was like, 'Nah, maybe I need to go and have a baseline test for autism because this is how I feel in spaces.'

So I spoke to my cousin, who's a therapist. And she was like, 'Oh, no, you don't have autism. It's PTSD. It can feel similar to autism in certain ways, but it's trauma from the way that we grew up, where you're from, your father, and all of those things.

The reason entering public spaces feels so fraught is because you're constantly looking for danger. You're looking for what could go wrong. You're finding the answers to five million different scenarios in your head until you've eliminated all of those scenarios, and you've mapped out what your every potential reaction will be. So everything feels intense because your mind is swirling, overstimulated. It's a different thing to autism.'

I've done a good job as I've gone along, though, in using some of those scars as tools, so nobody – and I say this with my chest – nobody within the corporate world of advertising can walk into the room like me, read everybody's energy levels, and understand how to get to where I need to get to.

Because, first of all, I don't fear any of you, man. I've been in enough knife fights. I've also been in gunfights and had people at my door trying to bring armshouse. So their snide remarks feel like tickles compared to actual danger. All of you are sweet, I can read you all like a book. I can make you feel like we fell in love or became best friends; it's like 'Oh, you thought I was feelin' you?'

'You thought I was feelin' you? It's just PTSD.' *[Both laugh]*

But me untangling all of that is trying to, like, completely remove myself and bury that old one.

Because the amount of peace and light that I've been finding while listening to my ancestors, elders, and real-life prophets – yourself included – has been astronomical. And even if you look at my creative trajectory in the past two or three years, it's undeniable, because I've done that stuff naturally there.

But across those past few years, I've also thought about how I'm going to apply that to my practice in all ways; not just in the work, but in the way that I communicate with people day-to-day. In the way that I communicate with myself.

Kelechi So in doing that, you're achieving one of the hardest things that intuition requires, which is leaving places that you've outgrown or leaving friendships that no longer serve you. They say that when you know better, you do better. I think that is part of the reason why sometimes people ignore their intuition, and don't let it grow. Because it's a muscle. You've got to train it to get stronger, and stronger, and stronger. So you don't even have to second guess it anymore. Intuition will never lead you wrong; it's PTSD that leads out of fear.

Kevin Yes, intuition will never lead you wrong; it's PTSD or trauma that pretends to lead, but instead holds you back in the same, familiar places out of fear. How can that be calling back to culture when culture celebrates our growth?

WHAT ARE YOU BEING LED BY?

Intuition

You don't have to have the same definition as the one Kelechi and I share for intuition. It's more important that after reading this chapter, you simply realise how important your intuition is. Advertising and all the related creative industries have enough robots and automated tech moving things along, without you adding to it from a place without soul. Truly creative work of any kind needs the essence of you; your softness, your light, and even the parts of you that you're still trying to heal.

As for the commercial side? The truth is, people want to be seen and feel understood in the content they consume. This will always guarantee a sale, repeat business, and all the other things accountants worry about.

TODAY'S TAKEAWAY:

Next time you need to make a creative choice, check in on what feelings you're experiencing at that moment. Then ask yourself whether what's stirring up is coming from a place of fear, or adventure. Are you being guided by a desire for safety, or growth?

Tuning in

Intuition only wants the best for us; it's eager to add to the culture it serves to protect. It will always guide you to the best insights and, in turn, the best ideas. The sort of ideas you want to make. As a custodian of culture, you already have all the tools you need. You just need to quiet down and listen to the answers.

Final tip: make sure you're in the right space to take in those answers – mentally and physically. My creative partner and I have several different environments we visit to find our answers. If we're annoyed at our current project, you'll probably find us in a CeX store; the visual of video games on shelves is always enough to calm us down. Conversely, if it's true peace we're after, you'll likely find us at one of several different galleries. Your external environment shapes your inner one, and vice versa.

10

RIDER

I've been a part of numerous collaborations or teams that were created to help change culture. To protect the culture, and enforce it. That has always been one of my main focuses.

Although those pairings were all set up with the best of intentions, the truth of the matter is that not all collaborations end well.

I think, naïvely, we can tend to believe that creating with a friend is an easy thing to do. Because, after all, they're your friend – you know one another inside out. You create memories and moments together. They're your safe space, and vice versa.

Nevertheless, none of that is the same as actually working together. All the projects I've been a part of have been successful; they either gave birth to new spaces or, for a period in time, gave people the respite they needed.

As an example, there was a time I ran the '90s hip hop, R&B, and garage night Bounty with a few people who – at the time – were friends. It ran for some four years, and was one of the biggest nights around. And then we stopped. I think, if I was writing this then, I'd definitely have some choice words to describe that break-up – but writing this from where I'm at now, I see why it had to happen. Hold on to that thought though, as I'll circle back round to it by the end.

After that period, I had a lot of self-doubt in my ability to collaborate and work with others. I mean, I knew I had the dedication; I knew I was hard-working. So I spent a long time doubting my personality, and how it was received by others.

I really overthought that for some time, and ended up shying away from people in general. As you'll discover in the following conversation, my favourite thing is to be a rider for those who need it. That's a strange one, because I'm definitely an introvert. But that's never affected my need and love for helping others.

The change that ended up happening for me was simply realising that I'd been working with the wrong people – wrong on the level of ego, imagination, and speed of thought. That's not to imply anyone was slow; I'm saying that everyone works at different rates, and at some points, I was too far ahead. At others, I was impatient at myself for not being quick enough.

I remember thinking of Bounty as a space to bring Black and Brown talent together. At times I would talk about starting a festival where everyone could come together and network, a space where all lived experiences of Blackness could hang out and get to know one another. Get excited by one another. This idea was laughed at. Not in a mean way – though it hurt at the time – but more from just not understanding the vision I was trying to convey. To be honest, the way I likely pitched that vision back then would probably have had me looking like that conspiracy theory meme.

Months later, Afropunk became a thing. I read about the festival, attended the launch, and thought, 'This is what I was talking about, so why was the idea laughed away?' Some years later, I decided to go into advertising for a while.

Looking back, I can see it was a way for me to exit social media and keep my head down. When Tom and I first became friends and creative partners, we took that pairing very seriously; we went on a double date where we met each other's partners, all while sitting through a 'Friday the 13th' marathon at the Prince Charles Cinema. I'd spent so much time thinking about working relationships that my obsession with vetting new friends and collaborators had become wild. What I found remarkable about Tom was how he thought that, even though at the time he didn't know the reason why, my wild was acceptable.

For those that don't know, in the advertising world a creative team is responsible for coming up with the ideas that help sell a product, or solve a creative problem a brand has. As an example: When Audi needed to make it clear that luxury was affordable to Gen Z, we created a game for them on Snapchat – their preferred habitat at that point in time. The Snapchat lens we made had almost three million plays within its first twenty-four hours online, and 275,000 prospective young customers swiped through to Audi's PCP finance page from the app. When it debuted, the campaign was one of the most successful of its kind on Snapchat.

A creative team works together to develop conceptual – and in our case, culturally impactful – campaigns. Depending on what is needed, and the type or size of the brand, these sit above, below, or through 'the line'. Originally based on an accounting principle, 'the line' is used in advertising to indicate which marketing space the brand needs to sit in to reach a particular audience. Above the line (ATL) is all about brand building – stuff like the big TV ads. Below the line (BTL) is more about targeting specific conversations, keeping existing customers loyal, or getting those who are thinking of buying past the point of conversion (that is, turning them from potential customers into actual ones). Through the line (TTL) is a mixture of both: if you've seen an idea pop up across TV, print, and social media, then that's a TTL campaign.

The team is made up of an art director, who predominantly rules over imagery, and a copywriter, who looks after the language. In our team, Tom is the copywriter and I'm the art director, although we have the skillsets for both roles, and naturally switch between them. We're hired as a team, fired as a team, and yes, interview as a team. We're paid the same wage; everything is 50/50.

We've been a team for just under a decade and only ever really had one argument. We've evolved past the roles of a typical advertising team, and now function as a creative team in a much broader sense – creative friends and scriptwriters. Even with this book, who else would help edit it than my creative partner?

At the same time, I've also founded both Pocc and 2Pocc with Nana – spaces that are specifically designed to bring together the creative global majority in different, safe outlets, while also providing a networking space that specifically caters to the UK, US, and Netherlands.

In short, collaborating requires the correct collaborator. Looking back, I can see that now. My thoughts do not have any regard for speed limits. Often, when creating, I will speak in the middle of thinking about something, and – back when doing Bounty – I would get annoyed at not being understood. Now? Tom and I are on the same wavelength. If you were to overhear us conversing while working out a creative solve, you would think we were talking gibberish, as we often speak in half sentences, or comic book and film references.

Same with Nana, our conversations are half words, half song lyrics, and dance moves.

The reason my idea for a festival didn't make sense to those I was running it past was because I was collaborating with people who, conceptually, think differently to me, or indeed, don't think conceptually at all. That's not to say I was better than them; I can't sit here and say that I really took the time to figure out their language. I'm saying that collaborating on a project and supporting a project are two different things. There are different roles to be played, and at that time I couldn't tell the difference between them.

What truly frustrates me about the breakdown of my working relationships – and friendships – with the others involved in Bounty is that because of my enthusiasm I forgot to check what role I was needed in. Now, whenever I start a new collaboration, the first thing I do is define my role and how I can best participate. Because seeing a project through to completion is a bonus; for me, the real goal is building true collaboration and community.

Once you're clear on what goals you're aiming for together, the real fun can start. (That's perhaps why those last few years at Bounty weren't enjoyable anymore).

"BEING A BLACK WOMAN, AND HAVING ANOTHER BLACK WOMAN TO LEAN ON, GENUINELY IS THE BIGGEST BLESSING TO ME."

A CONVERSATION WITH

AUDREY INDOME

Podcaster, presenter, and one third of The Receipts

ON COLLABORATION

Kevin I feel like you're a real team player, that you will help get the thing done and see it through. You're a rough rider. And in my head, that relates very closely to the idea of collaboration and communication within the workplace. But I do think, within the Black community, collaboration means a completely different thing; it's part of survival. The collaboration here is often from a space of reacting, rather than creating. On the other hand, I've now been working with Tom as my collaborator for the better part of a decade. In that time, bit by bit, I've realised that there's no need for a survival mode. We're just enjoying the creativity of working together, and that's the beauty of collaboration. I'm afforded this perspective and comfort because of the privileges Tom possesses as a white cis-het man. I'd be remiss not to mention that, as a pair, we also function as a diversity hire's wet dream.

Prior to that though, my experiences of collaboration in the creative industry had really sat within that 'crabs in a bucket' mentality, you know? Like, we will help to a certain point – and then we'll exit. But for me it's like, 'Wait, what else can we build?'

Would you say it's fair to describe you as a rough rider? And what does that mean for you in terms of collaboration?

> **Audrey** Do you know what? That is spot on. That's exactly who I am, in all aspects of my life but especially in my work. Obviously, when we do the podcast I'd say I'm the middle-ground. I've always played that role of being the go-to, in-between person. I think it's a personality thing. I do think rearing and upbringing has got a lot to do with it as well. I don't know how much of it is rearing versus just me being me, but I do think my upbringing had a lot to do with me wanting to be kind of, in the middle, or maybe not seen as much. Which sounds funny, considering what I do. But even in that space, I try not to be in the foreground too much.
>
> I think that it feeds nicely into my idea of collaboration, though. I thrive off it. I think I work better alongside other people. I don't know if it's a confidence thing. I don't know if it's because maybe I've never felt like me alone is, like, good enough, or my ideas are strong enough. But I do like that backbone of support that you get with collaboration, and just combining ideas. You get the best out of me when I'm amongst other people.

I get you. I like being part of a team and playing my position, holding other people down. There is an immense amount of joy that I get in the idea that when I'm no longer here, I will be described as loyal and a real backbone of the thing. That's something I'm really, really protective of.

I think I had to go through different stages of learning what collaboration is, because often you meet other creatives who are just vying to get their ideas out. To just make what they want to make. Or just, to make the cash. And that's never been my goal; I've always wanted to do the best possible work.

Sometimes those other creatives are saying, 'Well, I want to do this, and I want to do it this way.' And I'm like, 'That's cool. We can do whatever you want to do. Like, it's not that deep! But also, have you thought about this?' I'm trying to help them get to the best possible place and their ego gets in the way. And when I started working with Tom, specifically, he was the same as me. And I know you girlies don't believe in star signs, but Tom is also a Virgo, and we're born like a week apart.

And so from there, it was very much like, if I had an idea, and he was like, 'That doesn't make any sense at all.' There was a freedom in that all of a sudden, because it was just like, 'Oh, he's not trying to just rubbish the thing.' Or he'll take something from it and build on it, and vice versa. I think finding Tom was the moment that I really, consciously realised just how much I like being part of a team. And looking back, I felt the same when I used to work in retail, as well. I really enjoyed having a good boss, and like, having their back.

Audrey I was exactly the same.

Kevin Yeah, but I don't know where that comes from. I just really wanted my boss to do well. And like, I am going to be on time and I am going to be honest. All of these things. I would really war with my boss's boss if they tried it.

> I was exactly the same, like, exactly the same. And I think for me – I don't know if it's problematic, but – I do really enjoy the validation as well. I like being praised. And I feel like sometimes when you work in a team, it's kind of guaranteed. I'm not necessarily the most talkative in meetings, for example, but I do think when I say something it slaps. Do you know what I mean? Sometimes when you're like, on your own or whatever, you don't necessarily have anyone to be like, 'Yo, that's a dope idea.' I think that's another part of true collaboration that I really enjoy; the fact that people can validate your ideas, or just reaffirm them.
>
> I was a PA for a really, really long time. Before I was a PA, I was in retail, and I had that exact same mentality, like I proper used to ride out for my boss. I would hype everybody up about meeting our targets. And I knew that I wasn't necessarily going to do that full-time, but when I'm in a space, I like to give my all – it doesn't matter what it is. For now I'm here, and I'm gonna go in. And I also don't wanna be like a spare part in a team; I want to feel like I'm integral. And I guess it all links back to the idea of getting that validation or praise. Recognition, you know.

Do you think it's linked to pride in your work as well? Like, the fact that you actively don't want to make rubbish work?

> Definitely. Like what you were saying about Tom, just wanting to have the best outcome and create the best things? I feel the same. It doesn't matter if they didn't go with your idea, you're part of a team for the best outcome. I generally wanna be affiliated with things that are good and that are gonna leave a print. And I don't really want to do anything needy, if I have any control over it.

Do you feel like that's ever slightly backfired? And in a sense, I'm asking myself that question now, too. Because I'm one of those people who, I think when you first find me on the internet, you're not entirely sure who or what I am. But as you start to look, you see that I'm always sharing my creative knowledge. There are people for whom I've played a part in getting record deals, TV roles, or other jobs – I'll set up meetings, I'll link people up. Because my black book is everyone's black book, and I've always been like that. I can give you all my resources, and what you're going to then do with them is what only you could do. You're not stealing off my plate, as I'm already over here doing what I'm gonna do. There's no need for me to ever be in competition with anyone. And there have been people who've have stopped and said, 'Hold on a minute. He's the guy that put this together. He's why this exists.' I like that because it's always about the community and not the fame. But I'd be lying if I didn't say there were moments when I thought, 'Oh. You forgot to credit me.' And that doesn't feel nice. I like simple things, and a 'thank you' is one of them. It doesn't even have to be a public thing half the time, it's just letting me know that you appreciate the help.

I wanted to say all of that just to give a bit more context behind the question, because I guess for me I do sometimes feel like the way I like to work has maybe backfired in some ways.

> Yeah, all the time. And it's really hard. When we started the podcast, it wasn't like we planned to be representative of a certain thing so others can follow our lead. That would be a lie; we just wanted to get in the studio and chat shit, essentially. But then it turned into this bigger thing, and the longer you're doing something, the more you realise the impact of it, that it's helping people. That you're someone people can look to. I've always been very honest about my journey, and it hasn't always been smooth sailing. I've tried so many different things that have flopped and failed. But then I see it all the time, how people can take the things you say – your thoughts – and just repeat them. They don't even reword it, and I wish they would, because at least then I could sit back and think, 'Oh, is this just a coincidence?' instead of knowing you just stole my entire thought there. You know that they got it from you, and it's really frustrating. I see it a lot online, people just regurgitating things and projecting it as their own. It really winds me up.

You know what? On that note, I'm gonna take something back that I just said. About it being okay for people acknowledging my input in private, because, actually, whilst that is nice, it'd be a lot nicer if you did just say it out loud. I've got so many kids on the internet – whether they're directors or photographers – that have literally taken bits and bobs of what I've done in the specific way that I do it, and they're just running wild with it. You're all my sons and daughters, amazing, so where's the Father's Day card? Wagwarn for that? Am I a deadbeat dad? Did I not give you everything?

Sometimes I meet big, known directors and I'm just thinking, 'I would like to believe it's all a coincidence, and you don't actually know who I am.' But then they'll list off my catalogue, and tell me in private that they loved when I said this, or did that. So why then – when they're in those spaces where they're being asked to share what inspires or excites them – why is my name never coming off their lips?

Collaboration is a bit like love; it can really break your heart. But I have to get back up and just try again with a new team, you know? You have to get back out there. So with that in mind, how do you facilitate collaborations? How do you set up the space to create within your team? Like, for me, I've said this elsewhere, but I will learn your star sign quickly so I know how to start communicating with you from the off. I also know that, whilst I'm very much an introvert, I can be loud. When I walk into a room I can change the energy in that space if I want to. I'm really aware of the energy I'm giving out so that when we're collaborating, I can make you feel as comfortable as possible. Are there any specific approaches you use?

Audrey I think firstly, one thing that really irks me is when people want to collaborate with me and they don't even know the basics of what I do. It's like, you don't have to be a fan, but I need to feel as though you're sincere. It's work, init, and if we're gonna work together I want it to be mutually beneficial. But there have been so many times when people have put something forward and it's clear that you've just caught wind of this wave, and you want in. Even then, I'm not actually angry at that, but just do your research first. At least spell my name correctly.

I like to give people that respect. To me, that's just basic. So that's where I start: making sure that before I present myself to anybody, that I know a little bit about them, and that it's clear why I want to work with them. You know, that I've done my reading and this whole thing makes sense for both of us. And like, these things are really obvious but a lot of people just don't pay attention to that stuff. You say please don't DM me, here's the email address – and they still DM you. If you're not paying attention to those small details early on of how people want to be approached, then that's really setting the tone for what's to come later. How you choose to handle those initial moments really says a lot about you.

I remember one time I was watching this 'Breakfast Club' interview with Nicki Minaj. And she was fuming because they hadn't listened to her new music. You know, she'd come on to do an interview. And she started asking them questions about songs on the album, and none of them had any clue. And she went off on them. And she was just like, 'Y'all have got me up here and you haven't even listened to the album.' That was a real takeaway for me, just being aware of what the goal is for the person you're meant to be collaborating with. What have they got going on? Why are they here? What are they promoting?

Kevin I remember that interview. And she was one-hundred per cent right.

We're having meetings at the moment about script work, and the ones that don't vibe well are where you can really tell that they've read, like, four pages of the script before they jumped on the call. But we have the best time in the ones where they start throwing up all these little nuances, to the point where we have to ask ourselves, 'Did we write that?' It's just clear that they're really involved in the thing and have their own thoughts. That gets me really hyped. Immediately, I wanna do right by them; I don't wanna let them down.

I guess within that, the word 'kindness' is popping up for me. Because there is a real sense of kindness in true collaboration; you're choosing to give someone the space to have a voice alongside or even in front of you. You're helping them do the thing and it's just wrapped up in this sense of care. And that's something that I feel speaks to how Black women move through this world more widely: you've been through absolute horrors on this earth, and yet you're still the kindest, sweetest, most loving beings.

If I were you lot, I would've killed everyone else off by now. I'd have had enough. The Woman King, I'm telling you! I get it. Yet you still turn around and forgive, give, and nurture. I'm always in awe of that. That's why I'm so like, 'He said what to you? Give me the address, I will fight. Point them out.'

But do you have an idea of where that kindness comes from? Or the fact that kindness is intrinsic to collaboration?

Yeah, one-hundred per cent. I think the basis of everything you just said is that, as Black women, this shit ain't easy, you know. And that idea of collaboration, in that sense, it's a blessing and curse. Because that collaboration comes from the fact you're fighting such a big monster, and you don't want to do everything by yourself. So that sisterhood is vital. It's vital. You don't want to go into those spaces exposed and alone, because there are a lot of eyes looking at you; a lot of demons that you've got to fight single-handedly.

So the idea of collaborating with someone that looks like you, that can relate to your experiences, that can go in with you, kind of holding hands, is really special. And it's needed. And I do think intrinsically, it does come from a place of scarcity, of not being allowed access to these spaces, and it being quite scary. To go in on your own and do things – whether it be presenting an idea in public, or in the corporate world – that shit is scary. And I think that's why we have those little special moments where, you know, you walk into an office and you immediately make a connection with the other Black woman in there. Those kinds of moments are really special.

So I do think that kind of collaboration has come from a place of necessity for us, and not necessarily having the luxury to just be fearless with everything we want to do. And kindness is a huge element of it – to be able to say that I'm going to minimise myself a little bit for the greater cause. And I feel like that's such a Black thing; that's what we've been doing, and I feel like that's just what we know. There's this idea of a greater reward at the end, because you're essentially opening the door for other people. I think that's the greatest kindness you can ever give, to dim your shine for the greater good. Being a Black woman, and having another Black woman to lean on, genuinely is the biggest blessing to me, and I think that is then shown in our work as well. A hundred per cent.

But, conversely, I've had so many working relationships that have gone left. And I think one of the best ways that I've dealt with things is just like – it kind of goes back to what we were saying at the beginning – is this thing going to be good? I've had working relationships that have gone left and, to me, the product wasn't going to be good. So I've had to pull myself away. And that's the best thing I could do for the sake of the project. If it means that I have to sacrifice myself so this thing can go ahead, or so that I can go ahead, so be it.

I've definitely been in situations where this thing has impacted my mental health so badly, and I think one tip I would give is that it is okay to walk away – even if you do feel like you've put your heart and soul into something. If it's impacting you and your wellbeing in that way, then let it go. I've definitely fought to stay on things that just weren't making sense, to the point where it was starting to really impact my creative flow because I was so unhappy in the situation. But if you're not good, there's no way you're going to make a good product.

And I know sometimes that you can make the best things off the back of hard times, through adversity, stuff like that. Absolutely. But I feel like you can tell the difference between 'No, we've just got to fight for this thing; we've got all these obstacles, but we can knock them down,' versus the situation just outright being bad for you and your mind. And so, yeah, I've had to walk away from situations where it came down to me or the project. Or even, me or the friendship. And that's one thing that's been so hard for me – especially because of the way I was raised as a Black African woman.

You fight, you stay, you don't give up. So learning that walking away isn't giving up was one of the toughest things.

Kevin Yeah, same. Being from Croydon, I definitely had that fighter mentality, but there was a real moment for me when I realised that it's even more powerful to just be like, 'Deuces, I'm out.' And then on top of that, the realisation that you can do that in a really quiet, professional way. There's no need for a big wahala. That's been my journey – bit by bit – because collaborating should be the easiest thing in the world. If everybody's coming to the table without ego, then we're gonna make the best possible work. Don't get me wrong, there are hierarchies to things, people are in charge of certain things, and there are boundaries not to cross because those people have the skillset to best manage that part of the project, and vice versa. But that's just trusting in everyone to bring what they individually offer to the table. Collaboration should be easy. The moment that you find there is no ease, then you're probably in the wrong space.

We worked with someone once who firmly believed that chaos bred the best creative. If you're reading this, I do love you, little Irish man. But he would actively ignite chaos on a project, and it would mean that people would just start beefing with one another. Now, mind you, I would see all of this from a space of being the only Black creative in this office. So I'm always perched back, like, 'What is everyone doing?' And I would just see the circus and be like, 'Yo!' And they'd be like, 'Yeah, because when everyone's depressed and almost wants to take themselves out, that's when the best idea emerges.' And I would think, 'No, not me. There's got to be an easier, better way.' 'Cause this was like 'Hunger Games' shit, right in the office. It was wild.

Tom and I left there after a year, knowing we would never do that to each other. We check in on each other's mental health. We've always been like that and, within that, we've always got the best results.

I GOT YOU, BABE

Are you part of the team...

Be clear on your roles; it's very easy to walk into a situation thinking you're a collaborator with real autonomy and able to make meaningful business choices ... only for your 'partner' to be the one giving all the orders.

Be clear on what role you are taking, and who is responsible for what. Sometimes you're just meant to be friends, and that's okay.

... or just backing it?

TODAY'S TAKEAWAY:

When it comes to business, Tom and I have a simple rule: nothing will ever be more important than our friendship. The oath works. The point is that I couldn't make that oath with just any friend. You have to find the correct collaborators.

Biggie had a rule about this

Wanna support a friend? Do that: buy all their shit and show up to every show. That might be your role in that moment, rather than trying to force a collaboration where there shouldn't be one.

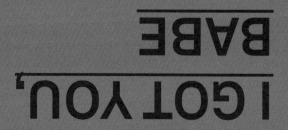

11

HOME

PART ONE:
DEFINING HOME

'The Big Idea' is loud and will not be ignored. It communicates a brand, and the products it sells, in a way that's at once utterly simple and endlessly compelling. You just get it straight away; no need for an explanation, no room for misunderstanding or doubt. In its very best form, the Big Idea is a statement from a brand that none of its competitors could ever make, claim, or call home.

Clients are always looking for something that they can own – a marketing edge that is bold and unexpected, that can also last far longer than that initial launch before whimpering away with a few supporting social posts. They're looking for a space to occupy that has strong foundations (wink wink); something they can future-proof so it grows and adapts with them. An idea they can confidently speak about and stand behind. I think this, ultimately, is a task of defining, not designing. With the former, you're working from the ground up before collecting the keepsakes; you're looking at the details of the brand that establish its story. Its history, its heritage … its very reason for being.

Doing this connects the brand to a core purpose, and regardless of how your sins weigh on whatever scale you deem relevant, we all long for purpose. Because of this, we find it a compellingly simple way to measure relevance.

Example: The Green Party has this attitude of being welcome-to-all built into its foundations, so it never feels as though they're judging potential voters for not being 'green' enough. This ensures that the Green Party's values feel like somewhere anyone who cares about the environment can call home, no matter how actively they campaign for change as individuals (if indeed they do at all). Coming at branding from a space of aesthetics without essence, however, is akin to the photoshopped, air-brushed images we all spot a mile away. They're just not real.

In part one of this chapter, the conversation with Paula shows the importance of honouring all of the elements that make a project – or home – authentic. I've said this before and I'll say it again: you can't make a pound with ninety-nine pennies – every single detail is important and relevant. In part two, my conversation with Africa looks at how you then protect that authentic space. Ensuring that what you've made is built to last is vital if you want to stand apart from the crowd in a meaningful way.

"EVEN WHEN THERE IS NO ROOM, THERE'S STILL ROOM."

PAULA SUTTON

Stylist, writer, and interior design blogger

ON HOME

Kevin So, one of the things I wanted to talk to you about, for me, kind of relates back to this thing we have in advertising called 'The Big Idea' – the thing that all of the other parts of the brand's story, personality, product points, or whatever hang down from. And some of those Big Ideas, or concepts, can go on and on for years, like when BT started off with the advert about that same guy who went on to meet his partner, and then integrated with her family. And it just kept going, whatever they were saying always came back to this clear space that we all became familiar with.

And for me, in order to sell those ideas to clients, I've always reinvented the question in my head and asked myself, 'How do I sell you your perfect home? What would you need? How many bedrooms? How many bathrooms? What sort of amenities? This, that and the third.' And a lot of people found this method quite weird, but I've actually got a great track record from it. And so naturally, when I was thinking about this idea of home, and what it can be, I knew I wanted to talk to you and . . . do you know 'The Vitamin D Project'?

Paula Ah yes, Africa. Love her.

Good, okay – so then I thought, 'I need to talk to Paula. And I need to talk to Africa.' And specifically, I want to talk to you about the importance of actually building a home; seeking comfort and creating that safe space. One of the sayings that I live by is that 'You only find peace in your grave and in your home.' I really do believe in that. But what does 'home' mean to you, and why is it so important?

It is the most important thing in my life, that sense of home. And it's actually been the framework for so many of my decisions over the years – including why I find myself in the depths of rural England, where I knew no one at first. My sense of home is all about gathering family and friends together, and so my space always needs the ability to have many people under one roof; whether that's in their own bedroom, on the sofa, or on the floor – it's all about making those places as comfortable as possible, for as many people as possible. Because all through my life, having parents from the Caribbean, you're always having family coming over from abroad. There were always people, there were always parties, and there were always guests staying over. And I've totally inherited that.

Even after moving to Norfolk from London, when we were just settling in and everyone else was getting on with their lives, my sense of home was still such that I had to be prepared for anyone to come to the door and need a bed for the night. So it's always been about comfort and having a place that was able to welcome whoever arrived with open arms. You know, my cupboards are full of tablecloths and napkins and cushion covers and everything. In fact, all the things I collect are based around entertaining, and looking after as many people as possible.

My heritage is Jamaican, and that's why I'm smiling so broadly, because I know exactly what you're talking about. Even when there is no room, there's still room. And I think that's often an inherent result of the histories of Black and Brown people – or in fact any marginalised people. Innately, whether we realise it or not, we're put in a position where we have to take up space – and that might be really loudly, or just as an impetus to do something, because it's the first time anyone in the family has done it, and everything in between.

And so, within that, I've been thinking about the fact that, at least for me, it's not just the act of taking up space and like, yes, making a political statement about inclusion. It's also about what we then bring to that space, the abundance of love we have to give. I talk all the time online about trying to find some kind of land where I can have my own moat. That's really my introverted side coming out; the idea of being in the middle of nowhere is my goal. But being able to fill that place – with people, with love – is even more of a triumph.

Paula I relate so much, because I do call myself an introverted extrovert. I'm a sociable recluse. I've got the side of me that is welcoming; no one can come to the door and be turned away. But at the same time, I need my space to regroup, too. I know you're a Virgo; I'm a Virgo too. Seventh of September. I don't know whether there's a connection there, but I have the exact same thing. I'm quite happy on my own, but when people are here, I'm the life and soul – you know, I'm Auntie Paula. *[Both laugh]*

Only now and then, I have to open the doors and have a party. My mother was exactly the same. But my father? Total opposite. My father was sociable, sociable, sociable. He was a politician – a diplomat of sorts – and his life was all about entertaining and making people feel good. He would often be the one to suggest a party, and my mum's automatic reaction was 'no'. But then the doors would open, the people would come in, and she'd become the life and soul, too.

No never really meant no with my mother. I don't say it as often as she did, but it was more of an initial response for her, almost as a protection. I think sometimes, when you imagine bringing people into your domain – because of the people we are, because you're probably a very generous host too – it becomes too big. So what scares you, and stops you from wanting to do that straightaway is often that ... well, if you're going do to it, you're going to do it large. You're going to do it big. And that can be quite scary. Until you're doing it, and then of course you're enjoying it.

But sometimes that perfectionism actually paralyses you. Because you're wanting it to be so wonderful, it sort of consumes you. I went through a stage, here in Norfolk, where I wanted the house to be perfect, everything just right. And that was actually my low period; it was a few years after arriving here, and I was just consumed by the thought that the children needed to be okay in this different space. And then the house became quieter, and I realised that I had become a little bit joyless; I needed to have people in my life more often, but my perfectionism was preventing that from happening.

I had to learn to relax, to chill out a bit, and remind myself that it's not about perfection, it's about communicating. How you communicate. That's why I do so much now, because my New Year's resolution – I think maybe four, five years ago – it was to say, 'YES!' Just say yes to stuff. And in doing that, 'yes' becomes this wonderful, joyful thing. Saying yes meant that my life very suddenly changed and opened up, and I was back to being me again.

Because of a few years there, I'd lost myself. Finding that again has been an amazing thing. Getting older is helpful. Getting older is a wonderful thing. It's something I bang on about a lot because there's such a freedom and openness to rebirth, to losing your inhibitions. And not caring – it's wonderful. It's a privilege to get older, and not everyone manages it.

Kevin I know what you mean. If I look back to when I first got into advertising – and even, somewhat, when I started in film – I was thinking so much about hitting all of these supposed checkmarks and meeting someone else's criteria. And when you do that for long enough, before you know it, you're just on auto-pilot. If you're not checking in on yourself – on what actually matters to you – then you'll look up one day and realise that what you're doing just isn't true to the essence of you anymore. I found that within my work where I was trying to make it perfect, as you said about your home. I'm not crippled by that anymore; I do the work, I put it out, and the response is the response. And there will be some lessons to learn in there for next time, for that next thing. That's what's more important, and that's how you get closer to what really matters to you. Like, what is the essence that you're trying to say? Does it need to be worded in that way? And if you lose that thread, you do look back and think, 'Am I even enjoying this right now?' If that happens, you have to come back to yourself and what feels right for you, in your space. Because that idea of perfectionism can actually just be another comfort zone that it's time to leave.

Absolutely. I've had several periods of my life where I've had to let go of that. My childhood was incredible; I had such a loving, wonderful home. And then, when I turned eighteen, suddenly my parents left to go back to the Caribbean. They'd spoken about it for years, as many Caribbean parents do, that they'd only intended to come here for a few years, but had ended up staying for thirty. So one day it was, 'All right, you've done your A levels. We're going now.'

Except I did terribly in my A levels. The world suddenly became more scary: Do I go back with them, or do I stay here and retake my exams? So suddenly, I went from one day having this very close, tight-knit family to being on my own, because I chose to stay. I love Grenada, but I'm a South London girl. At eighteen I thought that Grenada was a tiny island, something I wasn't ready for yet. And so my perception of home suddenly changed overnight. I was very thrown for a few years; I ended up going off to university in Bristol the following year, but for a while I didn't really have a home in England.

My parents eventually bought a place for my brother and myself, but he was older than me and had his own friends there. And so I had a feeling of displacement for quite a few years, until I was able to make my own home.

Going to Grenada and being with my parents was lovely, but I didn't feel that my bedroom there was ever permanent. Because I hadn't made it. So when I bought my first flat with my now husband, it was the first time in almost a decade that I felt I had roots again. And I do feel that that's one of the reasons why home is so important to me now. And that's why I show my home, and why I talk about the joy of home and the love of home. Because that five-year period of not having my own place was tough. I don't want my children to ever feel displaced and not know where home is. So it's been a very strong thing for me.

It's so interesting because your story has parallels to mine. I'm also from South London (as are Kelechi and Candice). I'm originally from Thornton Heath, Croydon—

Paula I was born at Mayday Hospital!

Kevin So was I!

Must be something in the water. *[Both laugh]*

So, I grew up with my mum, one younger brother, and two younger sisters. Our home was a two-bedroom flat. And it was a weird one; not everyone around us had their parents together. So when I was really young, we were almost a special family – 'Your dad still in the house.' Yet there were certain things that weren't happy, and being older now, I'm able to look at some of my dad's behaviours in a new light. We didn't talk then about looking after your mental health, self-care, or anything like that.

So yes, I grew up in South Norwood in that flat, but my home was my grandparents' home. Because as soon as I walked through that door . . . that, to me, was Jamaica. That was Mandeville, that was one of those spaces that my grandparents taught me about. There was always fruit – all the fruit, any fruit – on the table, everything's there. 'We've got leftover rice and chicken, what do you want?' Everything was always there. Even now, the colour orange is so important to me. Because any time you left my grandparents' house, my grandma would appear and say, 'Here's orange, take this with love.' Love, always.

Then I got older. At eighteen, my parents split up, and my father didn't really do what he was meant to do. So I became the man of the house out of nowhere, and I had bills to pay, things to contribute to. And I could see very quickly that I was just gonna get drawn into a narrative that I'd seen many times before. I'd be like thirty-five and still at home, trying to support everyone in the same way and not really going for the things I wanted to go for. So I left at nineteen, very quickly. I knew I had to. I knew I was still going to try and help, but I had to go and live my own life, too.

Since then I've lived in East, West and North London. But South has it for me; all the other areas are just really weird. Then I met my other half, who's northern; his family are from Croston – about an hour from the Lake District. My time became split between north and south, and I found myself spending more time in the countryside, experiencing things I'd never experienced before.

I always thought I hated the rain, until I was in the countryside. You get soaked? You start a fire and you're all around, getting dry. And my perspective started to change; I realised I can move outside of London. I do love South London, inherently, but I realised I need to be by water, by things that are so much bigger, and have been here for so much longer than me, just to humble me in the moment.

And what you were saying about leaving the home of your parents in a way reminded me of that. I love my mum and I want her to be in beautiful surroundings, but I don't know if, after that moment of leaving, I continued to look at that space as home. Whereas my grandparents' house in Thornton Heath is still home. Even details like their little green door, the number on the door, the way the street looks – these all turn up in my work, probably only for me to recognise, but they're my ways of paying homage to what home meant to me and continues to mean to me.

Absolutely, that's what you do. When my parents first moved over, they had an incredible scope of choices for how and where they lived. So when they came over, they started off in Hammersmith, and then looked to Notting Hill. And now . . . this is a folklore story – I don't know anything about this personally. But the story goes that they were buying a house in Notting Hill, a big, four-storey, stucco-fronted house. The ones that cost about £10 million now.

But this was back in the late '50s, and it belonged to a chap from Grenada, who they'd known about, who looked very smart and successful. He took them to look at this house, saying it was absolutely 'made for them'. But he'd left the keys back at his office, so they'd all have to go through the window. If they came back for a second viewing, he'd be able to let them in with the keys next time.

So they went through the window and took a look around and thought, 'My goodness, the streets of London really are paved with gold; we can afford this house.' So they gave the gentleman their deposit – this cash they'd been saving up – right there and then. My brother had just been born and they wanted their first family home, and they thought they'd be better buying it from someone they knew from back home. And of course, they never saw him again, because he didn't own the house.

So that was their first deposit gone, but they were determined to have a home. They saved up again, and this time they moved across to South London. So that's when they bought in Grange Road, Thornton Heath, opposite the park. I had the little box room at the front; my view, for the first eight years of my life, was just trees and green.

So when people say, 'Oh, you were born in South London,' talking about it as though it was purely concrete? For me, that just wasn't the case. My early years of life were just green, and I thought that all of London was green. It's interesting that you say you need to be near water, because I need to be able to see trees from my bedroom window. Even now, I look out of my bedroom window and I see trees, and that's because of my formative years. That's what London was to me.

So when people ask me why I'm in the countryside, it's because I had countryside in London. I was very fortunate in those early days. And as my parents' fortunes increased, our houses got a bit nicer, the gardens a bit bigger. Before they left, we lived in this very beautiful, big Edwardian house with seven bedrooms and an acre around it – and this is all in London, still.

My parents, as all of that generation did, came here with nothing on their feet. And I'm so proud of them, because they built on through all sorts of crap they had to put up with – especially in the '70s and '80s – the crap anyone who's Black or Brown is familiar with. But no matter where they moved, they always went for trees; a garden was so important to them. So you can draw a line directly from the day of my birth to where I am today.

Sometimes it is those little things that you see when you're young – whether it's water, or trees – that stay with you. You seek those things out later on in life when you need that sense of calm, that sense of peace. That sense of coming home.

PART TWO:

AUTHENTICITY

In the words of 'Sex and the City's Samantha Jones, 'Motherfucker's concise.'

'The Big Idea' comes in many forms, but the greatest ones are – almost invariably – simple, relatable, and (in my humble opinion the most important trait), honest.

Because if the idea is honest, then inherently it's also relatable. And by proximity, the brand is too. I've found that the most honest ideas are about showing up authentically, and wearing that authenticity. This has been the starting point for all of the Big Ideas, or homes, I've built for clients. Why do I call them homes, you ask?

Simple. Where else are you your most authentic self?

Before you dive into the next conversation, what I will say is that the purpose of this chapter is to make you think about your own authenticity, and how you may or may not have had to fight for it. How you've had to prove it. Apologise for it. Hold on to it. Marginalised groups the world over know what it feels like to be doubted through the lens of distrust, and if we're not careful, we can find we're taking on the weight of that distrust for ourselves, corroding the very qualities that we hold most dear.

In short, if you're going to help a client be authentic and honest then you're going to have to define what those words mean for you, and how you act on them. Especially in such an image-obsessed world as the one we're in today. If you're not practising authenticity in your own way of being, how can you honestly help others to do the same?

"THERE'S NOTHING I CAN DO FOR YOU."

A CONVERSATION WITH

AFRICA DALEY-CLARKE

Interior stylist, writer, and founder of The Vitamin D Project

ON HOME

Kevin I wanted to talk to you about home. It'd be easier to just say that some people online look at your home as an aesthetic. The truth is that they don't understand – nor could they ever fathom – just how authentically, and how richly Black your home is.

Africa But also, Kevin, I think it's a matter of confusion that what's nice and beautiful is inherently white. The idea that if somebody Black is doing something nice, it must be a white aesthetic, and that the audience we're speaking of just doesn't know about this aesthetic yet. So when you say they don't understand how Black it actually is, I couldn't agree with you more.

It's no secret how much time I try to spend near water, in nature, in the Lakes. Yet the conversations I have around that are very similar: 'Oh, it's just a very white area.' I've always believed that there's no way an area holding such beauty could not be for me. I understand the implication, and I'm not trying to be facetious at all, but at the same time, my favourite thing is when we take up space. I love that for us.

And what I love about your home is just the little corners of it. How very Black it is, that your kids are in a safe space where they also have fun. It's a space that they're allowed to live in, and they're allowed to manipulate in any way they see fit. It is their home, too.

You made a point about, you know, the home belonging to the children. And I think as parents, one of the things that J and I do not take for granted at all, is that we don't have our children forever, right? It is such a task for us to make sure that this home – for the next eighteen years or however long – creates everything that they need. I've found that in sharing that online, it's really affirming for a lot of other Black and Brown people. But it is so offensive! Kevin, I cannot tell you why that act in itself is so offensive to so many non-Black and Brown people.

I don't think I prepared myself for that. You know, we had very humble living accommodation. I choose my words carefully, because people love to throw them back up seven years later. We had a humble flat that we made into a beautiful home. Three flats cramped into a space of one house. I thought surely, you know, we're just sharing what we are doing within those confines. How can that not be encouraging to so many other people who find themselves in that scenario?

But, I think because what I share goes beyond faceless pictures – I share a bit of my mind, I share my lows, I share my highs, I share bits about my family – I think it just became really difficult for people to absorb the fact that this wasn't a facade.

But you can dig and dig and dig, Kevin. I'm never scared for anyone to find any skeletons. Because I've already shared it all. I think that it made people feel a bit uneasy that there wasn't a rug to pull out from under our feet, because there's continuity in our life.

I think that it's the continuity aspect that rubs a lot of people up the wrong way. This concept of home that we're talking about spills over into the idea of how we speak to each other, how we dress, what we buy, what we bring into our home, who we welcome into our home – until ultimately it becomes about our entire existence.

Because Instagram's a platform inherently about image, a lot of the time you start to scratch beneath the surface of the stories others are telling, and that continuity I'm talking about just isn't there. But with us it does all connect. And so when people throw the word 'aesthetic' around? I mean, you can use it, but it's not an aesthetic. It's a way of life.

Authenticity is what I always get from your space.

There was this programme called 'My Crazy Jamaican Life'; it was a wild documentary about how Jamaican men have five million baby-mothers and this, that, and the other. I remember the outrage at the time, because if I think about my grandfather, he didn't have five million baby mothers; he had seven kids with one wife, who he was married to for over fifty years. Growing up I'd watch him take as much pride in cooking and cleaning around their home as my grandmother. In fact, in all Jamaican households that I grew up around and within, this is what I saw.

So when it comes to your home and the conversation around whether your story is a fluke, or not real, I'm just like 'no'. This representation is all I know. This is normal. I see the comments on your page sometimes and it gets me so angry. I would say if you're not marginalised – if you are not Black, Brown, etc. – you would read those comments as nice enough. Seemingly polite, you know. But when you decipher what's actually being said behind those comments it's like, 'Oh, you really have a problem with this.' As you said, they just can't comprehend that this is a Black family in a very Black household.

With that being said, do you feel a need to prove your authenticity?

I had to let go of the pressure to prove that I'm authentic because I know that a lot of these people simply do not possess the lived experience to understand that growth is a defining factor in an honest life. So ironically, they conflate that growth with being inauthentic.

They may prefer me to continue to be depressed, but I'm not in that position anymore – the one where I'm sharing a bedroom with two children and my husband and have no windows. I don't need to be depressed; I still believe in all the things that I believed in then, I still buy the same things I did before, even now that I do have a disposable income.

But I had to decide that I don't need to prove my authenticity to anyone, because the few people who are insistent on challenging it aren't looking for personal growth.

In 2020, there was a lot of noise about wanting Black people to be able to obtain equity. We saw what it took from Black and Brown people, mentally, to educate and teach others. It was claimed that it's time for equity for all. And now we're seeing some of the results of, you know, levelling the playing field. But even with where we are at, Kevin, people lose their minds over it.

Meanwhile we're just minding our business, as we've always done. We're just now at this second starting to get paid for it. There's no back pay, no reparations, none of that. We're just now being paid for our time while still on the back foot. Nevertheless, this little shift has caused outrage, and this is where those accusations of inauthenticity come from. Those accusations are racist, with no uncertainty. They didn't actually want equality for Black and Brown people at all.

143

Their version of authenticity had to be through a lens of pain and suffering. As soon as the pain and suffering is detached, it's an issue. You know, it was very, very easy for people to praise our home and our surroundings when it was all clearly very humble. We're living in the exact same way now, just amplified. We were growing carrots on top of the bins, planning storage; this is nothing new. We've always been doing the most with the very little that we had. But now that we have more space to do it all, that's when it will cause offence, right? So now that there's been growth, less financial pressure, now that I'm more relaxed and not operating under the confines of, you know, literal slave masters, it's that that deems me to be inauthentic? I think it says a lot more about the other person. I don't waste any time explaining myself more than once to anyone. And I don't explain myself even the first time to people I don't know. Which is a lot of my audience.

Kevin Some of my films have gone on to show in various film festivals. And one particular festival offered to share feedback on the film I'd submitted. I don't know why I said yes at the time, but something made me say it. Anyway, that feedback came through this week, and it was all really positive. But one person was like, 'Oh, this film feels disjointed. Feels all over the place. And I can't make out the rhythm.' That's paraphrasing, but it was in that realm. And as soon as I saw those words, I knew that it was a white person with none of my lived experience that is saying this. I did not make that film for them . . . Like, I don't actually care.

> **Africa** I can't explain how much that in itself sums up everything I feel. It's so obvious to me that they do not know a Black person on a personal level.
> I'll give you an example. All of my children have very, very Black names. Not only do they have very Black names, they have names that are very specifically connected to the Rastafarian religion. And let me tell you about the way people will bend over backwards – literally do mental gymnastics – to work out what could possibly have possessed me to give them such different, 'random' names.
> Do you know how many Black people I know who have three children with the same three names as mine, that have the same faith as me? The people shocked by this just don't know any Black people. I don't owe these people anything because they have lived through the biggest Civil Rights movement ever – just in the last two years – and they have still decided not to widen their friendship circle.
> There's nothing I can do for you.

I turned down so much money in different places and different things in 2020. I knew it was a lie. I was like, very aware at the time that these corporate types weren't going to still be here in the conversation next year. 'I can't rely on you. And I don't want to rely on you. Because actually, I like how angry it makes you, if I'm honest. The fact that you knowing I don't need you makes you angry.'

> We knew that the only thing a lot of people had up on us was generational wealth, right? We had a conversation about this briefly, Kevin, before we bought the house. I knew what I was going to do. We knew what we needed to earn in a year to obtain that generational wealth. And we did it.

The whole family had to get involved. People might say, 'You shouldn't get your kids in this and that.' Whatever. If you could change your family's fortune in one year of joint effort and working together . . .? Kevin, I really couldn't have cared less. You think I'd rather have my kids living in the house they were living in before?

Me and my husband knew that we just needed that year of generational wealth to change our fortunes. I no longer rely on any income from social media to maintain our current life. I have two employees that are full time: my sisters. I split my salary between my sisters. I think a lot of Black people in my position do the same thing. It's never about self-preservation; it's looking after your family. And then that definition of family gets wider once your immediate family unit is taken care of – and that's where we are now.

But we knew we needed that year to get ourselves in a position that people literally wait on inheritances for. We were so fortunate to be able to obtain that in such a short space of time. So now I don't pander to anyone, you know?

We knew it wouldn't last forever. And we could have done it for a couple more years if we wanted to. We probably still can. I don't want to have the rug pulled from under my feet.

Now we've burned all the racists out. *[Both laugh for several moments]* I just want to say that when I am having boog days, I turn to your account – to see your kids, to see the space you create, where they have space to be kids. Space to investigate, to be scientists or astronauts, to play in the mud. To see that your kids have an understanding of sustainability, kindness and giving just brings me light on those days when I feel shit. Your home, to me, is the ultimate definition of a safe space.

That's what we've gone for, Kevin. My husband was raised to be the kind, amazing, wonderful person he is, and we had a conversation about what principles made us the adults we are. We always want to be better. I've got a long way to go. I think we both understand what things we would have loved to have removed from our childhood homes; to have got to our ideal adult selves sooner. And that's all it is. That's not a dig at anything in our upbringing at all; we just understand the barriers that are in place and which need to be removed. We're older than our parents were when they raised us. That is crazy.

We are trying to remove any single barrier that could possibly get in the way of our children becoming the best adults they want to become. And so we just choose our battles. Everything is kid-first. I don't think there's a single instance where mine or J's feelings will get put before what our child might need. It's literally just about creating a space where every single person can have a bit of respite. It doesn't mean you need to have a big house – we did it in our two-bedroom flat, we did it in our one-bedroom flat. It's just about compromise.

I do really feel it when I see that our elder three children have the space to show they're tired or frustrated, and then be emotional. I have to remind myself that I could never have dreamed of being able to let out my feelings in the home environment to my parents. That's a reminder to me that we've created a safe space.

That more than anything makes it easy not to just follow the trends. Cater for you and your family instead. The only thing that will never go out of style is following exactly what it is that your children need. And that means adapting spaces. That means that, you know, we might have a climbing frame in our front room for half the year – even though we've finally given them a playroom and we said all that stuff would only be in there. It literally is just following the ebb and flow of your family's needs.

We hold on to our confidence, because white supremacy will really try and chip away – especially as a Black parent – at your credibility in understanding your own child's needs. It happens to me time and time again. People catastrophise the way that I parent, trying to insinuate that a Black parent can't successfully raise their child. The people saying all that fully understand what they're doing, Kevin, and I have to really, really tune out the noise.

I feel like also J and I are so far removed from our culture, and I'm not embarrassed about that. You know, my mum is mixed race. She was only raised by her white mum. That means I have one grandparent who was born here. J's two parents were born here; we're third generation, right? Our children are fourth generation with one great-grandparent who was born here. And unfortunately, that generation is dying out. So what is our culture now? I feel like for a lot of us, those that didn't necessarily grow up visiting back home, this is a thing. Kevin, we travelled everywhere, but we didn't go to Grenada until I was fifteen. In fact, I went to Jamaica before I went to Grenada.

So I always try to encourage people to remember that, actually, it doesn't matter if you don't know your culture. Go and take it. You can create your own hybrid. How many of us are living and loving people of different cultures? That in itself can be a new hybrid culture. And it's up to you to bring that into your home. There's so much gatekeeping in the interiors industry of, you know, only a certain type of house being able to belong to a certain type of person. Well, if Victorian houses are only for white middle-class people, why were all my ancestors living in Notting Hill in the '60s?

Like, why should we not be part of the conversation now? So again, I think it goes back to this idea of authenticity. I don't need to say it; I can just do it. And then I'll see it replicated by others. I love to know that just by being present, I'm giving people the permission to do it themselves.

Kevin I spoke to Auntie Paula.

Africa Did you?

She was talking about where we're from as well. She grew up a few roads across from my grandparents' house and her explanation of like, loving nature and needing to be in the countryside was based on her childhood bedroom; the window looked out on to all these trees in South London. So the idea that she would then move to the country was inevitable, because that's what she grew up with.

And I never forgive any of those people who attacked her online. I have a very, very long memory. And that absence of any formal apology matching the level of vitriol she received? I think it served as a permanent reminder, as I said before, that there is a belief amongst some that comfort is simply not meant to be for us.

What I love about these conversations is that they all interweave. You can very clearly see the shared connections, the commonality of lived experiences. It's because we are living, breathing culture. We're more than just an algorithm. There is something that connects us in a deeper way; higher and grander than just a social connection. It's very loving and peaceful. And it's just really wonderful to kind of see, you know, the similarities beyond just the discrimination we face. This is why being authentic comes so naturally to us; the definition of true authenticity is a tool that works for all, not just for some. It provides a voice for all of us.

Home is a Big Idea

In short, just let it all hang out. When we're in the middle of creating something, looking for perfection can lead us astray, taking us away from the most interesting parts of the idea. There's a time and a place to cross the 't's and dot the 'i's, but that's definitely not when you're still building out your project's foundations. Once you are there – once you know the ins and outs of your idea and the brand it represents – I promise you that those worries of whether it's right, or if you should even be doing the thing, will just melt away.

Because the truth is, no one knows what they're doing, and no one can predict the future. What we can do, though, is make sure that the work we're creating is built on authentic qualities. That way, when it's all said and done, you know that you made the best work you could.

WORK, WORK, WORK, WORK, WORK

TODAY'S TAKEAWAY:

Don't be like Kate Nash

Lay the right foundations. When you next sit down to solve a creative challenge, ask yourself: who are you talking to, and why are you talking to them? Look at how the brand got started, and why they got started. Sounds obvious, but this is crucial for building out the journey the brand is taking its consumers on. It will help you tell the right story, and then create the right work.

Your job as a creative is about smart thinking, not fads. Ideas based on facts and real insights make this hard work a lot more fun. Why? Because, this way, everything actually adds up. Nothing should be more satisfying to a creative of any discipline than putting out that kind of work.

Authenticity: Do you have the right to be talking to that particular group of people? Is what you're saying coming from a place of authentic engagement, or are you actually working to put those people in a box, rather than give them the space to be themselves when they engage with your work?

Never stop asking those questions. Remind yourself of them, constantly. It's very easy to drift away from this kind of scrutiny, and this is when your sense of discipline (see Chapter 19) will really need to come in and help.

12

STORYTELLING

STORYTELLING

For me, the best storyteller in the world was always Biggie Smalls, aka Christopher Wallace. I've told the following story many times, but just in case you've never heard me explain it in full...

I was enamoured by the simplicity of Biggie's rhymes, because within those simple lines were the most vividly detailed stories. I studied his songs over and over again, wanting to learn how to tell stories the way he did. Eventually, to further try to capture moments like he did, I turned to photography and, for a long time, only worked with film as an ode to Biggie's process. He would freestyle all of his rhymes, holding lines in his head to work with, only letting them free once he'd already got everything in the right place in his mind. To imitate this, I became obsessed with film and rejected digital. I didn't want the option to look over what I did, delete it, and try again. For me, every image was a freestyle.

My thinking was that I couldn't rap like him, so I would snap like him. I developed an obsession – which I still have – for capturing all the detail around me. I constantly look for the most succinct way to explain everything I am seeing and feeling. (With that said, it should also be clear why Nan Goldin is the photographer I consider most personally influential to me.) Even the way I write now isn't just sitting and typing; these thoughts were all fully mapped out in my head before being put to page.

When you get into advertising, you learn different rules that all manner of creatives follow. Tools that help make your work the best it can be. One rule was KISS, an acronym for 'Keep It Simple, Stupid', representing the act – and even the art – of simplifying an idea to its bare bones. A bad idea will have a million layers or tricks to make it work. A good idea doesn't need all the bells and whistles to make itself make sense. A good idea is timeless. A good idea is honest and truthful. If a good idea were a person it would be Dawn Butler.

A bad one? Boris Johnson.

When I learned about KISS, I realised the philosophy behind it wasn't new to me. Biggie had been teaching it for years. The idea of pitching, or taking a client on a journey, can be really intimidating – but it needn't be. Instead, think about the best possible story you can not only tell them, but take them on.

Be a storyteller. Make it fun, emotional, and exciting.

The following conversation is with one of my favourite storytellers, whose tales will leave you feeling all the feels.

...And yes, I did just tell you that the technique I've used to write, sell in, and make million-pound phone adverts all came from the only Christopher we acknowledge.

"I FREESTYLED THE FIRST PART ON THE TOILET."

A CONVERSATION WITH

TERRI WALKER

Artist and songwriter

ON STORYTELLING

Terri Hey gorgeous. I know you've missed me, I dunno why you're pretending otherwise.

Kevin You know what? I don't have to physically miss you, because I have your back catalogue and I just listen to the music.

I love you so much. I've missed you. Look at this beautiful face.

Don't try to charm me.

[Terri laughs] Okay, I'm gonna stop. Let's chat.

So, I'm writing a book about my creative practices, and specifically about all the Black women in my life who have helped inspire me. Annoyingly, you're one of those women.

'Annoyingly.' You know, you're lucky.

You're lucky, 'cause you're sitting there like you don't know the heap of problems you've put me through.

What? Kevin! *[Terri laughs]* Me? For you? All right, I'll let you have your time. You have your moment. Go ahead.

I'll start from the beginning. 2003 was a really dark year. I don't know if I've ever explained this in detail, but that year I broke up with one of my biggest loves thus far. Sitting here today I can look back and say that boy is a eediat, but at the time . . . yeah. It was a very wild situation. MTV Base was on, and I guess I heard the – is it a guitar at the start of 'Drawing Board'?

No, that's the keys.

Right. And then there's like this humming – and I've never known what instrument that is – going bmm, bmmmm.

It's the bass. It's the bass.

Oh is it the bass? Well, you're the musician.

I'm just giving you the answers that you're asking me.

Okay, just take down the tone.

Bare attitude, you know. *[Both laugh]*

Anyway, that comes in, and then there's a sax or trumpet – so it was jazz.

Mm-hmm. Yeah, I know the bit you mean. It's the horns.

152

And then this woman starts singing and you're like, 'But he had no rhythm, and between the sheets that's a no-go.' I'm sorry, what?

All of that to say, I'd never heard a song written like that before. I'd never heard music like this before, but I could hear the jazz inflection in your voice. So I went and got your album, 'Untitled', and after I listened to the whole thing I realised that I'd never heard someone sing and tell stories like that before. I really felt like I personally knew you. I studied that album, it taught me – alongside my other influences – how to write my poetry, the stories that I wanted to tell, and it showed me the importance of expression. And by that I mean that there is no wrong way to express yourself in those creative fields. I was obsessed.

There really weren't contemporary artists I listened to that did that for me – certainly not at that time. There was Mariah Carey, and then there was you. Artists that I just thought were amazing, and I would fight people for them. And then, yeah, Amy came along. And you know how much I love Amy—

You know Amy was only a year after, right? Mad.

Yeah, I know. I was there. *[Both laugh]*

So Amy came along, and I was like, 'You love Terri as much as I love Terri,' 'cause I could hear you through her music. And I thought that was amazing, how this thing had been passed on and she was doing her own, new thing – but I knew that she loved you.

That's amazing that you could tell. That's crazy.

During that time as well, I was still working in the shop with that dirty boy – we were meant to be friends now. I would just play your album in the store, then we'd go on to Amy's, then back to yours ... twenty years later, the quality of expression going on there really inspired me like nothing else.

Ten years later, we inadvertently met. And you tried to link me with the biggest ginnal in the world – that woman who tried telling me I had to pretend I was white to be an artist.

Oh, God! I forgot about her. Bloody hell, yes. That was in New York, right?

Yeah. One awful lady. Anyway, you're obviously aware that we're not just friends by this point, we're family. Even though you get on my nerves.

Vice versa.

It's all good, our friendship lives in a space where we honestly hold each other accountable.

Always.

So yes, you get on my nerves. But the point is, you are one of the best writers in the world. The way you tell stories – weave all the threads together – is like nothing I've seen anywhere else. The only one I can compare you to is Biggie Smalls. Not to mention that your voice is just ridiculous.

Terri I'm getting emotional.

Kevin It's true. I was literally just playing your album, and it's not because I was about to talk to you – I play it all the time.

Thank you.

Don't. It's so I can pretend you're still that normal person I knew you as on the record.

Biggie Smalls, you know. You trying to give me a heart attack? That's big.

That's how it's always felt to me. Especially 'Love Fool'.

It's funny, that's the song that got me signed. You know how you're like me? When you've got to get something done and people aren't doing it, so you disappear and do it yourself. So, I disappeared. I disappeared from my management for about a month, and went to the States by myself. Remember Hinda Hicks?

Yeah, yeah. I Wanna Be Your—

—Lady. Yeah, so somehow we end up staying together in this house for about a month. I recorded 'Love Fool', 'Ching Ching', and 'Brand New Day'. I remember the first few lines of 'Love Fool' came to me on the toilet, and that's the song that got me signed to Def Soul. My whole career would've been a completely different situation if I hadn't gone out there.

So, wait, did you just say you were on the toilet when you first came up with that song?

Yeah. I freestyled the first part on the toilet. So basically, I had been in a relationship with this guy from East London who was a 'gangster', and he had me there as if I was one of his side-chicks, but I wasn't. So, when I bounced from London I was bouncing from him too. We were breaking up. Like, he didn't understand that I was there with him out of choice, not because I needed him more than he needed me. So that's what 'Love Fool' is about; you think you've got it going on and your shit don't stink. When people do certain things, it's not actually about the person they're doing them to, it's them revealing their insecurities. And that's where the middle eight of that song came from: 'Why you gotta be so insecure?' I remember thinking, 'Yo! That sounds dope.' And that was it.

[Kevin and Terri sing the song] But when you freestyled it, did you even freestyle the melody?

Everything. And I love that first album, I'm so proud of it. One of these reasons I called it 'Untitled' is because you can hear so many different influences from the people I was listening to. So that's why it was 'untitled'. I knew I was doing this thing but I hadn't found my voice yet. I didn't know who I was yet. So that's why I think some of the songs sound so different.

154

I think you definitely had your voice, it's that you were still finessing your sound. But you always had that beautiful jazz voice. Do you freestyle most of your songs, then?

There are no rules, there's no right or wrong. Nothing's ever forced; I follow my spirit. What I love to do is just go up to the mic and then freestyle a bunch of gibberish, then come back and listen to some of the things I just did. Sometimes I end up with a phrase, or even a melody from doing that.

You definitely do that in general. Like, I'll just be with you and you'll suddenly start being all, 'ba-da-da-buuum, ba-da-da-buuuuumm'. You're always vibing. I guess you're always in a state of freestyling.

There was a video, ages ago, that we filmed together. You just started randomly singing, and then you turned directly into the camera. I asked you what the song was and you were just like, 'I don't know.' *[Both laugh]*

I think it's because I've always trusted the process. And that's something I've always had, since I was a kid. My cousins would say, 'Oh, she always believes in love and justice, she wants everything to be okay. We're all one.' And yeah, I've always been that way, and I was allowed to be that way. So I'd always be off in my dream worlds, and I'd just explore them.

I think that's the reason why, when I'm in creative mode, I'm never scared. Even if I get it wrong or speak too fast, I know I'll get there eventually. I'm not meant to be perfect, I'm meant to be who I'm meant to be. I just need to let it come out and I'll figure out the rest somehow. It's taken me a while to work that out, but I always knew there was something uncontrollable that I just needed to trust and follow. And that's what it's always been.

I would love to talk to you about one of my favourite songs of yours, 'Whoopsie Daisy'. *[Kevin laughs]*

Some people. This is how I know the devil is trying to take me off track, you know. I hate that song. Do you know how much I fucking hate that song?

Me too! Do you know how much I felt let down?

Babe, do you know what? I remember I'd been getting all these amazing reviews, and then on that second album, someone just said, 'crash and burn'. And that's stayed with me. There are two songs on that album I really hate, and I didn't write either of them. 'Whoopsie Daisy' and 'What the Hell'. I would never write shit like that. I've never written songs about getting my heart broken, piss off. And those two songs weren't even written for me, I wasn't involved in the process at all. You can hear it straight away, right?

And the thing is, right, that happened around the time when I changed management, and so I was suddenly around these people who didn't really understand who I was, and didn't really take the time to understand my worth. They just said, 'You've got to keep the record label happy.' And that song was produced by the same team who did Jamelia's 'Superstar', and it was clear the record label just wanted me to copy that sound – but that's not who I am. And so that's why I'm there in that music video like a bad Beyoncé.

Kevin I'm sorry I brought that up, I am. But I did it for a reason; I think it's really important for people to understand what happens when you're removed — whether by yourself or by others — from the path you're meant to be on. And, I mean, you're a storyteller who wasn't being allowed to tell her own stories.

> **Terri** Oh my God, amen. And that's the reason why I left Mercury Records in the end. I chose to leave because I could see these people just didn't know what to do with me.

The label saw how good that first album was but, instead of letting you continue to explore how you use music to convey emotion and tell stories in the way you do, they just wanted another Beyoncé. Because that's what was popular at the time, and you'd proven yourself capable enough to, what, just be put into a mould? Mad ting.

But taking it back to when you were just allowed to do what you do — when did that start? When did you start writing songs?

> The first song I wrote that got released was 'Easy Lovin' You' for TNT. It had J2K, Wiley, Skepta, D Double E — all these people on it. The album 'Tried N Tested' came out in 2009, but I wrote that song back in 2001. It's wild looking back to see what I was writing then, but at the time I didn't even see myself as a writer because I kept being put in sessions with writers. So I felt like they were the ones doing the writing, and I didn't have a direction. But for 'Drawing Board', they paired me with Lou Francis, and she asked me questions about me. She wanted to talk to me about the things that meant something to me. And that's how I knew I could write — because other people would just write stuff and tell you what you should be singing.
>
> So, even with 'Untitled', I was in control of the concepts throughout — and I co-wrote some of the songs — though I wasn't necessarily in control of the process fully. But I wrote 'Love Fool', 'Brand New Day', 'It's All Good' and '4 Feet Under'.

But I guess even then, as you said, with the songs that you didn't necessarily write yourself, you still had control of the concept. You still had a way of ensuring that the story being told was true to what you wanted to tell.

I GOT A STORY TO TELL

We all do

Just tell that story in the only way you could.

TODAY'S TAKEAWAY:

'I Just Wanna Curse'

Biggie's last freestyle on the radio happened eight days before his death. The first round of rhymes he spat were amazing – obviously – but a little more subdued than normal, purely because he was trying his best not to swear on air.

When it comes to the second round, he hilariously starts laughing and then complaining about wanting to curse.

Biggie Yo man, I can rhyme all night, but I wanna curse.

Radio Host Ay yo, do your thing.

Biggie I wanna curse man, it's late.

Radio Host Do your thing, do your thing.

Biggie Can I do my thing? My man, my man.

He then begins to rhyme in such a powerful, passionate way. You can see he's having fun, with no holding back in the delivery. It's magical.

You can apply this to your creative conversation, whether that is a pitch or a conversation about pay – whatever it is, think about what's the most compelling way to tell a story in that specific situation.

13

FOCUS

I like rules. Love them, in fact.

Those that know me well will read that and think, 'I know this boy isn't starting this chapter off by lying.' They have this view only because I have never taken the time to explain myself.

I do like rules. I like a plan, I like order, I like doing the best possible work in the best possible way.

I like efficiency. For me, working in such a way allows me to see the mechanics of the situation, and more importantly how people turn those mechanics into living, breathing things – into culture. If the human condition is about the correlation between us all – effectively biology – then I guess I am a scientist. This makes sense as there is nothing more exciting to me than my calculations being correct.

Like, sex is cool – but have you ever predicted musical trends two years before they found a home in a subculture? And, in turn, four years before the mainstream then pretends to have found it first? In those moments, I am living my best Devil-Wears-Prada, It's-Not-Blue-It's-Cerulean life.

It's in this space where I am an influencer's influencer. I can't be categorised with the regular, hashtag-ad crew. No tea no shade, get your coin.

I'm just saying I live in a different creative space; if you are the pretty picture, I'm the one who decides where each pixel sits and how it comes together.

I am the one who tells your influencers what's cool and what will be cool. I am the one who evokes quiet revolutions here and there. I am able to do this because of my ability to focus.

Focus, like intentional boundaries (see Chapter 3), keeps you on the correct path. The same can be said for rules. Both go hand-in-hand and will stop you from wasting your time, following irrelevant trains of thought, and heading towards false discovery.

I do get it – why some would label me a rule breaker, or trouble maker – but my rebuttal to that will always be . . .

Trouble for who?
Whose rules am I breaking?

On closer inspection, you'll find that the rules I have broken only protected some and not all – the most powerful, not the ones in most need. Through this lens you'll realise I have never broken a rule in a single day of my life. What I break are structures of oppression dressed up as protective frilly things, restrictions, and illusions of inclusivity. They are distractions, and we all know what distractions pull you away from.

Ignore rules, and the focus they demand? Ignore principles (see Chapter 17) and morals, the very things that I believe sit at the centre of all creativity? I would never.

It is in these spaces of order that I am able to remain neutral, here for all people. When you are able to do that, you're able to understand what people will and won't need. You're able to hone in on the important changes that must happen. You can see each domino fall perfectly in place, and take comfort in effortlessly moving people into the exact position they need to be in so they can reach and experience their full potential.

Having an understanding of rules (rules that protect all of us, that are inclusive, that do away with privilege) means knowing that they're the perfect gateways to a rhythm. They provide a pocket of focus that brings real intent to your creative practice.

The world is a very loud place, providing the perfect conditions for miscommunication.

Your understanding of, not only your rules but everyone else's – whilst maintaining a clear focus – will guide you to the perfect result every time.

"STOPPING TO LISTEN, RATHER THAN JUST FREEZING."

A CONVERSATION WITH

LADY PHYLL OPOKU-GYIMAH

Co-founder of UK Black Pride and executive director of Kaleidoscope Trust

ON FOCUS

Kevin Something I always come back to when I'm trying to streamline my ideas, is the concept of focus. As in, like, really honing in on the specifics of the thing, and seeing if the work actually meets the criteria. Just really direct stuff like, who is it I'm talking to? What am I trying to fight for? Who am I giving my platform over to? I even think that last one with regard to big brands, because once I have a stake in their space, it becomes my space. And, more importantly, a space for me to then hand over to others.

That's been a big part of how I've approached advertising: using it to give a platform to those we really need to hear more from. But even in those situations, when I've been actively pushing for representation or the next step in a conversation, I've not always felt welcome doing it. Even if I'm surrounded by supposed allies. Particularly in fashion land when I was a photographer, I found that some of the white gay men I was in the company of were some of the biggest bullies. And I didn't get it. I thought, 'I should be getting on with you, because we're all meant to be part of the same community and you care about what I care about.' Very quickly I realised that I was living in a dreamland. So I've really got to focus all of you man out and instead just concentrate on what I'm doing.

I feel like that's something you'll completely get, just because of the spaces you build. In terms of taking up space in places where we're not encouraged to feel welcome, I feel like there aren't many that can rival you. You are immovable in the most beautiful of ways, so before we get into anything else, I just want to say thank you. When I'm doing stuff that specifically pertains to our shared community as Black and Brown queer people, I'm just trying to catch up with you.

Lady Phyll Do you know what makes that so beautiful to hear? That it's a Black gay man telling me this. I don't often hear from Black queer men. I'm never lost for words, but after what you just said . . . I'm feeling it close to my chest. So thank you. I'm grateful.

I'm just trying to be a mirror, trust me. It's a shame that me saying this is such a rare thing. But it's believable, too.

We're so in the midst of trying to survive that we don't even get to congratulate one another.

You're right. We're all just trying to survive in our own way, and I think that's also why I tried to walk around with a lot of forgiveness for those who maybe aren't speaking up when they could, because it is what it is.

In all honesty as well, talking to you now, I think part of the reason I feel this warmth towards you is because your skin tone is so very much like my grandfather's. So just seeing your face lights me up in such a way.

Okay, you're gonna turn me into a hot mess now. If I can focus now, are you asking me what focus means to me?

Yes. What does focus mean to you, whether as a way to stay true to your course, a way to communicate with others, or even as a defence mechanism for navigating bullshit – or whatever other meaning it carries for you individually?

162

I guess when someone else uses the word 'focus', my immediate feeling is that it's about stopping in my tracks and taking in my surroundings. Focusing means reflecting, absorbing, smelling, touching, feeling ... just using all the means at my disposal to really concentrate on whatever's at hand. When you focus, there's an element of embracing where you're at right now – and that might not be cute. It might be frightening – you might be in an unsafe space at that moment.

My life revolves around focusing on other people, connecting with them. Stopping in my tracks to understand and, more importantly, actively listen to what they're saying. Even if I don't like what I hear. Sometimes that does place me in really unsafe, uncomfortable situations. I'm not always allowed to just turn around and say, 'Why don't you eff off, man?' I want to deal with what they're saying to me. Because whilst what they're saying may feel harmful to me and my people, in order to learn and unlearn, I have to focus. I have to resist that immediate feeling of cutting them – or the subject at hand – off at the knees, and just keep it moving.

But I guess I've never really thought about focus consciously. It's just something you have to do as part of the everyday. You have to focus if you want to get things done. And yeah, for me, most immediately that tends to mean stopping to listen, rather than just freezing. It also means blocking out all of the other white noise when it matters.

Yeah, I think that's definitely how I feel about it. I didn't know what the answer was going to be, but I knew it would let me highlight how remarkable your focus has to be. Because you're being so calm and peaceful in yourself to do that, whilst nevertheless being prodded and pushed and poked – left, right, and centre – by this small, clapped island's ways.

You know, you've said something there that I want to reflect on a little bit more. Everyone believes that I'm this really calm, peaceful person. That I create harmony wherever I am – that I'm really diplomatic.

I tell you what, inside it's not like that. But it's about the spaces that I'm in; what I do. I can't be erratic, I can't swear from the top of my lungs when I want to. I cannot just shout out and tell somebody about themselves. Sometimes I really would love to, and I have an outlet for that. But if the changes that I want to see – not just for me, but for our community and the generation after – are to happen, I have to be aware that the people I'm speaking to often hold a level of power and privilege. They have access to the corridors of power. And they're not gonna hear me when I start telling them about themselves; they're going to shut me off.

So I have to focus – stop, stay calm – and think about what I want to say. It's that code-switching, which does frustrate me. Audre Lorde talks about code-switching and how Black women, in this anti-Black world, often have to be somebody different from who they are. It's frustrating. But at the same time, I get it. Because if we hadn't stopped, reflected, and stayed focused on the bigger picture, UK Black Pride would not be here today.

We've never sold ourselves out, but you've really got me thinking about this word 'focus', and how calm I have to stay in spaces where sometimes I just want to cry.

Kevin I think that's why your job is harder. Not just because of the privileges that I hold in being able to present as like, a straight Black man. But that, within that, I'm able to choose violence in how I use my words, if I want to. And in the past few years, I have managed to get into this great space of delivering that violence, but in a way where my point is still heard. I don't have to bite my tongue, but I'm still diplomatic, I'm still planning.

I think, In turn, part of that shift in how I express myself comes from understanding what you, and others like you, do. I understand that you have to know what game it is you're playing, to be able to play it in the way that gets you that authentic result.

There's a bigger mission at play, and I guess that's what you're saying. If you're focused on the bigger, positive shift, it comes at a cost in the present.

> **Lady Phyll** It's a really challenging one, because of the capitalist world we live in. Things need funding. Whether that's for international development, UK Black Pride, or for our refugees to literally be able to eat. We're asking people for money to fund things that are trying to make a genuine, positive difference – yet it still feels like you're going in there with your begging bowl. Sometimes just asking for the bare minimum.
>
> But because of how you had to ask, you feel like you're not even dismantling the structures that you really want to dismantle; you're not decolonising what you want to decolonise because you're still working within this framework that continues to perpetuate the same harms and the same wrongs as before. It's just done in a different way. So I guess I've learned now that I'm at a stage where I feel confident enough – I'm stable enough – to turn around and tell somebody, 'Actually, no, we don't need your money.' Because of their unethical practices, or because of how they conduct themselves. And I can do that now, without feeling terrible about it.
>
> And I guess that in itself is a privilege, right? Even within that, my definition of 'focus' is different to what my daughter's might be. I've already got my foot in a door, even if it isn't necessarily the house I'd normally choose to walk into. But it's somewhere I know I can gain some control of the situation, somewhere I can take charge. Because, actually, they need me more than I need them.

It's interesting, because I've been talking about this recently with some people who say, 'I want to be like you, making these big corporations accountable.' And first of all, yeah, I'm here for that energy. But I also want you to be safe. As a Jamaican, I one-hundred per cent believe in and endorse the idea of vex money. I have the means to be like, 'I haven't got time for this back-and-forth, I'll just pay for the thing myself.' And that might be funding a film, or putting out my affirmation cards, giving talks – whatever. And in the case of stuff like the cards, I'm able to then put the proceeds back into my art, which allows me to be increasingly free in how I operate.

But getting to that place has taken me a very, very long time. To get to that position of privilege took a lot of work.

> And now you're actually focused on your own craft, right? So you're able to do that because you want to be accountable to yourself; you don't want to fall into all the red tape and the bureaucratic systems that weigh us down.

You've focused, you've taken the time to think about what it means if you don't take money from over here, and what that means for the amount of effort you have to put in over there.

The thing about when you do things like that, is that you're also focusing on your own mental health and wellbeing. Sometimes I worry that, 'Oh my gosh, am I gonna literally combust and crack?' because I don't want to speak to that MP, or I don't want to speak to that minister. But there's a bigger picture here. I have to think about what hope looks like, and what the end goal is. And that's what keeps me going. So there's a different level of focus in my mind, which is having that big picture view, that sense of a longer-term purpose.

And you're good at it as well. I've learned to be a good diplomat in the right settings, but fundamentally I'm a ride or die kind of person.

I'm a very deep thinker, to the point where I can stay up all night strategising about how we're going to get from A to B; creating several theories of change, all so I can master this next meeting that's coming up. It's not something that I only learned to do consciously, I think my parents handed it to me. I'm a Ghanaian woman born from Ghanaian parents. They've always had to be, and always have been, ever so diplomatic, polite, and courteous. I think it's something from when they came to this country. The streets were not paved with gold and they were beholden to a system that was not their own. So I learned that diplomacy from them I guess, but then I come in with that radical edge that cuts through to the matter. I know what you want to hear. And I'm going to tell you what you want to hear, but in a way that is meaningful and intentional for what I need to get out of this. And we're not leaving the room until I get what I want to get.

Listening to what you've just said, I realised that I think for me, whilst I'm not about the small talk, once we get into the deep, dark stuff – like, why you wanna kill your ex – I know the problem then that we're dealing with, and I can work with that. I can be very charming and diplomatic to get to that space, because that's vital information for me. My focus becomes super sharp then; I understand where you're really coming at it from, at a real place of individual need, and I'm then able to look at how I can manoeuvre within that to get the thing that gives back to my community. If you're a corporation, and, at the end of the day, underneath it all, you're just chasing profit, fine. Personally, I'm not for greed, but now I know what you need and how what I need has to fit into that.

Where I struggle, and where I'm trying to improve, is that I can't get past that angle of, 'What is your vice?' What star sign are you, by the way?

Oh, I'm a true Scorpio.

There you go. It makes sense, because Virgos and Scorpios are very similar.

I want to say something to you that not many people understand. Sometimes it depends on who you're speaking to with me. Are you speaking to Lady Phyll, who is UK Black Pride and does that diplomacy in certain spaces? Are you speaking to Dr Phyll Opoku-Gyimah about Kaleidoscope Trust and my human rights work? Or are you speaking to Phyll Opoku-Gyimah? Because those three people are very, very different. No one in my family would ever call me Lady Phyll or Dr Phyll. My closest friends would never call me Lady Phyll, but if we're going to an event and it's about UK Black Pride, they'll be like, 'Here we go, Lady Phyll's out tonight.' And so I behave in different ways. So within that, my focus is different in different spaces – for different people. I'm sure that every one of us – especially as Black, queer people – has … I don't want to call it an alter ego, but we have that slightly different version of ourselves to hand.

You said it yourself when you talked about being charming and diplomatic, and I can just tell that I'd love to be in those spaces with that version of you. Because we'd be able to just bounce off one another. But it's about having different ways of channelling your energy to suit different spaces, and it's okay for us to do that when we live in a world that does not see our Blackness or our queerness as great. It does not see these aspects of who we are as things that can co-exist alongside each other. So, at different times, we're going to have to use a different level of vernacular, or articulate ourselves in particular ways.

I've been called everything from a 'Bounty' through to 'too radical', or 'too white'. And I don't get that last one, other than to think that you're reflecting on my pronunciation – how you place me based on my pattern of speech – and deciding that only white people can be seen in that sense.

Kevin That says more about what that person thinks about Blackness.

Lady Phyll Right? Come on.

Let me hurt some feelings … that says more about how that individual feels about their mother's skin tone. Because there is nothing under the sun that is too white for me. I will do exactly as I please, knowing that my Blackness is my Blackness, just as your Blackness is yours. We are all on our own journey, defining what these things mean individually to us. We should be able to come together and celebrate how each of us owns that for ourselves; that should be the vibe.

But why do you think we can't do that? It's because society plays us off each other. And we fall into this blueprint that was set out for us, yet never had us in mind. My whole ethos for life is about connection, community, and celebration, and seeing the joy that brings. But sometimes I've had to stop at connection, because there's so much deep-rooted trauma that we're unable to get past. There is healing that needs to take place first, but unless you call it and you name it, you can't do that healing.

What you were saying about those three personae you embody is really interesting to me. Because it's made me think about which one my energy has brought to the table. I always try and bring a certain energy to the Black women I'm interacting with; I'm lucky to be in your presence in that moment. I've never forgotten my first home. I'm very aware of the burdens, as you've said, specifically placed on Black women and so I never want you to feel like I'm wasting your time. But I guess, within that, I'm intrigued to know if that energy encouraged a particular version of you to be in this conversation?

166

I understand what you're saying. When we first started talking, it was probably Lady Phyll. But then you broke down a particular barrier; I felt that acknowledgement of me as a Black woman. I heard it. So now you're speaking to Phyll, because you keep on showing me that it's fine for me to show up. We can be messy, we can just speak – we're comfortable.

Thank you. And just to say, I love how that idea of using different approaches comes back to what are effectively different types of focus. Because there are people who will hopefully read this, know that they do that too, and hopefully realise that yes, they can do advertising. They can do all these things. These spaces are for you – they're for us – as intersectional as you are. Black, queer, trans – we have all the skillsets on lock, do not let these people fool you with gatekeeping methods. You, as the essence, are enough to fill up any space.

You talked at the beginning about democratising spaces within advertising, and I love that. We use the word 'decolonise' a lot to talk about rethinking these structures, but democratising them is not necessarily a concept you hear.

It comes from something I first learned in photography, and you see it often in advertising now. These places will suck up culture like a vampire, and use it to push product. We've really only just started talking about how they use Black Twitter to mine our language and jokes, and just use them to sell things. But coming in and being able to actually own that space, and give those in culture this brand platform to push their own voice, it turns it back into a place where these voices in culture are getting more out of it, too. They're not just being rinsed without credit.

That reminds me of some of the experiences I've had with the creative industries through UK Black Pride, where they would literally extract our talent and knowledge in return for peanuts. We got the bare minimum.
You see what's created at the end of it and just think, 'Damn, that's all come from us.' Funnily enough, the best experience we had was with an agency that had a Black woman at the helm, and we were given a lot more space to say what we wanted the creative to look like. But it took us a whole year to be clear on that, and negotiate for that. We had free rein though, to say, 'That's not going to work. This needs more money, because we need this person to be paid. We need the make-up artists to be Black.' If you want creative work to centre Black queer voices, they really need to be at the centre of it from the beginning. If they can't offer us that, and ensure that the talent we bring on board is paid adequately, then it's a no from us.

We're all smart enough now to know the game advertising is playing, and what you're talking about is the holistic approach I always go for. Because when you see work that has that authenticity to it, you know it was made by Black and Brown people who actually care about your existence – who want to ensure you're being spoken to honestly, and with knowledge.

I'd love to hear more about your approach to advertising, because it's not my specialism.

Kevin In a weird way, that's such a lovely place to round up. Because you've literally just told me all of the ways that you focus, that you have different languages of focus. And within that, you're not only part of the culture – you've literally given birth to it, over and over again.

For me, creative advertising at its best serves the culture, not the other way around. You set the blueprint, and a holistic approach to advertising should honour that.

BE WHO YOU NEED TO BE TO FOCUS

Different types of focus require different types of characters.

There is no shame in code-switching, as long as it's for your benefit.

I think we sometimes approach the subject of code-switching with shame, as if us dumbing ourselves down to get the job done reflects on us poorly. It doesn't.

Start thinking about it like this: between yourself and the person or group you are code-switching for, who is the one actually capable of speaking both languages? Who understands multiple cultures?

Be who you need to be to get your answers – to get the details you need to succeed.

TODAY'S TAKEAWAY:

One size does not fit all

Find what level of focus works for you, and curate your work rate and load around that. Make your capacity for focus work for you in the right places.

For instance, the long task of sitting with a project from start to finish is nothing to me. I've worked on projects for two years straight, then got the results I set out and predicted I would get.

What I'm not good at is the small-talk of the thing – the millions of catch-ups in between. So rather than have hour after hour of catch-ups, I limit those meetings to thirty minutes each, with at least an hour in between. Make your focus work for you.

14

TONE OF VOICE

In simple terms, a brand's tone of voice lets us, the potential consumer, know just what that brand's about. The tone lets us know what to expect; it reflects the brand's personality, ambitions, and values so that they better connect with us.

My favourite tone of voice from a brand is Oatly: 'Like milk, but made for humans.' You can tell so many things about Oatly from the jump. Oatly comes across as a smart and honest brand. The tone sits in a place of light humour and polite truths, but nevertheless makes a point. They stand for something. They're an intentional brand, knowledgeable on the subject at hand and proud of it. But most of all, when we read that slogan we're left intrigued, excited. A traditional, older brand wouldn't use a sarcastic, sassy tone like this, so we know that Oatly are new – young, even – with matching ideas. They're compatible with Gen Z and Millennials, whilst Boomers are welcomed, but not necessary.

As a creative in advertising, you'll have to follow a brand's tone of voice so your ideas fit perfectly within that brand's current place in the market. For example, let's say you're tasked with creating work for Monzo Bank. From the neon orange cards to the fun typeface, we're able to quickly see that this is a more relaxed brand, appealing to a certain kind of consumer. The vibe is, 'money's not scary and everyone's welcome.' The same language, ideas, and execution you would use for Monzo, wouldn't work if your client was, say, Coutts, a more traditional bank. Yes, at times they might indulge in artist collaborations or limited-edition designs, but they'd never give you Nu Rave realness.

You may be asked by a brand to come up with a tone of voice from scratch. This is one of my favourite things to do – helping a brand, big or small, understand who they are. For me, getting to the core of a tone of voice is about establishing both the intent and the essence of the brand. By looking at what the brand is trying to do within the context of where it came from, you'll find the elements that make that brand unique.

As a simple starting point, look at yourself as a brand. How would you promote yourself and engage with your audience? The social media girlies will tell you to find your niche. Personally, I think there are a few steps before that. The main ones being:

- Intent: What's the end goal of all of this?
- Essence: What's the most authentic and honest way of meeting that goal?

It's about what makes you you. I'm not saying you then go and pour the fundamentals of you into your project. It's about creating a framework that is memorable for you to use in everything you do.

In the words of RuPaul, 'If you can't market yourself, how in the hell you gonna market somebody else?'
(Well, almost.)

171

Apart from providing a framework for looking at tone of voice as a product of both intent and essence, taking the time to understand yourself will help inform the kind of work you want to make. Myself and Tom have always preferred comedy. Real comedy – the type that doesn't rely on using trans people as a punching bag. I'm looking at you, Dave ... Comedy – done right – is smart and informative. It provides a space to be funny and sassy (obviously), but it should also make you think. You can see, then, why Oatly is a brand I admire.

Regardless of the kind of creative content or art you make, you have your own individual tone of voice that is informed by who you are. Your voice is a product of the media you consume and, as a creative, your voice also helps inform that media. Capitalism is a mean girl, and we all love and adore her. No matter the amount of abuse she throws our way, we keep coming back and worshipping her.

Throughout this book, I have touched on the ways subcultures create popular culture. We have content creators who, with nothing but their smartphones and some homemade props, are speaking to millions of invested viewers – daily. Yet when those creatives are invited into big, shiny buildings for the chance to collaborate with brands, they're paid pennies for their worth and treated like fools.

I, myself, went through this. A lot of effort was put into making me doubt myself and the skills I arrived with. Because of this, I didn't really look at my own foundations to discover what it was I could bring to the table. The process of eventually finding my own tone of voice in my work – let alone then combining that with Tom's as joint creatives – was a struggle.

I've always loved who I am, don't get it twisted; it just took me a second to realise that the skillset I showed up with was good enough. It wasn't less than, just because I hadn't had it certified by attending a lecture at uni. This is the sort of situation where the following conversations may come in handy.

My ability to pitch and tell a story, I learned from road. Problem-solving? Road. My understanding of people, and what makes them tick? Road. Regardless of the trauma along the way, there is no way I can't accredit my skills to the things I learned from my upbringing. None of the offices I've been in taught me this skillset. I've picked up experience. I've won and lost, for sure. But my core skills – how I experience and, further, enjoy the world – were things I already showed up with. I came with my own natural talent that I was then able to finesse over time.

When you look at it from that standpoint, it becomes crystal clear that these corporate spaces were lucky to have me – not the other way around, as they'd have preferred me to believe. The following conversations show you my essence and intent. I hope they help you look and smile at yours.

"WE'RE FROM SOUTH, IT'S INGRAINED IN US."

A CONVERSATION WITH

RIVAH

Radio DJ

ON INTENT

Kevin My thing has always been: 'But I'm from South. You can't par me – I've been through things.' I'm from Thornton Heath, I'm from Croydon. There is a certain way that you just cannot deal with me; it's just not going to happen. Because worse comes to worst, I'm just gonna turn this whole room upside down and do the time on my head. I feel like you carry that within you, too.

> **Rivah** I mean, so much. South for me is . . . I was literally thinking about this the other day . . . why don't we have our own flag? Because I'm sorry, but South is the best place ever, and it must be insufferable for everybody else to see that, but it's just so warranted. We have every reason to feel this way.
>
> I remember we talked about this a few years ago, and you said that you felt respected in South London. And I feel the same; I feel safe in South. I'm in the moment, yet I'm also constantly surrounded by nostalgia, which is just so comforting. I trust it, I've done everything there: school, college, uni.
>
> All of it has been in South. It's built me up in so many different ways, and I think it's where I learned how to fight. It's prepared me for being someone who's thorough, too, and that's probably the best thing, because it's produced a very thorough individual in me. When you meet other thorough people, you just recognise it right away. That's why I love going to New York – going to Brooklyn – because you can recognise that they're thorough people, and they see it in you, too.

Because is Brooklyn not Brixton?

> Brooklyn is Brixton, babes. It's crazy!

I remember the first time I went to New York, and when I found my way to Brooklyn I was genuinely like, 'This is actually Brixton.' There is no difference apart from the accent. And yes, I agree that it's definitely made me thorough too. I don't fear anyone, I know the rules. And as much as people say South is wild, and that the people have no behaviour, we actually do adhere to rules. We are focused.

I think you was at Bounty – maybe Livin' Proof – when I first met you. Somebody tried something with your friend, and the next thing I know you're wading through the crowd to fight some man. In that moment I knew that, a) you were from South, and b) I was gonna back it. So I run after you through the crowd and we don't find the guy. From then on, I feel like we've always spoken the same language.

I feel like people from South are able to talk to anyone, to understand and have empathy in any situation. So we're able to read spirits and energy effortlessly, problem solve effortlessly. When I was growing up, South felt equal, like everyone was poor, everyone had the same type of yard. It definitely felt like that in Junction and Pond. It felt like there was a much greater sense of equality if that makes sense?

> Just amongst each other? One-hundred per cent. When I think of people like my cousins that live in West, for example, I'd go and visit them on Latimer Road, Ladbroke Grove. And it would always just be so insane to me that they were living in, like, literally one of the blocks next to where Grenfell was – but then you'd have these million-pound houses in the very same area.

People always say that's the charm of West London; the fact that everyone can mix, and it's all really nice. But I'm thinking, 'I don't know how this works.' It just used to blow my mind.

Whereas in South, everybody – socially, economically – we're about the same. We're all kind of dealing with the same things. And that brings balance, I guess.

It's true and yeah, I definitely feel like that's a part of my DNA in everything I do. What effect does being from South have on your work now? Do you think it shows up in any of your practices?

I don't have to prove to you that I'm hard, or I'm a bitch, or I need to be sass – any of that. Because we're from South, it's ingrained in us. We've had to do what we need to do. So when you're with people, you're just your authentic self. I don't have anything to prove. I proved it all a long time ago. There's always a level of authenticity and treating people with so much respect. And always, if I can do something for someone, I'll do it, there's just no ego. And that shows up in so many different ways with work when I think about it.

There's a feeling of fearlessness as well because, if push comes to shove, I will actually fight everybody here, I don't care. So I'll take a risk or ask a question that maybe others wouldn't because I'm always sticking up for myself, and making sure that I'm doing that for the people around me as well. Just looking out for everyone. I think that is definitely part of being from South, because that's what we're taught. *[Kevin clicks fingers]*

I've definitely found it difficult because a lot of spaces don't live up to the values that I hold dear, attributes I would say are very South London. So I'm constantly disappointed in certain spaces because I'm just like, 'Well, why would you do that? That's not fair. That's not equal.' Or else, 'Why are you lying about the project? Just tell me if you were feeling it or not.' It's really not that deep – and I don't think people realise when I say that, that I am comparing it with situations that have been deep. Whether that's knife crime, turf war, or whatever – I've seen the end of the world back-to-back a couple of times. And it was in Croydon, it was in Thornton Heath, it was in Peckham, it was in Streatham. All of those things have happened, so I'm not being heartless, I just can't take your tears seriously. Do people often accuse you of being heartless?

Yeah, I've definitely been accused of being nonchalant about things, like, 'Do you even care?' But it could be worse; things could be really bad. I think, in the beginning, I didn't want to succumb to the pretence of feeling like something's the end of the world just because that's what's expected of everyone in that moment – when actually, it's really not that. We're gonna make it work.

When I look at our peers that are in the same scene as I am, there's a lightness that we all have. Especially my friend James Messiah, for example. James is a poet, and he is the most carefree person in the world. James is always laughing. When he's faced with anything that's heavy, he's always just like, 'You're gonna figure it out.' It's always just really light. The same with Kush. The same with Charlie. Because we've all suffered some kind of a loss.

When I think of how aggressive growing up was at times, I think having them around me the whole time whilst I was growing and working has been a real help as well. Just being able to turn to them and remember that we're all a product of our environment, in the best way possible.

Kevin Yeah, it is really that feeling of, like, 'You lot are screaming and crying about this make believe devil, but I can actually show you the devil.'

Rivah Exactly.

One song I love, deep, is 'My Hood' by RAY BLK.

I like that song.

At a caff, not a café.
And Stormzy:

> *Coming from the land of wings and chicken fillets,*
> *Where you're from, man won't be able to read but he can bill it.*

The way he says that just sounds so familiar, so warm and inviting. Just the best of things. There's an energy to his hustle. Do you find that you hustle harder than most people around? Do you ever look at people and think, 'Where's your get up and go? Where is your drive?'

I feel like the way we hustle in South London, as people, is very similar to the fact that a barbershop can also be a nail shop, and it can also sell a shoe or a bag. There's like three things going on in that shop, basically. And that's very us.
So yes, I'm DJing, but I also want to do this; I need to do this. So I've got three things going on at the same time. And that makes me feel great. And the second I finish doing one thing, I need to move on to the next. I need at least three or four things spinning at the same time.
And that is basically what I think about when I think of those shops. It's just like yeah, you cut hair, and someone's getting a pedicure in the corner. Someone's shotting a handbag and a trainer, it's all going off.
Just going back to that thing you said about being called heartless. I used to take it to heart when I was a little younger. It's actually not a nice thing for someone to say. You know, in saying that, you're actually being the most insensitive 'sensitive' person. It's an awful thing to say to somebody.

For me, it's because we actually would die for the right cause, or to protect the things that we care about. We really would go to war. So when you're saying something like that to me, you're questioning my loyalty.

That's really what it is. Because it couldn't be further from the truth. I think that as you get older and evolve emotionally, you're then able to look back and be more confident in yourself, so those accusations don't hurt as much. You don't take them to heart as much.

176

I definitely had those conversations with myself, where I've had to tell myself that I am the definition of 'ride or die' (see Chapter 10). So if I am questioning something, it's from a place of honesty. I'm not about turning a blind eye. I'm just trying to make sure there is integrity, that everything being done is at a hundred per cent.

All of the magic that I bring in to projects comes from the essence of me being from South, and me being so empathetic and open is because of the community in South. I can sweet-talk anyone, and I can turn any situation around. I can do it with my eyes closed while standing on my head.

"IT'S SO MAGICAL WHEN YOU MEET SOMEONE ELSE WHO KNOWS YOUR STORY, JUST BY HEARING THE SMALLEST PART OF IT."

A CONVERSATION WITH

REMI SADÉ

Writer, podcaster, and talent consultant

ON ESSENCE

Kevin So, today I want to talk to you about essence. Specifically, I want to talk to you about South London, and how that shows up in everything that we both do.

> **Remi** Shut it! Kevinnn! Come on, I'm listening.

I remember the first time I properly met you, you did a couple of things that really stayed with me. Firstly, the way you walked into the room and scanned it made me think, 'She's from South.' And then immediately after, you said, 'Yes, goody.' So then I knew you were Jamaican, too. And then when you spoke about where you're from and how you were raised, you really took the time to make sure every detail was included.

But it wasn't a thing of you, like, reading out your resumé. It was very obvious to me that you were sharing your love language, really getting into the details of who you are. That's my love language, too. If I'm taking the time to explain every single nook and cranny of the story about where I'm from, then I'm really trying to tell you about who I am. Low key, I'm also giving you a warning. 'These are my ends, and this is what I'm about. So let's see.' I really recognised that in you, too – straight away – and I knew that it was because you're from South. There's nowhere else that matches that kind of energy.

> Yes, SW9's finest. I completely agree with you. Do you know, it's really interesting that this whole idea of 'essence' is what we're gonna be talking about. Because lately, I've really been thinking about a lot of the choices I've made in my life, and what my life looks like now compared to what it used to be. Just measuring all that up. And, obviously, I'm raising a daughter who's not gonna be a girl from South in the same way that I am. As someone from ends it's an interesting thing to notice – that absence of South in somebody who you really see as a full person.
>
> It sounds weird, but I think there's a certain roughness that South gives you that you're then able to polish as you grow up. It gives us a sheen. In fact, the only thing I can liken it to is that process of crystal polishing. You start off with this rough stone, but by putting it in the polisher it comes out shiny and smooth on the outside. But if you were to cut through, it'd still be rough and solid the whole way. To me, that's what it means to be a girl from South. Specifically, a girl from South who grew up in the late '90s, early noughties. She was a specific genre of woman.
>
> And I always say to people that I'm more of an experience than a description, so dating apps aren't really the best place for me. Writing it all out is so reductive compared to the fullness of our personalities and characters. But it's tough sometimes, because that essence is also made from an understanding that our grandparents are from the Windrush generation. We were grown by the stories they raised us on. A lot of us grew up in multigenerational households and, even if we didn't, the elders were never far. We always had younger cousins, too. There was always a cousin or friend's older sister who'd just had a baby that we were also helping to raise. Those two things alone teach you so much, on so many different levels.
>
> The other thing is that, when you're from South, immigrant culture is what you live and breathe. So even if you yourself have one particular heritage, you're part of a community who're from all over. I think South London really broke me bad when it came to multiculturalism; I had the

understanding of us being a minority within the UK in a theoretical sense, but it wasn't until I was a little bit older that I started to understand it in a lived sense. In South we were surrounded by people who, even if they weren't from the same culture as us, had been through similar experiences to our grandparents' generation. So when you'd ask bossman in the shop how he is, and he says, 'You know, it's hard, but thank God,' you know what that means. Or when he says, 'I'm trying to get my family to come over,' your grandma had already told you about that time when her sister sent for somebody. So you understand.

We also know how not to talk too much. That's a really big thing. Sometimes you just need to be quiet and observe. When you mentioned about me scanning the room I laughed, because I didn't think that was one of my 'markers'. Personally, I didn't grow up in an estate, but I had a lot of friends from Stockwell, Tulse Hill, Somerleyton, and Aylesbury Estate. And the thing was, you'd always scan the entrance and exit of any building as you came and went. Once you're in that environment, you assess your safety in that environment – even if you're somewhere that you've been a hundred times. Because there's one day when something could be different. And then, there were always the specific ways to walk into a place, and the ones you just avoided.

Kevin One-hundred per cent. And you were told to be in at a certain time, so if you thought you were rough and stayed out later, you knew something was going to happen because you hadn't listened to the elders. So even that double-checking had an element of you thinking, 'Is this curse now gonna come to life here? Because I'm fully not meant to be here right now, and I've been told so.'

Remi But also, prayer was a big thing – regardless of whether you believed or not. That was neither here nor there, everything in our community was either solved with prayer, or else caused by a lack of prayer. And again, that was shared across cultures. You might have been Christian, but you still knew when it was Ramadan because of your Muslim friends. 'Ah bruv, it's that time. Okay, we're not gonna go chicken shop after school.' You also understood the spiritual undercurrent to life; everybody was always telling us, 'If God spare life.' You say bye to your granny and she replies, 'If God spare life. I hope it go.' There was always an understanding of something esoteric, beyond ourselves.

The other thing is, if you grew up in South you had white friends who understood that if you said, 'Rah, my auntie dreamt about fish,' they'd say – regardless of whether they're from the culture or not – 'Oh, who's pregnant?' There's a lot of talk now about Black British culture and where it comes from, and I will go on record and say it's a direct result of Caribbeans and the influence of Caribbeans. Specifically, I would say Bajan, Trinidadian, and Jamaican people. I think what we consider now to be Black Britishness is maybe the grandchild of what the kids of the '80s or '90s experienced. Like, bashment culture comes from shebeen culture, which comes from the fact that our grandparents couldn't afford to go to the rave. And if they could, they weren't always able to get in, or it wasn't safe. So they would throw a dancehall in their house. And then their kids grew up understanding, 'Rah, my mum used to throw a shebeen. Now we can go and rent somewhere.'

Soundclash culture comes from MCs holding up a dance in somebody's house, and that being, you know, like a sound system. All of that kind of stuff. So to me, there are two sides to this idea of essence. There's my personal experience, but there's also that wider look at where we are today. And we don't get enough respect for what we brought to culture, specifically the understanding of Black girls having sauce in this country. We always used to look to African Americans for that essence – that sauce and community – but now they're looking at us, recognising our own progression. And I think that predominantly comes from the spread of South London culture and music; those two are the big things. Also, when we say South, we don't mean Richmond. Because some people now will be like, 'I live in South London' and it's like SW16. Wimbledon.

No, you lot are in mookooland. You're a mook, calm down.

Like, Tooting is probably as far as you can go southwest. Even Clapham South you wouldn't consider. But Clapham? All right, cool. So now, if people say they live in South London, I wait for them to say something else so I then understand what version of South London they mean, you know? It's bittersweet now, because I feel like we're almost antiques; the place that we knew does not exist anymore. In some senses, that essence we carry is no longer about a geographical location. But we're able to take that into so many different environments that we never thought we'd end up in, as well as ones we've created for ourselves. And that's an even more powerful space to be in.

We definitely are relics of that time. But as creatives, yeah, we are absolutely running and doing the ting – regardless of the field. That's not to say we get the ratings or credit that we deserve, or that we even realise for ourselves that we should be in those spaces. I remember conversations that you and I have had where I've been like, 'Go and ask them for your money and just do the thing, because you've got the skillset.' It's ridiculous that it takes that, but that's a wider conversation on society in general.

That's a really interesting point because, recently, I've been doing headhunting in advertising and creative spaces. Still doing my own freelance thing too, obviously. But it's interesting that you brought up my . . . I don't know, I don't even wanna call it impostor syndrome. It's beyond that – just the raw question of 'Can I do it or not?' Because now I'm looking at the market from a different perspective, and understanding more of what people ask for against what they have to offer. Now I'm able to look back at my career and understand that I have all this experience – five years building up very specific skills – that other people actively aim to gain just by building somebody else's dream. It's shifted my sense of what I'm worth and what I can do. Not even what I think I'm worth, actually, because I also think that coming from South brings a level of delusion to your self-belief that you just have to have.

It's more the fact that we're led to think, 'Oh, I only know this thing, and maybe one or two others, so I'm just gonna run with that.' But actually, people will go for stuff that they just aren't qualified for. It's really interesting looking at how Black women speak about their professional capabilities online. We'll say we can do two-hundred per cent of something whilst acting like it's a hundred per cent – as if we're on everybody else's level. I don't understand. Because I look at it and I'm like, 'No, you're a whole magician.'

Kevin Whole wizards hold everything. And I would say that the reason Black women do that – and, in fact, I think that we as a people do that – is because we were so close to our grandparents, right? I really don't know anyone in our generation who doesn't ride for their grandparents. We were so close to them; we grew up in their embrace. And because of that, the restrictions that they felt are ones we've now taken on ourselves, even though times have changed. And that's not to say that actually everything's roses now, not at all. If anything, it shows that the way people try it today is just a fresh version of what came before.

But yes, Black women really are magicians. And in fact, when you mentioned that specific type of Black South London girl from the '90s, that really warmed my heart. Everything I do is based on that vibe, the fierceness. That's a big part of why this book is called *Black Women Always*, because it was those Black girls you're talking about who really gave me game on every single thing. Me being gay wasn't a concern; all I got from them was open-arms acceptance. Even when I was warring with other boys over their stupidness, these lot were fully taking off their earrings and getting in the fight. Like backing it fully and not even blinking. That's always been my experience.

Remi And you would also see those girls on Saturday with their granny outside of Safeways. Do you remember Safeways in Brixton, by the arches?

Please behave, of course I do.

With the trolley, and very respectful as well. You know, 'Hello, how are you?'

And calling all of their elders Mum and Dad. So versatile and multifaceted with their communication. But South makes you adaptable in a way that goes beyond code-switching.

I have so many memories of what you're talking about; that whole energy of just backing it. Remember when Stockwell Park was still called Stockwell Park? I remember my older sisters taking me out of my pushchair there, because there were some school kids who were like, 'If it's peak, it's peak. Either you're gonna back it or you're not gonna back it.' And so the pushchair was parked to the side.

But there was also a really strong sense of respect. I remember watching 'The Wire' once – not that South was like that at all. But that respect I'm talking about turned up in one specific scene where this gangster's grandma got knocked off on a Sunday. And all the sides were like, 'But it's Sunday, and you knocked off her crown.' That was too far; even the person who the guy had done it for was like, 'Nah, we have to discipline you. The man was taking his grandma to church.'

And I do feel like growing up in South really gave us our own code of conduct and respect. You didn't feel like you were growing up in London; you felt like you were growing up in South London. It's not like we just stayed in

South, but it was always home and it always will be. Nothing beats coming back from abroad and walking out of the steps at Brixton underground station – no matter the time of day, there's always the noise and the bustle. Over there's a man selling incense saying, 'I ain't seen you in ages.' Rah, I didn't even know you noticed. You get a real sense of, like, 'Welcome home.' And it's so magical when you meet someone else who knows your story, just by hearing the smallest part of it. And if you're both in a place to be able to say, 'Yeah, we made it. We made something. And to meet you here in itself is a privilege beyond working with any person.' To see one of your own in spaces like that, when so many of us questioned if we would even be okay, is beautiful. Our hard work paid off, it wasn't in vain. I think that's really powerful.

Sorry, I just got lost in the poetry of everything you were saying. Because I know exactly what you mean, but I'd never had the words for it before. So thank you.

I want to ask you about how all the things we're talking about show up in your work now, but actually hearing what you've just said has reminded me of something I wrote.

Read it to me, let me hear it.

Do you want me to read it to you?

God's rhythm housed in patterned Mosh, Patrick Cox's and exposed ankles
Chops and gold rings, gold clowns on gold chains and gold bangles

Versace Blue Jeans floats atop of cocoa butter
Make magic with no effort from passed down trauma and clutter

Milk tokens gave birth to banquets
Phone cards and JR Hartley before bandwidths

Nestled in front of the universe and tender headed
Blessings bestowed upon me by Black women, my leverage

Gold tooth caps with Nike emblems, A-line skirts, lipstick plum
No future, but a shot at legacy eggs us on to be young dads and mums

Underestimated soft tones, I let them name call, they thought that shit hurt
Gangsters move in silence and some of us also lift shirts
In reality, my limp wrist produced great right hooks
My love language? Something of a mix of Ramsey and Fen and bell hooks

While you were having lunches with Mel and Sue
We were selling food while selling food
£3.20 per hour for the perfect cover
The narrative alleviated the stress for our mothers

I know my worth
The industry is – light work
Explain Crypto to someone accustomed to notes in socks
Or the irony of representation found on a dark and lovely perm box

I can, you can't.

Inherently intersectional, that's why culture sits at our core.
Black creatives are advertising's favourite whores.

Remi That was so beautiful. I felt a lump in my throat from the moment you said chops, and that was very early on. It's a memory of home, man. It's such a memory of home.

Kevin Thank you. Let's bring it all back to how exactly you think the essence we're talking about shows up in your own work? Like what you said about having an essence that you've polished and refined over time, what does that mean for how you do business now?

I think I'm still understanding that, but I think the number one way in which it shows up is that versatility; we cannot be boxed in. Career-wise, that means I've tried a lot of different versions of storytelling. Whatever medium I can use, I will. And I guess the other thing is that I'm not just trying to tell my own story, I'm trying to facilitate people telling their stories, in their own words, too. And it's important that I do that collaboratively.

And you do see the other side of that in advertising, right? A lot of brands don't understand the importance of translation. The issue isn't that the conversation is necessarily wrong, it's that the attempt to translate it authentically just isn't there. It lacks that true heart. Two people can speak their truth but if you do not understand my language, and I do not recognise yours, we are not communicating. And a conversation is not communication without translation, and communication is the element of advertising that brands struggle with often.

The other side of it, for me, is that I'm always trying to learn the structure of the business from all the angles. It's the same as when we used to assess the entrances and exits growing up. It doesn't matter how long you're going to be in the building, you should always know. And if something changes, you should always try to know; you should always try to be alert.

Yes, as Tom is my witness, in every agency we've ever worked at, I will make sure I learn about everyone else's skillsets. Then, I'm more fluent in their language and understand how they communicate what they mean.

If I could just sit down all day with somebody in advertising, and they paid me to literally give them all the ideas on how to communicate, have conversations, and find talent, I'd love that. And I mean, like, new talent, not somebody who's just gone to drama school. To be able to sit with people and just ask them their story, how the product or brand really works in their world – I think that's something that, in most advertising I've seen, is clearly not tapped into. I don't think a lot of people know how to do that.

But again, it's that idea of collaborative storytelling that I'm really passionate about in my own work now. The truth is though, when I first started, like most of us when we're building our careers, I looked at it purely from the point of view of what my strengths were, and how they could get me what I needed. So when I originally started writing, I did it because there was nobody else providing their experiences of new parenthood from the same demographic as me; a Black student aged 22.

So I was going to be raising my baby on a student loan. I wasn't going to be doing it on my husband's money, or my parents' funds, or anything like that. And I had moved out of home very young, like a lot of us do. There was no fallback. I didn't want to give advice, nor did I want to be inspirational. I just wanted to give an honest account of one person's perspective. Because my motto at the time was like, if one person reads this, and it helps them in any way, then I've done something good.

But I can see how you've naturally moved from that space into one of collaborative storytelling, now that you have the means to. Do you think that – maybe subconsciously – you run towards storytelling in that way because this is what our grandparents did? Storytelling always saved their lives, and that's perhaps something you want to pass on?

Entirely. To be honest with you, I didn't even set out to do it as a career; it took me about two years of doing it to realise that's what it had become. It was so removed from what my idea of a career was in other spaces.

But I also grew to understand that it was really important for our voices to be heard. It took a lot of learning, but I know I don't want to be front-facing. I'm good at it because I'm good at communicating. But actually, I enjoy strategy. I enjoy research. I oftentimes take on freelance jobs that have nothing to do with being an influencer; it's all about research. And I will send a nine-page document back with like 11,000 words covering five key questions. And they're like, 'Wow, you really looked deeply into this. Thanks so much'. And I'm like, 'Yeah, the reason why, is because you are gonna take this information, and you're gonna give it to a strategist, who's then gonna come up with something else that they give to the creative making the ad, and I want them to have as much information as possible so that it lands accurately.' It is so powerful when you feel seen by people who you never expected to see you. I remember the first time that I saw rice in a Christmas advert – it will never leave my mind. And it was a Black family having Christmas dinner. And you know that, Kevin – whether we are African, Caribbean, Black British – you know that we eat rice at Christmas.

We eat rice at Christmas, we have coleslaw at Christmas. We have plantin. Not plan-tayn. Plant-in.

It's important to include us visually. But it is much more important to include us culturally. Because if you only include us visually, in my opinion, what that means is that you're just ticking your box. You're just making sure that you really quickly did a thing, or seem to have done a thing. But when you sit down and you have these conversations and you take the time to really understand somebody, then you know the work you make is going to ring true.

I think ultimately though, it's even more than that for me. Storytelling is so powerful. It's archiving. I feel like I'm an archivist of people's stories.

Yes. You're honouring their essence, because you know how important it is to honour your own.

YOUR LOVE IS A 197, TAKING ME TO PECKHAM

(It used to be the 312)

I don't know why they swapped the buses around, but they
get you to the same destination. All of that to say, sometimes
you will have to use the essence of the project as
a Trojan horse for your intent.

TODAY'S TAKEAWAY:

It's killing me, this bus should be so dirty

The work you do is not always going to be fun, but by
understanding your intent and finding the truth, or essence,
of the subject matter, you'll find that the experience
not only becomes bearable — it actually reveals itself as
worthwhile. Not just for what you'll learn from it, but for the
satisfaction gained from controlling the work in a
professional, easy manner.

(Shout out to the Whitehead Bros.)

15

INSPIRATION

INSPIRATION

To say I would raise hell for the two women in the following conversations is an understatement. For their protection and comfort, the levels of violence I'd happily enact would make the devil hide.

By now, you have an idea of the kind of place Croydon was in the '90s. You have an idea of how that environment forced us to utilise violence when needed. Economic disparity slows time, enabling the pain of your circumstances to feel like an eternity. The language of poverty, wrapped in ridicule like barbed wire on fences, slices your eardrums, leaving you deaf to words of hope. The only words that might make it through are prayers from our grandparents and, if you're as lucky as me, some friends who are down to ride for you. No matter what. We just knew we had to move and get out of the situation, by any means necessary.

Often people talk about crimes in inner cities as if they are not a symptom of a bigger issue; as if cause and effect are not rules of science. Croydon is no Virgin Mary – we were definitely fucked and left to figure out raising ourselves.

Some of the stories in these conversations took place in 1998, when Labour had been in power for a year or so – this is after sixteen years of Tory rule. I'm no historian – this is based off my lived experience – but for further reference, I suggest reading through *Faith in the City: A Call for Action by Church and Nation*. It's co-authored by Wilfred Wood, the bishop of Croydon from 1985 to 2003, and it sheds light on those forgotten inner-city spaces, affected as they were by recession and unemployment. The report caused a massive political argument, one that the church and the Tories are still salty about to this day.

During those times, Bush and Ashley – who I talk with in the following conversations – held me down in a way that I find hard to describe. They have both individually saved my life multiple times.

I'm a product of my environment. I've healed and grown. I'm a bigger fan of peace and harmony for sure, but I'd hate for you to think that I would not pull those old skillsets out of retirement – while sending my maturity packing – and act a fool to defend these two women.

Now that it's clear why these two women are so important to me, I want to let you in on a fact: these two women are magic. The work I make today is imbued with this magic. I make magic. If I don't call what I do magic – if I don't believe in what I do – then I don't believe in those that inspired my actions. Then I don't believe in how they've shaped my practices and, yes, saved me. Sometimes just from myself.

Influence in your work is important. Mine ranges from Biggie to Nan Goldin. What Ashley and Bush are to me are more like muses – inspiration and, at the same time, reminders of everything that makes me, me. The results of that inspiration can always be found in my work.

"YOU'RE JUST LIKE ME."

A CONVERSATION WITH

BUSHIRA ATTAH

Mother, and Kevin's right-hand woman

ON FRIENDSHIP

Kevin My first question is, why did you come into that lunch room and fight me for no reason?

Bushira Oh, gosh. Why?

I'm joking. We don't actually have to start there, but it does make me laugh. I will say that when I first stepped into that burger shop (see Chapter 1), I didn't understand what was going on, because everybody was ignoring you. And you were whispering and, like, tiptoeing around.

It was almost like you were trying to be annoying for everyone, and everyone already knew your game. But because I'd just started working there, I didn't understand what was going on. So you'd be like, 'Ohhh, I can't lift the nuggets,' and everyone was just looking at you like, 'Just do your work, please.' I'd be like, 'Nah, she needs help.'

And I don't know if you remember, there was that guy called Nasa? Anyway, he was like, 'Bro, don't fall for it, don't fall for it.' I was like, 'What do you mean? She needs help with the nuggets.' And then before I knew it, I was kind of doing your job. And then I thought, 'Hold on a minute. You're actually taking me for a mook.' From then, I was just obsessed with you.

Pretty soon I thought you were a genius for the way that you saw things, and how passionate you were. And still are.

And especially with regards to defending me; you always waited to hear my side of the story and, even if I was dead wrong, you'd back it, and it was only later, one-on-one, that you'd say, 'That was some bullshit, I'm telling you right now.' But you'd always give me time and space to really explain myself, and hear it from my mouth first.

When I came out too, you just took it very casually. You didn't bat an eyelid or have anything to say about it. You were just like, 'Okay cool, are we going out tonight? Because I think I can get the lesbians to buy us drinks.'

From the moment I met you, I was just in awe. I thought you were the coolest person ever.

Oh my gosh.

No, really.

No, stop.

You was! Because you just did this tomboy thing in a time when lots of other girls were trying to do tomboy too, but weren't really about it. And you were like, 'Nah, I am a tomboy, and I'm sexy. And I'm about it. What?' And I just remember how all the other girls were jealous of you, but knew they could not tell you anything. They were between a rock and a hard place, and the only option to keep it a hundred was to be within your circle.

Without you providing me the space to be myself, whilst also having you challenging me when I needed it, I wouldn't be the person I am today. No way.

You know what? You make me sound like such a superhero.

But you were, I mean we can get into the evil side if you want?

The evil villain. *[Both laugh]*

But what were your thoughts on our friendship in those early days? Because, to be honest, I feel like we really didn't have anything but ourselves and each other.

And this is what I explained to people; I was the female version of you, and you were the male version of me. I don't know if you know this, but I was a loner at school. You do know I don't like people. But when someone's real? You just know, and you connect. All I saw was me, that's all it is. And the fact that we had that familial connection through your uncle and my brothers, it was just like we were meant to be. That's the only way I can explain it. It was just love from day dot, you know? We were inseparable from the first minute. Everything you said – all the superhero stuff about me – it's just you. Loyalty. Maybe I love myself too much, you know?

[Kevin laughs] I'm laughing because it's true. Maybe we just love ourselves.

Nah, maybe it is that. But when you find someone real, you just know. And that's what it was all about. Like, at the risk of sounding cliché, you want someone to treat you how you would treat others. That's you. That's all I can say.

I don't think there will ever be another time like there was during those years. There were so many things going on culturally. The women and young girls of that time were definitely the forerunners of the conversations that we're having now in terms of expression and freedom. That was the first time, not literally the first time, but the first time it felt like the girls were really saying, 'Maybe I'm not going to get married. I don't want to get married. Maybe I just want to go and work and earn money for myself, actually. Maybe men are the fucking problem and it's got absolutely nothing to do with us lot. Because you lot are actually moving mad.'
In terms of music, everything we were listening to was from London, so we started to feel like we had our own identity. Up until that point we all thought we were from Brooklyn or wherever your favourite rapper was from.

Looking back, yeah, that's so true.

Like, not to snitch on people I grew up around, but you'd know what some of those American rappers were talking about. Like, we'd lived it, too.

See, I think that's another thing that really linked us, because only a select few people were that real, and understood it. So people talk about it and sing about it, but they didn't understand it.

Yeah.

It was true for us. It was real.

Kevin You're right. A lot of people ran around screaming 'Ride or die, ride or die!' and then they weren't even willing to ride, let alone die. That really used to frustrate me because those people didn't have to shout and claim that was what they were about. I really enjoyed the fact that people were absolutely petrified to talk sideways about you in front of me, because they knew it'd be a wrap if they did.

      Bushira One-hundred per cent.

We were the menaces of Croydon. I'm going to say it. There's this reference to you in the film script Tom and I are writing, and it's based on something that happened one time at the burger store you and I worked at. I went outside and these two girls were pointing and staring at me. And we didn't even know why, because they never got the chance to explain themselves. But they were being a bit funny on the sly. And I remember you. We had just finished our shift and you had your large cup of still Fanta with your ice, and you came out and saw I was upset. You asked what was wrong, and I said, 'Oh, it's them over there.' And like, you didn't even wait, you just walked over very calmly, took the cap off of the drink and just poured it on the girl's head.
      Do you know how much I fucking love you?
      Because I can't confirm if their behaviour was to do with like, the whole gay thing. And specifically, with the fact that they couldn't get their head around the fact that I was gay and road. They didn't know what to make of me. But that wasn't my problem.
      I don't know what them lot thought I was going to be, especially with the way that they all tried to bully me one way or another. If I'm a monster, they created it – because I could have just been happy in my little corner. I'm happy with peace, you know. I'm happy sharing everything I've got. I'm happy helping everyone. But that maybe wasn't the best environment for me to be growing up in, because I wasn't necessarily allowed to do that. So when you just swept in like that—

      You make me sound like a monster to people.

Nah, listen. The gays who read this will be looking over to their best friend and saying, 'This is the level I need you to get to.' You're gay best friend goals. I've just got so much admiration for you because you made my life bearable. You really, really did.

      Vice versa. Everything is a path, and we were meant to meet each other that time. Because remember, everything was the same. We may not have the same exact stories, but it's like we were living the same life.

I'm gonna get emotional now, too. One of the ingredients that made us work right away was that we were always gonna be a hundred per cent with each other. And that was a rule. And I knew that at any point, if I ever tried to turn around to you and lie to you about anything, I would be doing irreparable damage. I knew that. I probably could get you back in my life, but something would be missing. So from the get-go I knew I would always have to tell you the truth, which isn't a problem because I hate lying and I'm too lazy to remember where I hid everything.

That must a be a Virgo quality, you know. Too lazy to lie. But do you know what's interesting? I've now discovered why I don't like lying. Apparently, when I was really young, my dad used to say to all of my siblings that I'm not a liar; I don't lie. So it's probably stuck with me through age because I hate liars. And then, you know the music we listened to? I took it to heart. I took it very, very seriously.

So loyalty, respect, and discipline. I was very influenced by the music. On top of that, remember that I went to a girls' school and I never had good friends. I think you were my first real friend. Just seeing the things they were keeping up at school, and I wouldn't be able to understand it. I just didn't get all their snakey behaviour. And I said I wasn't gonna be around people like that. I wanted to be around people who were like me. So really, it was just being around disgusting people. That's all it is. And listening to so much rap music.

[Kevin laughs] I think in hindsight, you were my first real friend too. Because at school I'd had that one bredrin Colin, ginger kid, but then he got shifted for something and had to do time. So him, maybe, but then when that happened all the other boys that I did roll around with just, like, disappeared. Within a week or two.

That's what I'm saying. It's all fake and what you're saying resonates with me so much. Like you could be alone in a room full of people. That's how I was in school. I always felt like an outsider.

Yeah, for taking the idea of loyalty seriously. And you're right, we really did take the music seriously. It was a miracle no one pushed us to the limit because it would've been a wrap. 'That was for Bush.' But again, it felt like some kind of divine power was watching out for us, 'cause there were a lot of near misses – times when something bad should have happened, and it didn't. I think there was always space for intuition within our friendship, too.

There were times when I wanted to do something and you didn't want to, and so I'd be like, 'Well if Bush isn't going then neither am I.' And vice versa. And then we'd come to find there'd been some kind of madness that had happened. The thing is, a lot of what we were going through at that time, we just weren't having the conversations that people do now. I always felt like we were very emotionally intelligent, and that scared a lot of people.

And the behaviour, too. We've got so many different facets to our personalities, and it stops people from being able to box us in. I guess for them it is quite scary because it's like, who am I going to get today, this hour, this minute? Remember the jokes, though, that would come of that? Like, I'd get angry at work and just leave – so you'd leave too.

Yeah, calling us back, trying to get us in. But I mean, there was some mad shit going on there, it really was a time before HR was a thing. Remember we'd just draw our holiday pay without ever going on holiday? They'd just add it on to your pay. Oh, or we'd do fourteen-hour shifts. But I had some of the best times at that place.

Them days were fun. They really were.

Kevin They were a fairy tale; they were dangerous, but they were fun. And it was like we knew that we deserved better. Like we were watching a live comedy show and waiting for the other shoe to drop. Like, for someone to turn up and say, 'You guys shouldn't be here. No one should have to do this.' But that day never came, so we were just left watching all this madness saying, 'What is this?'

Remember when that guy was sleeping with two of the other staff, and when they both found out they decided to have an episode of 'The Jerry Springer Show' on the shop floor in front of all the customers, just fighting over this guy? They had to be broken apart, their uniforms all torn up. All this over a guy with no skincare routine.

Bushira Oh yeah, I can see his face, but I can't remember his name.

Then there was that other time someone got into beef with someone else over a girl, and he just pulled out his thing and basically pistol-whipped him. And my main thought was just, 'Who knew you were packing? You just seemed like a lovely, sweet guy.'

Remember how many fights there really were on the shop floor? And the shooting?

Yeah. That was a real turning point for me (see Chapter 18 for the full story).

You see the way people talk about Croydon now as this dangerous place? I don't get what they mean. But maybe it's just because of what we had to live through.

Yeah, because I'm like Croydon is a lovely place now. You can't tell me any different. It was so much worse than it is now. But, on a certain level, I'm so thankful that I went through those things because I feel like now I can go anywhere.

Yeah, because back then, you'd see something in Croydon every day. Every single day.

When I changed school it was really interesting, because I had to learn how to act around a very different kind of people. But I think that taught me a lot about sitting back, observing, and just listening to what's going on.

I'll talk to anyone. Someone might say to me, 'Why are you talking to them? They're a weirdo.' No one's a weirdo. I think everyone's interesting. Everyone's got something to say.

That's the thing though, like we were saying earlier, most people like to compartmentalise others. And if they can't box you in, they don't like it. But why would you wanna do that, or be box-shaped in the first place? How do you not understand that by learning about other people, you're effectively learning more about yourself?

There you go.

Sometimes I have to interact with people just to hear their thoughts on the thing, because yes, I might not agree or do it the same way, but in listening to them I have a better understanding of them, and also of what it is I'm actually about.

You were also the one that really made me realise all of us could be destined for much bigger things if our skillsets were actually used and governed in the right way. Like, when I hear about UN ambassadors going to different places to try and make peace, in my head there's no reason why you couldn't do that job. But were we ever told such a thing? I've seen you fully talk people off of ledges. People who were going to go and seek bloodshed. You've literally saved lives. And the thing is, yes, Croydon is getting better, but there are still kids that aren't being shepherded in the right way. They haven't got someone like you telling them they've got the skills.

And now you're talking about my passion. The youth are my passion, which is maybe why I've got many children.

Why do you think it is your passion?

I think it's going back to what you said. I always knew there was more. You knew there was more. Because, and I say this with no disrespect, a lot of the people we grew up with weren't very smart. No shade. But I used to think everyone was on the same level of intelligence. They're not, unfortunately. So the reason that I'm like this about the youth is because the ones that are smart aren't given the chance to know any different. Society pigeonholes them. 'You come from the ghetto, you stay in the ghetto. Your parents didn't do this? Grandparents didn't do that? Then stay here.' Essentially, producing a generation of slaves.

It's modern-day slavery. But I can see something else in these kids, and that's why I'm so passionate. Because if I can change one person then that, at least, is something to me. I'd like to do more, but yeah. This is the thing, right, you got asked to leave Ashburton and I was expelled from school. But in terms of grades, I was in the top set.

I'd do the work, and then I'd read a book because there's still an hour left. And yeah, I don't mind reading a book. But I've read all these books already, so what am I gonna do next? I'm gonna play about and cause problems because I'm bored.

Chaos. [Both laugh]

But they're still doing these things these days. I speak to teachers and they're teaching to one particular mindset in the class, without thinking about the others. So whilst you're building one up, you're doing it at the expense of others because you're not flexing with the rest of the class. Like, that has to change. When is that going to change?

It's funny 'cause someone asked me something at a talk that ties into that, about how I try to encourage growth in my business and, you know, make sure it's a place where people feel fulfilled. I think at Pocc I try to let people do the things they're naturally good at. Our head of growth, Jordie, she enjoys costing up jobs and creating budget, etc., so we give her space to do that, whilst minimising the time she has to have, like, conversations with negative clients or whatever. Not that she can't handle them, but for me I can do all that in my sleep, and I'm happy to step in and take that on so it's smoother for her. I guess it's still drawing on our topic of friendship – that's how I try and run the business.

And in terms of school, really and truly a lot of the subjects that are force-fed to them now . . . you have to ask yourself: Are they really as important as we're making out?

> **Bushira** Yeah, because they're asking these questions about trigonometry, and how is that even relevant?

Kevin I've never used any of those things. I tell you what I did need. I needed you to explain about taxes.

> Do you know there's grown people – aged nineteen, twenty – who don't know how to operate a bank account? I don't understand. But then, we just taught ourselves this stuff.

Do you think some of that also comes from wanting to know how to best play the game against a system that's determined not to lift you up? Like, knowing how to work that system? Because otherwise the system will continue to rob us, by accidentally-on-purpose leaving us in the dark. As a society, we minimise the damage neglect can cause – but that neglect is planned. Like, I found out the other day how unbalanced the funding is between boroughs in South.

> They're all like it. Like, because Kingston's upper-class, they're going to put more money into their schools to keep that level up. They put the money where they're going to gain the most, with the least amount of work. Look how many private schools there are in Kingston. How many in Croydon? And look at what extracurricular activities they're offering in Kingston's schools, and what they're doing in Croydon.

That's why I loved it when we were talking about your kids the other day, and you said how they go to five million different activities.

> 'Five million.' You're just like me.

But that genuinely excites me because I know exactly why you're doing it, and why it's so important. Whereas others will just think, 'Is that needed? Are you all right?'

> I knew you got it, and that was everything for me.

It's because we didn't have hobbies. Not one. Except fighting. But it wasn't for nothing; I always saw us as the Robin Hoods of Croydon. Like, 'I'm sorry, who did that to you?' And then we'd go and avenge those people.

> That's one thing I still can't stand. I hate bullies.

196

I hate bullies too. We really did go through a lot. What's your fondest memory, looking back?

Ah, that's gonna be hard. Give me a minute. Because when I tell the kids about any of it, all of it brings me joy. I can't pick out one thing. I can tell you the thing I'm most grateful for from you. Do you know what I'm gonna say? Shania.

Really?

Yeah. You really were her other parent.

Oh, wow.

Because other people used to try to use her as a prop.

Yeah. You know what it was – I think for both of us? I think it was the first time we met someone outside of our immediate friendship group – you know, ourselves, Ashley, and the others – that we felt like we could pour everything into, and we weren't gonna get burned that time. Because we'd poured so much into other people who had failed us – and we knew they were gonna fail us, but we did it anyway.

I have so many moments I look back on. I've already said one that turns up in mine and Tom's film script, but honestly we have a whole character who is, basically, you. Her name is Rose and I can't wait for you to meet her.

You're making me blush.

"SOUTH LONDON VERSION OF ... DAWSON'S CREEK."

A CONVERSATION WITH

ASHLEY MADEKWE

BAFTA-nominated actress and keeper of Kevin's secrets

ON FRIENDSHIP

Kevin When I think about one of the key processes behind how I try to bring a real sense of connection to my work, I really bring that back to the biggest inspirations in my life. And, you know, looking at those inspirations, thinking about their beauty, and then tapping into that in my work. Trying to bring some of that magic to the work itself.

Specifically, I look at the most important friendships I have, and what makes them so strong. I look at the relationships I've made with you, along with Bush. I really think it's us. We could run around and say that we're family, but that seems too much of a meek, small word. When you use the term 'friendship', it implies how much we've endured together. How much shit we put up with from each other and still stuck around – all of those things.

Ashley It's a choice.

It's always been a choice. I think when we first met it was like, 'Okay, great. You understand that this is Sunnydale, this is a hellmouth that we are working in and we need to get out of here.'

SOS. *[Kevin laughs]*

Also, I think there's something to be said for having friends in your life that you've known at different stages. I know it's about time, but it's also about stages. The idea of who you are as a sixteen-year-old, versus who you are at twenty or thirty. The sixteen-year-old brain is very, very different from the thirty-year-old's.

And that's why I think many people don't have friends from that time in their life, because you grow and change. And that's okay. But if you're able to keep a friend or two from that time period, then good luck hiding from the mirror of yourself.

Yeah, it's true.

Congratulations, you will grow.

Yeah, 'cause sometimes I try to come back to you and tell you things and you're like, 'Are you all right? Who are you talking to? Don't lie to me.'

Why are you lying?

[Kevin laughs] You almost have physical time capsules walking around with you that you can open just to remind you, like, 'Don't be silly.' And that works both ways because – and I think we both do this for each other – like, I might be down on myself one day and you'll remind me of where we were, and what's been built to get to the point we're at now.

Like, don't disrespect yourself and don't disrespect me because why would we be friends otherwise? Which is really funny because it's something that I say to Tom all the time. I'm like, 'So you think I'm friends with dickheads? Are you all right?' *[Ashley laughs]*

Like, why would I have you around me? *[Both laugh]* When we were working in Sunnydale, never in a million years was it in my head that I could go off and do advertising.

Ashley No.

Kevin For you, you were always clear and set on acting.

> You knew you wanted to be in a creative field, but you didn't know how to get there. Which I think is why so many people from where we're from don't get to live their dreams. Because there's no roadmap for them.
>
> You didn't have that. With acting, it's slightly easier because you can at least go to a drama group, or a drama school, or try to get an agent. But with advertising? So much is unknown.

My clear path was really you, and our friendship. Like, 'I can't be dusty, because she's not.' *[Both laugh]*

You were the first person I'd come across who believed in everything being possible, like, 'You know what, I believe that can happen and I'm gonna try to make it happen.' We used to have this running joke of owning a flat on Bond Street above the original—

> —Original Gucci! Above the original Gucci store. I think they're moving back now.

You were – and still are – always focused. 'Cool, I want that Iceberg hat. So I need to work this amount of hours. Boom.' You have always been just A-B-C-Execute. That was just the bedrock of our friendship.

> Yeah, 'What's everyone doing? What's the plan?' I mean, it's hard when you don't have opportunity – it's lack of opportunity, really. Lack of access. There's not this plethora of opportunities where we're from, unfortunately. I think having a dream made me very lucky, and then going to a free performing arts school made me very lucky because I got to be around like-minded people of my age, and be inspired by teachers who were like, 'Yes you can.'
>
> But the thing you're saying about friends pushing you, I completely see and understand that because I had that with you. And I had it with one other person, Nicole Charles, who was also from South London. We would always be reading. I wasn't one to read non-fiction but Nicole would be like, 'Today I'm reading the history of theatre,' or, 'I'm working through so-and-so's autobiography.' And I was like, 'Well, I'd better be reading that too, I guess.' So I think it's about community, opportunity, and inspiration. If there's a lack of all that then how we gonna move?

[Kevin laughs] I'm laughing to myself because I realise that we really were a very South London version of some of the characters from 'Dawson's Creek'. *[Both laugh]*

Because it was just a moment where like, yes, Nicole was always reading things. You were always reading, and then there's me. I really have never enjoyed reading. Obviously later on, being diagnosed with dyslexia, it made sense. But I did love words. I would read the dictionary to work on my vocabulary, while at the same time still being interested in all the things within our culture.

I think we both loved words and didn't see a need to separate those two worlds, so we'd read about it, but also Shakespeare.

Well, why does one have to exclude the other? I do think that the BRIT School was a great level-up for me, because there were people there from all over the UK. Not everybody came from Sunnydale. People travelled quite far to go to the school, and that just made for a very different mix of races and cultural groups. Do you know what I mean? All of my musical influences came from the people I'd grown up with, so I was very into R&B, hip hop, soul – and still am. But then, being around those other kids who were listening to Nirvana and No Doubt? I was like, 'Wow, this is a bop too.'

That happened to me, too. When I left, or got asked to leave, Ashburton and went to that mookooland school. I went to that school with some serious I-want-to-fight-everyone energy. And every pupil in that school was like, 'Do you need a time out?' *[Ashley laughs]*

They all declined the wahala and were like, 'No, I don't have time for this, I've got to go and learn the flute.'

In the BRIT School, there weren't cliques. There really wasn't. I mean, yeah, you maybe hung out within the drama strand or the music strand. But within your strand, no. Like the emo kids were hanging out with the hip hop kids and vice versa. And we all informed each other's stylistic choices and culture.

Agreed. If I didn't go to that school, I don't think I ever would have discovered Green Day or Nirvana or whatever.

And then we'd both connect back at work, and I'd be like, 'I heard this . . . have you ever heard the lyrics to this?' Let's not get it twisted, we were still listening to Mariah all day, every day. But in between there was this exciting exchange – and that happened with films, too. And then there was that whole year where I was addicted to 'Meet Joe Black'.

A year? You still watch 'Joe' like that now.

I know because it's amazing. It's just incredible.

Sure, but there are other films.

[Kevin ignores Ashley] My dream is to one day be able to remake it and actually get someone to do the Jamaican accent correctly.

I know you aren't dragging Brad Pitt on his Jamaican accent. *[Both laugh]* He tried. He tried.

He tried, and you know what? In places he was all right.

Ten out of ten for effort.

Yeah, bless him.

But look, we've got sidetracked. We've set a bit of the scene for our friendship, but I think a big part of why it's something I try to build into my work is because it comes with this extreme loyalty. I've talked elsewhere about how I think that's a real South London thing (see Chapter 14), but I think for us in Sunnydale, loyalty really meant, 'Are you going to jump over and fight with me if this kicks off?' Which was really important at that time, because really and truly we were fifteen years old – we were scared kids – and as much as we were confident and wanted to do all the things, we were really scared.

As we grew up, that loyalty became more a thing of recognising that we were gonna keep each other on track. Like, even when things are really hard, just constantly reminding the other of the mission. When I talk about friendship as a sort of conduit for my work, I really do mean it in that sense of building a deep connection in the art I'm making.

You always did such an excellent job of making me feel included – you always took the time to stop and ask how I felt, and then try to find the middle ground. I would love to know if you felt like I gave that back to you? Imagine if you just said, 'Not really. It's been a disappointment all these years.' [Both laugh]

Ashley Yes. At this time, I wanted to tell you this friendship is over. Thank you for meeting so I could tell you. [Kevin laughs deeply]

But, yeah, I do feel that you gave that back to me. You've always been someone who's more on top of trends, so it makes complete sense now that you're in advertising. Back then, who knew what you were gonna do with that information? But I think you've always had like, I don't know, access to it in some way. Which is funny because you would think that, as, like, a Black gay man, you would be on the periphery of it. But people have come to find out that it always starts with Black women, or being Black and gay, and then it just trickles down to everybody else from there.

Kevin Yeah.

Black women and Black gays are first, always first. Always creating – the creators of all the trends. I don't think the mainstream knows it, but it's true.

Yeah. We didn't know that growing up either. It's really funny because I felt like we had confidence in it. We didn't know why. We just knew that we should.

Yeah. 'What he said was right, we don't know why but it is. Yeah!' [Kevin laughs]

We fucking know. I think you've always been a trendsetter? And I've enjoyed, like, getting to reap the benefits of that.

I think you set trends as well, though. Like . . . what's her name from 'Mean Girls'?

Regina George.

That's it. Minus her actual character, you know, her being a complete psycho. You know when they tried to cut the circle out of her top, on the boobs, and she puts it on and she's like, 'Huh,' and walks around? Then everyone else started doing that? Literally, you would do that in Croydon and like two days later it'd just be the thing. [Both laugh]

God, that poor workplace.

We've worked together in more than one store.

You know what? Yeah. The burger restaurant.

We used to serve flat Fanta. It was a real thing.

It's a beautiful thing. I feel like within our friendship and our friendships with others, we have always been humble. Like we never thought – apart from when it came to trends – that we knew better or more than anyone else.

Yeah, that's a good point. I think that's something we watch out for as well, respectively, in our roles within film. You can come into the process wanting to overexplain everything, or like, really put a pin in it. But I think the best work leaves room for others to come in and make it their own – at whatever stage of the process. Whether that's the actor seeing the script as a map to their version of the character, or else leaving room for those watching to bring themselves in. You don't have to give all the answers. You have to trust in others to show up, and give them room to do that.

That's the root of true friendship, right? It's always fifty-fifty, it's always about understanding everyone is equal. It's funny, I apply that in general. I don't get intimidated meeting anyone. Sometimes Tom and I might be somewhere and we bump into a publicly known figure, and I suppose the standard response would be to get starstruck. But I just think, 'They're gonna go and have a shit, now.' *[Ashley laughs]*
Like it's not that deep, everybody is human. I feel like I learned that from you as well. It's a big, discerning feature of our friendship. Everybody is equal and everybody has their own talents.
Some friendships don't last because people will try and hold on to the version of you they'd like you to be for all time. But you're not allowing any space for growth or change when you do that. Honestly as well, sometimes it's about being able to have really difficult conversations. And we've had those too, like, once in a blue moon. Being able to say, 'You know what, I don't like the way that you're dealing with me. I feel like you were disrespectful then.' And it's a case of knowing that you're my friend and you're not gonna lie because you want the best for me. So you're telling me this from a really honest place, because it really is affecting you, and I need to take that on board. Whether I fully understand the why of it or not, the fact is I've done something that hasn't sat well with you and I need to respect that.

I have more fond memories of us working in the bar than I do of anything else. Actually, that's not true. I have many fond memories of us working in the burger restaurant, like going off on our break like a little bit early so we could watch 'Sunset Beach'. I love that kind of stuff. Doing the kids' parties…
Do you remember the first time we went to Cookies & Cream?

Yeah. I think that was really instrumental, because it allowed you to see what kind of a protector I am. I put my fun to the side to make sure I was where I needed to be to protect you – or indeed any woman – so they're secure and able to enjoy themselves.

Ashley I really cherished all the hours we spent in the car, literally on the road to nowhere, for no reason. Just listening to music and knowing every nuance of every song. Again, mostly Mariah. But we burnt out two Lauryn Hill CDs, 'Miseducation' and 'Unplugged'. Anyone else in the car would just have to get in line.

Kevin I loved the driving. Remember I had a ban on Brighton because of that dickhead boy?

Yeah, Brighton no more!

No more. We didn't go to Brighton for a year. Then one day, you were like, 'Yeah, we're going to Brighton, because this is ridiculous.'

Before the ban though, we really just used to drive to Brighton. Why did we do that? *[Both laugh]*

No idea, you'd just come and scoop me up. And then, other times, we'd go specifically to the twenty-four-hour burger restaurant in Wandsworth.

But why were we driving to that place? We, who already worked in another branch of that same place? Why the need to go and drive somewhere else to get more of what we just had for lunch that day?

When you deep it, there's a whole drive-through branch in Thornton Heath. But no, we had to go to Wandsworth. The cheese is special there.

[Ashley laughs] We just wanted something to do. That summer when we worked in Covent Garden – we weren't working at the same place, and it was more than a summer, but I think of it as summer all the same. I remember you, me, and Adam walking down Neal Street, and the manager of the shop I was working in – Offspring – he was like, 'Ohh, is that you living, yeah? You and your crew?' Now I think about it, I think in the moment, yeah, it was like I was walking with my crew down Neal Street, feeling like we owned the world.

We had left Croydon so like, 'Yeah, we living!' *[Both laugh]*
Then you was at RADA, and I was seeing you in that building, meeting your classmates when I picked you up for lunch or just to walk after school finished.

What about the fact that we had cell phones, yet we wanted to be pen-pals. So we would write each other letters?

I've still got all my letters.

I've still got my letters.

Imagine, in the same postcode, but we used to just write the letters. The envelopes were the gayest, when they came through the post box; they had, like, all of the sparkles and stickers.

Where did I get that stationery from? It was like some special Japanese stationery.

It was super cute.

Hello Kitty stars and bunny—

—rabbits, and wizard stuff in relation to that author who shall not be named. I was still living at home, and my mum would always ask, 'Why are you two writing to each other? You see each other every other day.'

You would send mine to RADA, so I could make use of my pigeonhole.

People really thought we were off living a life of weird and wonderful things. These times, it's like, 'Nah, we just went to Wandsworth to get a—'

'—quarter pounder. Just cheese—'

'—with BBQ sauce'. Driving to Brighton to do exposure therapy on me, so I'd get over my annoyance with that boy. *[Both laugh]*
Then you did some British TV stuff. We had a moment where we didn't talk for a while. Which I think was really healthy because it allowed us to—

Erm, we lived together after I left RADA.

Oh my God. We did live together. You were doing loads of plays, and on one of them you met Iddo. While working at some make-up store.

Yes, B.

Yes! 'Never be too . . .'

'B never too busy to be beautiful.'

That's it. Charlotte managed that store, init. Big up, Charlotte. You did another play and then you got 'Secret Diary of a Call Girl'. And then we did have like a year or so off, as our lives were changing in different ways.

At the time it felt like we weren't talking for ages. But in hindsight, it wasn't that long.

Yeah.

I don't think you came to the apartment that I lived in with Iddo at all.

The one in North?

The first one, in Belsize Park?

I didn't. I came to the other one. We had Christmas there and watched 'Elf'.

Ashley That was my second one, yeah.

Kevin At the wedding, I gave the best speech. Better than the two funny Davids, and a man, like, rubbished them. My speech was about my retirement because I remember meeting Iddo and thinking, 'Oh, he will take a life to make sure you're safe. I don't have to think about it.' I love Iddo anyway, but I really, really love him because of how much he loves you.

He's a good one.

I used to have worries. I don't think I've ever said this out loud to you, but my main worry about not surviving was like, 'But who would ride for Ashley as hard as I would if I wasn't here on this Earth?' And then I met Iddo and realised I could die now. *[Both laugh for an extended period]*

Not us laughing at your death. I'm just moving to get a jacket because it's so cold.

Is it cold or are you saying that as somebody who lives in LA with constant sun, so now you're just being extra?

It got cold this week. I woke up this morning and inside the house it was fifty-eight degrees. That's pretty chilly, no?

No.

Converted to Celsius?

One second, let me ask the internet.

Yeah.

Yeah, fair enough. It's fourteen degrees.

Yeah, I was like brrr when I woke up.

Not brrr.

BRRRR.

BRRRR. *[Both laugh]*

You know the Madea thing about the trunk and the roots? And the leaves? I've realised that I really am not one for leaves.
Like I don't really have many 'leaves' as friends. I've only got roots now. I like roots and branches, but I don't really have any time for the other stuff.

Same. Neither of us has ever enjoyed small talk.

Hate small talk. I hate it so much. It's one of my unattractive qualities in that I don't want to go and hang out with new people because I just want to get straight to the good part, and you can't. There's no shortcut to the good part.

Yeah. You wanna tell me why you're damaged? Sure, let's go. I'll take notes. Like, let's figure it out.

You've got childhood trauma?

Yeah, me too. *[Both laugh]* Neither of us have ever liked small chat. Or lies.

If I know someone's lying or being dishonest, I'm always that person who pulls at the thread. But apparently that's not the polite thing to do.

That's how people get popped. Spider-sense is going off and you're just ignoring it.

'The Girl with the Dragon Tattoo', the serial killer at the end ... he's like, 'You knew something was off with me, but you were too polite to say anything.' I'm paraphrasing, but it's like, don't be too polite. If someone's standing too close to you, move and be like, 'move'.

I spoke with Kelechi, and that conversation was about intuition (see Chapter 9). We got to a place of discussing how we started to separate intuition from PTSD. How has that been for you? Although, you are a witch.

I've always been a bit witchy. I can speak to the PTSD thing. Being a mixed woman, coming from South London, I come from an environment where people are confrontational. So that has been my communication style. And then, going on to film sets, I would sometimes enter the space with that energy but it wasn't serving me. I also felt like I was looked at younger than I am. So people would always treat me as younger than I am.
     Your PTSD, your past trauma, will have you confused – like, are all these people treating me badly? Or am I expecting them to treat me badly? They move mad, and thus I'm moving mad at them. You know what? Sometimes it is the former. Sometimes they are treating you badly. But nine times out of ten, it's not. Not like I'm old, but in my later years, I've really enjoyed moving with kindness. Killing with kindness. And being just as kind, generous, and humble as possible. So only when it gets right down to the end of the road am I like, 'Boo! Hi, you didn't know that I actually had this in me as well.' It's the better way. 'SURPRISE!' *[Both laugh]*

Looking back? The drives, the letters, all of it was self-care.

Therapy sessions, yeah.

Mariah was our therapist. And Lauryn Hill.

You have not done therapy if you haven't like, listened and shouted along. REBEL, REBEL, REBEL! *[Both laugh]*

Kevin It's true, it's true.

        Ashley Wow. Repent. The day is far too spent. *[Both laugh]*

WAKE UP, WAKE UP, WAKE UP.

        We must destroy in order to rebuild. Wake up, you might as well. Are you? Are you satisfied?

[Kevin screams and laughs] I'm so gonna listen to that now, a therapy session.

        I still haven't done any therapy.

I've been looking.

        Me too.

I said this to my cousin the other day – I need a therapist smarter than me because I would just take the piss all day long.

        Yeah, you have to audition them for sure. I'm not into online therapy, I need to be in the room.

A room that is nice enough for me to sit in, so then I'm jealous of the furniture, and I'm jealous of all the books.

        Give me something to aspire to.

That's what I want.

        Yes, furniture that I'm jealous of. How would I know you've made it otherwise?

This is what I mean. I need to see that you've got your life together via sofas that people should not be sitting on because they cost so much. That's how I know you've got it together. Not me doing a video call and I can see you're in a studio with your four cats? No, no, smelly cat lady. Have a blessed day, but it's not what I need. I need Hannibal Lecter's level of grandeur while you help fix my brain. And I want to be scared of you, like, 'Wow you're really smart. You could get away with any kind of crime if you wanted to, but you're using it for good. That's beautiful. I'm glad you're my therapist.' This is one of the favourite parts of our friendship though, like saying—

        —the inappropriate thing, out loud. Yeah.

You're one of my greatest safe spaces, that's the only way I can describe you.

        Twenty-five years.

Wow.

INSPIRATION

Which one?

Both. But remember, if your work is purely
bound by influence then it may just end up
being a copy. Whereas inspiration will give
birth to new ideas, bridging that gap.

OR

TODAY'S TAKEAWAY: Salon pro

I'm not going to overcomplicate this.
Whoever or whatever you decide to be
inspired by – just make sure it's something
you treasure. I've found that the stronger the
bond, the stronger your work.

INFLUENCE

16

COMMUNICATION

I can't help but think about *The Alchemist*, Paulo Coelho's novel, and its protagonist, Santiago.

I often think that maybe we're all Santiagos – especially those that call the Windrush generation 'Grandmother' and 'Grandfather'. I think we stumble out into this big, wide world with the goal of finding our own treasure; taking up space both for ourselves, and in honour of the space our grandparents didn't get to claim.

We search all over for this treasure, accumulating knowledge and experience, only to realise that our greatest treasure will always be the words that our grandparents and other elders already gave us growing up. I've been in some impressive rooms, but none of them compare to the mismatched decor of my grandparents' front room. Remember what Kendrick said?

I didn't know shit, the day I came home.

I promise you, the only prayers that ever worked for me have been from my grandparents.

Even now.

Respect to a whole generation that spent their time manifesting protection instead of gold for their grandbabies. We are grateful.

Where we're from, the idea of wasting words is an affront to nature. Our words should never go unheard.

The following conversation is a picture of younger voices remembering the voices we miss the most.

When you walk into that workplace, fuck a code-switch. Speak only with chest, please.

Don't deny your co-workers the opportunity to see what magic your elders taught you.

"I'VE NEVER SEEN KEVIN SPEECHLESS!"

A CONVERSATION WITH

CANDICE BRATHWAITE

Sunday Times bestselling author, journalist, and presenter

ON COMMUNICATION

Kevin I feel like you have a really unmatched energy for conveying your message online, in a way that seems to come very naturally and authentically from within yourself and yet is translatable to an audience that covers multiple backgrounds. In fact, it's not even that it's just translatable – everyone walks away feeling like you were speaking directly to them and them alone.

Candice I know that every time we hear these conversations where someone is like, 'Oh, you're really good at this thing,' the first response from the person being interviewed is always, 'Well actually, when I was a kid ...' But it's true, when I was a kid I was really quiet – too quiet. I would say that both my biological dad and my maternal grandad took the lead in raising me – particularly my grandad – and my grandad is severely dyslexic and blind in one eye. He stopped going to school at fourteen, so when it came to institutional education he wasn't the highest achiever. Because of this, he always felt – or understood, rather – that because he couldn't read, write, or now even see properly, that people were always trying to trick him. He had a fear of this.

Out of fear, he would stand over me, be like, 'Nah, form your letters better. Speak up.' He had this really great relationship with my Year One teacher, Miss Coco. She was a really stocky Ghanaian woman, and he would make Miss Coco give me the lead in every single school assembly. I'd be like, 'Grandad, I don't like this. I'm up there shaking.' He told me I'd have to reform myself and stop shaking, like, 'This is the task at hand and you will shake like a leaf until you don't.' So that was that. Up until Year Four, I was always leading the assemblies, and I just found myself getting better and better at speaking my mind.

It was solely him who would tell me that I had to understand just how important my voice is. So he'd put me in wild situations, like this time during the OJ Simpson trial. I was about six or seven, and we'd just got Sky for the first time. Of course, the US is on a different time, but that didn't stop my grandad pulling me out of bed at 2 a.m. to watch parts of the OJ Simpson trial. I'd come down and sleepily ask, 'Grandad, what are we doing?' And he said, 'You need to witness history. You need to have an opinion on history.' For a long time I just thought he was being extra, like, I'm not even ten – what are we doing?

But now I look back and realise that it just put me lightyears ahead of my peers. Because I never felt uncomfortable voicing my opinion, especially amongst people that I was 'supposed' to have respect for, people who were older than me and therefore supposedly more knowledgeable. Take that experience of me at six, and then imagine me at fourteen, fifteen. And then put me in a room with aunties and uncles who are abusers – of course the mouth is gonna run off. My grandad had me watching the OJ Simpson trial; you can't chat to me. But in that, the difficulty became being a Black kid in a space where you ain't meant to hear a Black kid's voice.

Seen and not heard.

You know what I'm saying? And then people would just look at me in shock. And then it would get even more peak because there's my grandad in the corner – till this day – always willing to back me up against what they see

213

as disrespect or rudeness. But I see it as just standing up for myself. That's really where my skills in communication are rooted.

Kevin It's really interesting, because my grandmother couldn't read or write either. She was one of twenty, and my grandfather was one of thirteen. My mum is one of seven, and I'm the eldest of thirty-five grandkids.

Anyway, she couldn't read or write. But I had no idea, because I would walk up and down with her and her voice would not tremble. She really thought that she was low-key the head of the mafia, very quick to tell you about how her sons will tump you if you try it with her. Short, beautiful, kind, light-skinned lady. I miss her so much.

She was really vocal in her opinions, but – and I've mentioned this elsewhere – she was the only one to say to me, 'If you want to cry, cry. If you don't let them know, they will say you enjoyed it. Don't it?' And I'd always say, 'Yes, Grandma.' So she really taught me to speak my mind and have an opinion. And I was allowed to be loud in that house.

I had such a sense of freedom at their house. 'Shall we play scientists? Okay.' And she'd let me put whatever I wanted into the jar to see what would happen – eggs in orange juice or whatever. She always used to have a jar of raw pickles that only me and her liked, so I'd run in and know exactly where they were. Just all those little things, and us having our words for all those little things.

Hearing you talk about your grandad, it's really dawned on me just how much of an impact this little lady had on me; this lady who couldn't read and write. She really shaped how I talk and carry myself through the world. So when I'm racing somebody up on the internet, best believe that is Gloria in spirit telling you about yourself.

I think we both come from a culture where you must be seen and not heard, where you're not allowed to have an opinion. There's no autonomy on your own body, or what you do and don't want to be saying. Where everybody praises that one book with the white superhero in it who died and came back to life.

Candice I'm so done with you. *[Both laugh]*

Is there a key moment in your life where you feel like you really stepped into the power of your words?

Yes, I'll tell you when that point was. I don't think I've spoken about this publicly – if I have it's clipped, and certainly not often. My dad died when I was twenty, and it was a really sudden death. He had a cold that turned into the flu; he was all right on Wednesday and he died in the A&E waiting room on Friday. He was on his way to an Arsenal match, but he pulled into the A&E as he didn't feel great. He went into cardiac arrest, they took him into a little cubby room, and he died in there. That's how quickly he died.

Just to set the scene to come: I was my dad's only child. My dad is of Jamaican heritage, and my mum is from Barbados. That's already a problem, because she was this small-island girl. My dad wasn't the greatest partner to my mum, and that was something I've had to evaluate as an adult with my own husband – because you could be the dopest dad to me, but you were a shit man to her. And how does that now affect how I see you?

My dad was one of two sons. He was seen as, like, the Messiah, whereas his brother was the one that could do nothing right. My Jamaican grandparents are distraught, not just because their eldest son has died, but their chequebook too. This is their golden son, who has supported their lives thus far. So now everything's crashing down for everyone very, very quickly. And at that point, I hadn't spoken to my grandparents in around five or six years. I was becoming a woman, working on my relationship with my dad and how I felt about him. And that affected how I felt about them. More to the point, everyone's silently bitter because I didn't make a public show of taking my dad's side.

Long story short, at that time in my life I see myself as a child caught in the crossfire of two families who absolutely hate each other, but have no regard for the sole pickney who's lost her only father. Bare madness happens leading up to the funeral, and on the day itself I get to my dad's door only to be told that I'm only allowed in for a specific amount of time.

So I say, 'Everybody's gonna hear my voice or his body goes on fucking ice today. How you wanna do this? Because as lickle as I am, I will turn over a man's coffin.'

Honest to God, it was like something from 'EastEnders', and I've never spoken about this before. They were just doing mad dodgy things though, like there were all these floral arrangements saying 'Son', 'Husband', and 'Brother'.

Where's 'Father'?

Not one. It gets worse . . . I make my own way to the church after all the cussing. His wife said, 'Do you wanna ride in the car with us?' and I said, 'Do you want me to kill you here now as well? We can double this up, two for one. Get the fuck outta my face.'

And I know people reading this must understand that, as good as I am at communicating, I cannot describe my pain. It's a valid pain, and I'm still working through it with a therapist.

I get to the service, and I'm not on the service sheet, bruv. *[Kevin says nothing; Candice laughs]* I've never seen Kevin speechless!

I am not on the service sheet. By now I'm at the point of fainting. I don't know what to do, but I have to make a choice. The pastor finds out he has a pickney – in the middle of the service; it's like the DJ's just scratchin' up the ting. He says, 'My, my, my. Things are not going to plan today. I've just learned that our departed soul, Richard Brown, was a father, and his only child is in attendance today. And it would be remiss of me not to give her the time she so rightly deserves on the podium.'

So I said, 'Wow, it's my time to shine.' And I remember my outfit was banging – purposely – because I knew in my heart that would be the last time certain people saw me, if not on TV. I was sitting at the back of the church, and I walked hella slow to the front. And I remember placing my hand on my dad's coffin as I stepped up the stairs. And I don't know what spirit rose up in me that day, but you see when I did done chat, yeah, you could hear a fucking pin drop.

All I knew was that this was my only moment to really voice my opinion. And my God, I didn't hold back. And so for me, as much as we can do this writing of the books and all of that, I think when I really do deep it,

I looked at them all and thought, 'You're gonna hear something today.' And I really looked at my dad's coffin and was like, 'You're about to see the embodiment of everything you taught me…

You taught me not to have any fuckeries. You taught me to not let people play in my face. You taught me to have my say, by any means necessary. So I'm sorry it's at your funeral, old man. But here we go.'

And that was that; I didn't even go to his committal. Just to add a little salt to the story, they took his ashes and dashed them without me. I don't even know where his remains are, blud. *[Candice laughs; Kevin is still speechless]*

Kevin I mean, I cussed at my grandma's funeral; I really thought I had a moment, but yours was some 'Sunset Beach' shit. I felt like nobody was really pulling their weight at my grandma's funeral in the way they could have been. So it was me and two of my uncles, every day. It was a really tough time because I wasn't really myself. I remember one day I was heading off to work, and I went to get one of those bikes you can unlock with the app outside my flat. Turns out it wasn't working. I was in such a daze I just left the bike and got to work another way. Sat down, and Tom was like, 'Erm, where's your laptop?'

I'd left my bag with the laptop in it in the bike's basket. But actually, I knew it would still be there because I knew my grandma would be watching it. And only by the grace was it still there when I went back. And I'm not like that normally. Not to say I don't make mistakes, but I'm very much Olivia Pope – I have a backup plan for the backup plan. But it was such a messy time.

I remember, during that time, I badded up the priest as well. She tried to say something slick at some point, and I cussed her out in her house. She made some kind of joke and I was like, 'Oh, you're a comedian? Is this time for a joke?' I just had her up, I wasn't in it with anyone. And my uncle said, 'Lord God, you really are your grandmother's child. Can you please behave? Stop cussing everyone out.' And I said, 'No, I live in truth.'

And then, when I got up to the pulpit on the day itself, someone's phone went off. Boy. I was cussing. But you're right, I just thought to myself that from this moment on, I'm going to do exactly what I want and say what I want. I'm not going to bed with anyone else's luggage. This is how my grandmother stays alive. You will all know her mouth via my mouth. I had spats with some family members over the service sheet. Like they said, 'Why is your picture there?' Because, when I asked you for pictures four weeks ago, none of you sent anything – so mind your business and mind your front. I just walked off, didn't even wait for the reply.

It was a really weird day, because the people that I'd begun to really choose, to be honest, were there as my family. So Tom was there, I remember Nana showing up later on crying. And I asked her why, because honestly she'd never met my gran. And she was like, 'It's because I'm pregnant!' *[Candice laughs]*

And as she said it the rain stopped and the sun came out. That was my grandma, just laughing at the whole thing. It felt like a real day of awakening. Something just arose in me that made me think, 'I'm carrying on this legacy.' I'm going to talk my truth, I'm also going to be really kind with my words, I'm going to be really intentional, I'm going to believe in my words, but I'm also going to allow my words to be questioned by the right people, in the right circle. And my words will never be torn down by people who can't even speak my language.

Because there's a real thing for us as Black and Brown people, where our stories have been erased. So we have to sit around and tell each other our histories to keep them alive, because they're not in books in the same way other histories are. Grandmother to grandchild, and so on and so forth. That's the way that we keep things alive.

With that in mind, I really admire the way you communicate with your kids. You've been very vocal about moving out of London to give your children a different experience. I love the way that both you and your husband interact with them, in so many different ways. And it all comes down to this sense of ensuring that they know, 'This is how we got to this.' And although everything is good, as it should be and deserves to be, you've let them know that there's been hard work involved to get to that place.

Candice I'm raising them at the highest point of discord with all the family I know – or the family that God gave me. Which is really uncomfortable and difficult, but also extremely necessary. Because unfortunately, so much of the family I was born into aren't ready to transition into a space of supporting, enabling, and encouraging my children in the way that I believe will be the best for them moving forward. And sometimes you just can't have your foot in two camps, right? You have to make a decision.

For me that was leaving London, leaving that negativity, and marching forward in building a new community. In doing so, I had to realise that my children have to be vocal in the building of this too. Especially my daughter, so that she not only recognises the power of her voice, but really has it click into place. For so many years we'd ask her where she'd want to eat that day, and she'd say 'Wherever you want to go.' Or, what do you want for Christmas? 'Whatever you'd like to get me.' Eventually it got to a point where – I remember this, it was a couple of years ago – Bodé completely lost his temper. Which he doesn't do often. But he slammed his fist down on the table and said, 'Enough. Enough trying to make everyone happy. What do you want? Where are you going?' And she was a little taken aback. But since then, we've seen such a change in her, understanding that she may upset someone but then she quickly gets over it.

And I needed that to happen for many reasons. Not least because I'm really coming into the strength of my womanhood, unsupported by those who we would usually say should be supporting us. And that could end so badly for me if I didn't have the likes of you and certain other friends, or if I wasn't able to move in the spaces I move in. And so, being able to encourage her like that from inside my house, I know if my eyes shut today, you ain't fucking with that little girl. I know I've given enough to her that she can pull on it. She can be like, 'Nah, do you remember when Mum was like, don't do this? Don't do that.'

I've told this story many times, but I think she really saw that when she was four or five. My father-in-law was around. He's Nigerian, and he called her from her bedroom to come and take his plate. She was so young she bumped down the stairs on her bum – very little. She came into the living room and she sat at the edge of the sofa and was like, 'Grandpa, I have a question.'

'Yeah.'

'I was upstairs building Lego, and do you know how far my room is from the kitchen? And do you know how close you are to the kitchen?'

I guess people who know what staunch Nigerian men are like, know this whole process. Myself and my husband are listening to this conversation in the kitchen. And my eyes have met with Bodé's, and he can see that if this don't go the only way it should go, someone's getting dashed out – and it ain't my yout.

She said, 'You know what, Grandpa? Now that I'm here I'll take it, but I really don't like the fact that you've called me out of my room to take your plate to the kitchen.' And he said it was about respect, that he's older than her. And she said, 'If Nana had called me, Nana's got a stick because of her leg, so I'd help. But last time I checked, Grandpa, you're good. And you got this plate from the kitchen.' *[Both laugh]*

I'm telling you, she's no more than five. Long story short, Bodé came in and took the plate and sent Esmé back to build her Lego. Him and his dad had an argument for about half an hour. But do you know what? The man just left our house yesterday, and every time he comes from Nigeria now, do you know what he does not do? He doesn't call none of my pickneys to take nothin'. Seeing that in action made me think, 'Nah Candice, you're on smoke. 'Cause even in difficult situations, this one can handle herself.'

And now they live a life that I don't particularly understand. I'm invested in it for them, but I'm learning that there's a new way of fighting in those sorts of spaces – in private school. I'm watching her do mental chess with her bredrins and it's wild.

Kevin While eating sushi.

Candice Listen! With the chopsticks that Auntie Remi sent via Amazon, because Esmé's now vexed that we're saving the planet and YO! Sushi aren't sending the chopsticks no more. But that's a different conversation. And you know what? I like it, because now I'm learning from them.

Because – and I find this to be very pertinent in the Black community – there are no conditions around my love for them. And now I'm almost thirty-five, I find parental love in our community to be very conditional.

'I love you until . . .'

'I love you as long as . . .'

'I love you if this bill is paid . . .'

'I love you for respecting me . . .'

'I love you if we just harbour abusers.'

But I look at mine and think, even if you do the worst thing in the world, this is it. Because I'm in this for life. I can't explain the beauty of our relationship, because there's nothing they don't tell me.

You're right though, there are these conditional aspects within the community. I've been thinking about this, and there's healing in forgiveness. Forgiveness isn't really for the person you're forgiving; it's for you. And so, in trying to understand these things more, I feel like more time, you can just point back to white supremacy, and how the society we live in condones only the right type of Blackness for you to be let in. That trickles down – right down – into the way we perceive love, and the right type of Blackness within the Black community. It really does.

And even in the space of how we communicate with our kids, I think you can really see that in the way we communicate physically. Like, I got a box when I was growing up, and for the longest time I thought my children would get boxed. But then I got to an age when I realised, 'Box who, for what?' They are pickneys to me, so I will figure out another way. I'm not putting my hands on you. Instead we will have a conversation. I will remind you who's paying the bills and giving you the things – and why I'm doing this for your safety and protection. And that's not me throwing my mum, or any of my elders, under the bus. It is what it is. I come from a certain generation where that was the thing. And, I mean, we're still trying to teach these kids the same kind of safety because the world is a dangerous place. Racism hasn't gone anywhere, it's just evolved.

And as a side note, I've said this elsewhere, but I'm not interested in having that conversation anymore. It's not that I don't care about racism – if you say something untoward to me, I will wipe your mouth clean off. But my time is done; I just want to enjoy my life and achieve the things I need to achieve. What's important is the example we set for the next lot of kids, so they can continue it for the ones after. So, like, how do they enjoy this sushi with the environment-saving chopsticks, and learn all the things that they want to learn? How do they move through the world and understand? I'm not going to be drawn into pointless arguments against pronouns. As if I would oppose my children ever being who they really are? There are other things to be worrying about, you know what I mean?

And I think that's the beauty of mothers like yourself, who are at the forefront of this new communication, online. Because you are the architects of this new language – of finding new ways to both explore and express how we're feeling. I see it within your kids, and how they're able to articulate themselves. It's magic.

Tell your stories

We need all the stories.
The world would die without them.

CHAT
WA
YOU
NA
SEE

17

PRINCIPLES

You know, you just get to a point where it's fun to win or lose. But you can only get to that point when you're excited by what you will learn, regardless of the outcome.

It's about doing the work to get better – not simply to have just done it. For those in advertising, a reminder: If you'd wanted a job that wasn't going to challenge you, you wouldn't have chosen to pursue one of the most stressful careers out there.

In this conversation, Mpho and I touch on how growth is a principle – something I'd never considered before. Principles are immovable elements that sit within our very core.

The idea that growth, and striving towards growth, is a concept that I subconsciously practise daily is something I would have never been able to articulate before this conversation, or add to my CV after.

There was a point in time at that first agency when all the creatives had had enough, including our very own Tom. (We were friends then, but had yet to team up.)

No one felt like they were getting their work out the door. Although I knew it at the time, I never said it, but the truth is everyone's work was rubbish. Including my own. I mean, I had ideas – I knew culture – but I hadn't yet perfected how I personally brought those elements together. And I knew I had to stay. I knew I had to learn and get better.

By the time I did leave, myself and Tom had delivered our first television commercial (TVC) while, in our spare time, we dedicated our skills to charity spaces that needed help raising funds. Whenever we had a second, or got pushed out of a project, we made our own opportunities. Which led to our own projects. We were carving out our own way to progress.

We had a plan when we left that place; we knew our next agency needed to be a small one. Because if we wanted to keep getting better, we'd need anything but an easy ride.

That first agency had somewhere around three- to four-hundred employees, so it was very easy to get away with being mediocre, with doing shit work. In large spaces like that, someone else will always pick up the slack. Or else, you can always take money from one retainer and redirect it to help another, financing your mistakes away.

Smaller spaces? You need to have your shit together. At our next agency, there were less than forty people. In that sort of environment, there's nowhere to hide. That place came with its own issues, but we did well in our time there. We were well-equipped on arrival – we'd lost enough to understand how to start winning. More importantly, we were no longer afraid of losing.

"IT'S NOT LOSS ANYMORE."

A CONVERSATION WITH

MPHO MCKENZIE

Artist, songwriter, and co-founder of MUVVA music

ON WINNING AND LOSING

Kevin There are many reasons our friendship is great, right? But I do think a big element of it is how much we've won and lost, and then were still able to get back up and say, 'Yeah, cool. Boom. I've learned something too. I'm a new human. What've you got for me now?' And then we get shot again, and we're just like 'Was that it? That tickled. What else you got?' *[Both laugh]*

Mpho Yeah.

I think I knew that was how our friendship would be from when I'd first met you. Just to set the scene, we started getting to know one another when you still had the tea shop in Brixton Market. I'd been asked to take some photos by Jessie Ware and she was like, 'We're gonna go and take them there.' So we did, and me and you became fast friends. I was really depressed at the time too, and I can't even remember why.

I remember.

Do you?

No need to go into it.

Then it was a deep thing. But I remember only having met you maybe twice before that, and then finding myself in that tea shop, just bursting into tears in the middle of it all. And knowing that it was okay to do that. You just came and hugged me, and it wasn't weird or awkward. I didn't even realise I was in the shop until I was in it; I'd just taken myself there on autopilot.

I've always thought about that, the fact that I just inherently knew the shop was a safe space. It's something that I come back to a lot, not just because of the many years that have passed in our friendship since, but because whenever I bring up your name, everybody knows who you are. In fact, it came up the other day with my assistant's manager while we were doing work on this book. She said you taught her how to sing. Her name's Leanne.

That is wild.

Terri Walker, too. Was talking to her the other day for the book. Everybody knows who you are.

It really made me think about what we were going to talk about for this chapter, because I don't know anyone else more willing to just jump in, help, and support than you. And what's more, to do it from a genuine place, ready to be burned. Like, 'I've taken you as far as I can. And now you've dashed me away. It's cool, I've got a whole toolbox of remedies here for that nonsense.'

So I want to talk to you about principles, because I think if there's anybody out here really understanding the human condition – what it means to be an artist, taking time away to reinvent yourself, helping others along the way – it's you. You make it a matter of principle to invest in everyone else's growth, as much as you do your own.

I don't know why you're tryna make me cry, like minutes in. But I guess that speaks to the nature of our relationship. I feel like you've always seen me. Right from the start, too. But you've seen me in all the other ways as well, when I've been, like, hiding behind bullshit or whatever, do you know what I mean? That's really valuable to me. We don't talk all the time, but I feel like even when it's just liking a post or whatever, it feels like it's me seeing you, beyond what you're actually posting, even if I haven't been about and in that conversation. And I feel like you see that, if it makes sense? I could just be making it up.

No, no, no. Like, there are certain people around me who hear me when I say, 'I'm just trying to get the thing done,' and then disappear. I'm concentrating. There are some who say they get it, and, nah. And there are some who really do. They know I'm tired of talking about the dream; I'm finning to shut up and do it. So when you do pop up and like a post or something, I feel like it's you reminding me to do the thing, like, 'That's good, keep going.' Because it's difficult. We are doing things that have never been done before in previous generations of the diaspora. We don't really know what we're doing. We do know we're trying to tear down the thing, but the only blueprint we've ever known is the thing that we're trying to set fire to. So yes, when you click a like, I know it's much more than just that.

Yeah, I'm glad that you receive it like that. I think to go back to what you were just talking about there, it comes back to the fact that you take what's in your environment as a seed and soil. You take what's in your environment. But the job of actually stepping into – standing firm in – your principles is quite lonely. It can be quite painful.

I remember I made a decision – it was when I had this flipping rasclart boyfriend. I went for a local thug, basically. As we do in South London. And it was a heartbreaking relationship. Four years long; he was in and out of jail, very abusive. All sorts of shit. But while I was in that relationship I was really learning about myself, and I remember when it was over I said to myself, 'Okay, it's better to love and lose than to never love.' I must have been about eighteen or nineteen. And I made that decision. And I think that's what you see – me trying to live that on a daily basis. Whether that's in the relationships I have in my community, my marriage, with my children, via the creatives I work with, or in the work itself. So I can feel that I love my work, and the journey it took to get there.

Now, when I'm thinking about, like, releasing stuff and actually putting stuff out there, again I remind myself that it's better to do it and lose, than to not do it at all. And to get back up again, and keep going with that sentiment. I feel that decision set me up to really lean in to not just growing, but searching. Like, in some kind of fucked up way, searching for the most painful thing – because that's where I'm really gonna be tested. I'll talk to my therapist about that one. Even the tea shop was a real journey, just getting up and doing something at a time when I was so struggling with so much – feeling lost – but still trying to create a space that was safe for me first, and then for anybody else who came in.

I learned not to be afraid of shifting my own perspective on myself, actually being open to that. I really value that idea of growth as a principle.

225

Kevin I never thought of growth as being a principle before. And I agree one-hundred per cent. But I've just never worded it like that. You just shifted my universe.

>**Mpho** I think it is. Like, growth is inevitable in some sense; we're all moving towards our death. So it's about how you value that process – how you treat that experience – that will determine how it happens. And how that then impacts the people, the relationships, the world around you.

You could really see that philosophy in the tea shop; you somehow poured yourself into the physicality of the building. I can't explain how it felt when we used to walk through those doors. It was like everything went from black-and-white to colour. The weight went off your chest, the air was just better to breathe. I'm not even sure you didn't have, like, a stream of unicorns in the back. It was just magical.

Anyone that needed it could walk in, take it and be with it, while you were there, kind of healing yourself also. I thought it was impressive at the time, but more and more I realise how you were like, 'No, you devils really tried it in this industry. I'm finna go feed my community – literally and spiritually – and just get myself back to where I need to be.' That's really huge. Most people wouldn't do that. They'd just disappear, or remain bitter on the sidelines.

>What's funny is I thought I was disappearing. I was like, 'Fuck this, I'm just gonna bake cakes.'

Yeah, but I don't think you was. And that's just my view. And I'm not trying to argue the ting with you. But, you were known to be signed. You were this ting in Brixton and everybody knew of you. And then you put yourself right back in the middle of Brixton like, 'Nah, I'm doing this now with my sister.' All while still doing music. I'm just looking back and I'm like, that is a big, bold move. More time people wouldn't have that energy to throw themselves back into the public in that way.

And then when I filmed you in that documentary about your career, at that school in mookooland? Just watching you talk about the song-writing process with those kids. I remember you had a piece of rubbish, like a drinks can or something. You scrunched it and made a beat, then asked the kids to read what it said on the can. They took a few words, and then before I knew it they had the start of a song. I just thought, 'What kind of witchcraft is this?' I think that does go back to that sense of growth as a guiding principle. Going from singing, to the tea shop, to teaching. You were saying we move before we said 'we move'.

>I think that, for so many Black women, there is that idea of growing in order to grow your community, your children – but also to grow some kind of power against how the system is continually trying to undermine you. I feel like there's this subconscious sense of responsibility to take all of that on. And so sometimes you're putting more energy into trying to ensure that other people are growing, than you are into yourself. I see that a lot. A lot of Black women serving the bigger-picture struggles – and obviously, inevitably, they are learning and growing within that, but it's secondary.

So while that sense of responsibility is an amazing thing, it undermines us. Then at some point, if you're lucky enough, you recognise that, and say, 'Actually, for this second, let them all focus on me.' And then everyone else can feed off of that. Do you know what I mean? Like, 'Let's change the perspective on this and do it that way for a minute instead.' I feel like that's where I am now. Everyone else's growth is gonna be a product of my own – not the other way around. And everybody else's strength is gonna be a product of mine. Because otherwise, everyone else is gonna be nurtured, but I'm just left exhausted and burned out.

I feel like there's a shift towards that happening. But I do wonder, when I hear these young people on Instagram talking in that way, whether they really are conscious of it, whether they do really mean it. I don't mean like, the 'self-care Sunday' stuff. All of that is important as well. But I mean like the deep, internal recognition of your own personal development. The internal process that allows you to actually be strong when you come out the back end of whatever else it is you're fighting.

I would say they're not. I believe in their self-care; I think they're looking after themselves and I wanna see that forever and forever. But I would say no because, ultimately, sitting here talking with you, I know it's true that you have to have experienced loss in order to understand what winning is. And sometimes you have to lose in order to understand what the disrespect is. Now, I'm also a big believer in the idea that we are not here to suffer, and that's why I'm very militant when it comes to my enjoyment and happiness.

If at any point you try to interrupt that, it's armshouse because you're taking the piss. I'm glad they know about self-care, because we never knew about self-care when we were younger. We didn't even have a name for it. But, respectfully, they're still kids.

I think the sense of time you're talking about is an important thing to recognise here. The thing about learning how to really care for yourself is that it takes time, doesn't it? You have to take time to get what caring for yourself actually looks like. And then when you're living in this jancro Babylon state of capitalism, when you're just trying to survive, time is such a precious commodity.

Which is heartbreaking, especially when you know and understand that time – as we often think about it – doesn't even really exist (see Chapter 1). It really, really doesn't. But then, on the other hand, you do need that space away from the incident itself to be able to gain perspective.

I think that's why the construct of time exists, isn't it? It's to allow us to have some kind of, like, perspective on our lives. So that we can grasp a sense of what's happened to us.

But I do think there are moments when we take the concept of time as a communication device, 'I'm going to meet you at this time.' We both understand where we need to be.

Mpho Somebody made a decision to create, like, seconds, minutes, hours, days, weeks, and months as they currently exist. And they don't actually work. It's more fluid than that. That construct doesn't really hold. But it was the invention of that denomination of time that was the beginning of capitalism, because then you can say, 'You are going to work from this time till this time. And this is what that is worth.' It's mad, init?

Kevin It is a mad ting. It very much is, how we use time against each other, and against ourselves like, 'Well, I have to do it in this time, I have to.' But then in my head, I truly believe – and I don't know if I'm going to lose you here, but I don't think I will because you're as wild as me – I truly believe that everything is happening all at once. So let's say I'm into – I don't know – the colour red. In a really, really big way. I'm just drawn to it. Come to find out, twenty years or so down the line – in a future that's actually happening concurrently – that I've got this big red house, and my kids are happy on this big red slide. The reason why I'm attracted to the colour red is because I've already got the colour red. So I'm just attracted to myself at a different point in 'time', and vice versa. The future is calling to me, and the past is calling back; we're just eager to meet each other. And so that's what the journey is.

I love that idea. I love that.

It's cool, right? Like, that sense of you sticking to your principles is actually you speaking to yourself across time. But to bring it back a bit, how has that idea of principles – of growth as a principle – played out in your career as an artist?

I think that it is the determining factor of how much of an artist you are actually being. To speak to the point you're making, I feel like you get called to be an artist; it's something that's inside you. But, you know, you still have to actually do the art, and you can prevent yourself. You can find yourself getting stuck, and I've been in that place. But it will continue to call you; it will haunt you. And I think holding on to your principles creatively then becomes more about letting go of other people's perceptions of what your art is, and who you should be within it – and instead, getting more and more clarity about who you are. And I think that that allows you to just get increasingly more freedom in your own creativity.

Yeah. Do you feel like you've done that successfully?

I feel like I'm doing it. I feel like it's becoming. And I feel like that's a more recent, real understanding. It's interesting, because I looked back at some of the footage from when we shot that film, and it's amazing seeing how much I've changed. There are things that I said that I'm like, 'You don't believe that anymore. That's not what you think. Some of what you were saying was just, like, your pain, and you've grown through it to a point where you can look at it way more objectively, and understand the lesson that you needed to learn.' And I'm really excited about that, and what it means for everything I do. Because I feel like if you don't lean in to that, then you stay in a place where you don't get the benefit. Because there's no hindsight if you're just stuck where you are – because there's nothing to look back on.

I feel like I know what the answer to this next question will be – we've kind of been leading up to it – but what, would you say, is the most important part of being creative?

> I would say authentic connection. That you are authentically connected to the work that you're doing, and you believe in its ability to authentically connect with other people. Actually feeling that, physically, in your solar plexus.

It's about following your gut isn't it? Staying true to your personal beliefs. Not compromising on your values for the sake of a quick fix. And that, again, comes back to that idea of being open to loss. Because staying true to yourself might not work for somebody else.

In the times when you have 'lost', for lack of a better word, how did you feel about it?

> I was about to give some trope quote, like I said before, 'It's better to love than lose,' but I think being honest about how painful it is is important. Because losing hurts like fuck. But being able to say that it hurts, while still being willing to continue – even when you've got to fight yourself to go through the process of what that's like – that's strengthening. Like, not me, more like Xena the Warrior Princess. But it's like the archetypal hero's journey, isn't it? You can't get your superpowers without facing the adversary. You know what I mean?

That's not how the story goes, is it? The losing is important. I feel like for everything I never got, for everything I lost out on, it wasn't mine in the first place. I wasn't meant to be there. And I've always come back stronger and better and learned from it. When you look at it like that, then, for me, I feel like I never lose.

> You don't.

And I don't lose because I'm always learning. It's a little bit like the Hulk and his power: the angrier he gets, the stronger he gets.

> Black Panther's got it as well, isn't it? His suit collects the kinetic energy.

Yeah, so it's like you're not actually being taken down by the losses; they're just momentum for you to build on and get bigger. The more that I've accepted that point of view, the less I've lost over the years. And that's not through rose-tinted glasses, it's just that I think viewing it like that really eradicates the ego. So then I approach every situation calm and chill. What will be will be, and I'm gonna put my best foot forward. Because the beautiful thing is, when you get the 'yes' for the thing that you really want, you don't remember all those other 'no's.

> Yeah. The minute you change your perspective about loss, it's not loss anymore. I guess that's the thing about time. It's like 'everything is everything is everything,' as Lauryn Hill would say.

GET WHAT YOU CAME FOR? MAYBE. LEARN SOMETHING NEW? ABSOLUTELY.

If you're growing, it's worth it

In the words of most Black mums from the '90s: 'Don't let no one's son tek you for a eediat.'

What I mean by that is, I'm not saying you should suffer for an opportunity. If any situation treats you unkindly, or disrespects you, then leave. There's nothing to learn there.

What I'm explicitly talking about here is the work. It may not always be what you envisioned, but are you still able to learn something from the experience? It could be as simple as that particular company's processes, or you taking note of what it was about the work that you ended up not liking – so you know to turn down that kind of work next time.

TODAY'S TAKEAWAY:

Don't be prang of the experience. Go through it, and let it turn your stomach on its head.

Going through the thing

is not the same as

going with the flow

Let it, if needs be, attempt to break your heart. It can't, and it won't.

18

SELF-CARE
BEFORE
SELF-CARE

SELF-CARE BEFORE SELF-CARE

I do think there are instances where the pursuit of self-care can be dangerous if you haven't taken a moment to work out why self-care is needed.

For example, if you are tired, run down, or need to rest, before you even consider what kind of bath salts and bombs you need, is it not worth looking at why you are so run down in the first place, and how you can change that?

While working at that job that I was too young to be working at (see Chapter 1), as you might remember, an argument broke out between two boys in the queue. The disagreement was about who was next to get served. It escalated, and one of the boys shot the other boy in his stomach.

As you can imagine, the burger restaurant erupted into chaos; lots of screaming and crying.

Me? I was unmoved – in all honesty I didn't care. I was more concerned with who would clean up the mess and what time I was leaving, because I had an early start the next morning.

As predicted, after a very long, extended shift, I got home and very casually told my mum about what had happened. She was in shock. At the violence? Yes. But also by how unbothered I was.

I brushed it off as nothing to worry about; the truth was, I had seen much worse things in that town.

I remember thinking I could temper her reaction by telling her that the restaurant had given us the next day off.

She stared at me blankly.

I followed up with, 'It's a paid day off.'

She continued to look past my banter, her silence cutting away at my nonchalance. Second by second, layer by layer.

When she finally spoke, she said, 'This place is broken, and if you stay long enough it will break you.'

I wouldn't get the full weight of her words until years later, but in that moment I knew she was right. That a paid day off wasn't going to be enough to process what had happened, or at least process why I was so desensitised to it.

Self-care is great, needed, and important. It's just that there are moments when we have to start at the heart of the thing, to learn what that self-care even is.

"I'M DOING IT FOR ME. BECAUSE I JUST FOUND ME."

A CONVERSATION WITH

SELMA NICHOLLS

Casting director and founder of Looks Like Me

ON SELF-CARE BEFORE SELF-CARE

Kevin I can really see it in your face; you look different. In a good way.

Selma I feel different. I went away on a week-long cruise last year. On my own, no kids, as it was adults-only. I went to Mexico and the Bahamas. It was fantastic. And for the first time, I wasn't Selma the founder, or Selma the mum. I just found Selma, and it was really overwhelming. I'd forgotten who I was, so it was beautiful, this life-changing rebirth experience.

Okay, that's amazing. And this sounds cheesy, but as soon as I saw you I could just tell that a weight has lifted off your shoulders – there's a visible sense of freedom to you. And I'm really interested in talking more about this, but first of all, I want to say thank you. The contribution you made to our short film, 'More Time', was ridiculous. It brought me to tears. I know how hard you work being the founder of your own business, and for you to part with that amount of money means that you really believed in what we were doing. That just rocked me, and ever since I've been trying to figure out how I can repay you.

No, no. It's not for that. For me, it doesn't matter if I give you a look, a loaf of bread, or £100 – the only thing that's needed is a thank you. Then go make sandwiches for the community, for your family, with that bread. You don't owe me anything. I know the power of gifting and giving, because a lot of people have shown me love and belief through gifting too. So the gift must continue; I can't hold on to everything. And I must pass it on to people that I believe in and love. That's what I've been shown, and what I want to continue to show. The gift was given because you're doing the work not just for yourself, but for others too.

Thank you. It's weird, because I'm in a space now where it's becoming really apparent what a difference believing in me makes to what I'm doing. It's becoming much clearer in the way that people deal with me when I enter new rooms, and that I don't necessarily want to do all the black flips to earn that belief anymore. Like, there's enough out there now to show that this is what I do, and if you're on board great, if not, peace out. It's not an ego thing; it's just about mutual respect for each other's time.

And you've always been someone who exudes kindness in abundance, right? So I want to talk more about this holiday, because when I just saw you, I was like, 'Oh, this is to a new level.'

It's interesting, because last year I went for coffee with Nana. When she saw me, I was just in a completely different space; there's such a juxtaposition between now and then. Last year was the end of a seven-year cycle for me, both for my business and for me as a female. I knew I was in a space of transition; I could feel that something was changing. And right then, nothing was working. Last year was my worst year ever; everything I touched said 'no', everything I wanted, I didn't get. I was like, 'What is going on?'

My background is in dance and movement. That's what I studied. And last year, Looks Like Me, my casting agency, turned seven. Looks Like Me was birthed, really, to help me with my parenting. I built it to help build up my daughter Riley-Ann, and make her see herself through a creative form – rather than me simply saying, 'You're lovely, you're this and that.' Right? In a way, I suppose it was intended as a mirror to show her what the world could look like. So, seven years on, the child is now flying; she's great, she's formed. She can speak up for herself. She's away from home on tour. So then I'm asking, what is this business really about now? Why am I doing what I'm doing?

And then I realised that the process of creating Looks Like Me had given me a genuine love of casting. But then, I'd formed a box where people only saw me as casting for kids, or only casting for Black people. How could I shift that, and show people that, actually, I just love casting? I have a skill, a creative way of approaching it, and it's what I want to do. So how do I articulate that? That was a struggle for me, figuring that out in a way that made it clear to clients that they shouldn't box me in. Because I felt very boxed in. But equally, everyone knows the story of how Looks Like Me was set up because of Riley-Ann. So I thought, park that. Who is Selma? And I didn't know.

The Selma before 'mother' was like eleven, twelve years ago. That was a completely different person. Then you have mother Selma, founder Selma – but where is Selma now? If you'd asked me what I liked doing, I'd be telling you stuff from 1999. In an interview, they asked me what my favourite film was and I said 'Boyz n the Hood'. Like, what? C'mon, Selma. I'd lost who I was.

I had the opportunity to go on this cruise, and I was a bit nervous so I brought along a friend. But being real with you, Kevin, prior to booking the dates, I also went in for some cognitive behavioural therapy. As I said, everything I touched was saying 'no', so I just felt that I wasn't good enough. What else could I do? I can't beg people to work with me, I can't email people every month – I'm not going to be that person. And I don't want to get a job in a whole other field just to pay the bills. So what am I going to do?

It was really starting to eat at me. Meanwhile, I was going through a long interview process for a job – nine interviews over four months. It got down to me and one other person, and I went for the final interview. I felt like I'd got the job. Then a day later, I get the phone call: 'Sorry Selma, we're not taking you on.' And yes, I'm used to rejection. But this felt different; this company has a rooftop venue, and it felt like I'd been pushed off the roof, hit the floor, and I didn't get up. I felt broken. Normally I jump back up.

I knew something was going on, so I booked in for the CBT. At the first session, she asked me why I was there, and I said, 'I'm here because I don't feel like I'm enough. I don't feel like I'm lovable, and I don't ever have the capacity to love outside of what I do as a mother and a founder.' So I went on a whole journey through that.

Anyway, I go on this cruise. And every day – I'm not lying to you – between ten and one hundred people would say to me, 'Oh my God, beautiful lady! You're shining like a light! You're enough.'

I turned to my friend and I was like, 'Are you hearing this?' And he said, 'Yes, everywhere you turn, people are telling you you're amazing.'

And I'm not talking to anyone about this stuff, right. I'm just saying, 'Good morning,' 'Hello,' holding the lift door, or whatever. And every night I'd start to cry, because it was too much. It was really overwhelming. 'Why are they saying this?'

Later, on the way to Mexico, there was a storm. The ship was rocking, and when I say rocking, it was like 'Titanic'. I was sleeping with the back doors open – it was hammering down with rain, thunder, and lightning. The heavens had opened, and I just thought, 'Okay, I accept it. I am enough. I surrender.' No lying; the water's licking me, and I just wanted to get on to safe land. So I surrendered; the tears were flowing, but I was calm.

And after that, whenever people said anything nice on the rest of the cruise, I just accepted it and thanked them. It was like I'd let go of all this armour, to reveal myself underneath. It was just beautiful. I started gravitating to all sorts of different people and it felt like I was having real soul-to-soul connections with them. I just flowed with it.

Once we got back to Miami, the head of experience at the Standard Hotel – where I was staying – gave me something for my birthday, and asked me to say hi again before I left. So on the day I leave, I find her to say goodbye. She says, 'Thank you for making the time, I really appreciate it. This here is my friend, the brand director of the ship; I told him you had a life-changing experience, I can see it in you. You came one way and you're leaving another.' Then she told me to search for a song on YouTube when I got home, and when I did, I saw it was called 'You Are Enough' by Sleeping At Last. Like, how did she know?

I was bawling all over again, but then I remembered that as I left, she whispered something to me: 'The Standard has magical powers. It's a magical place.'

A week later, I'm back home and getting into the swing of things, only to find the head of experience had sent me another song. I asked her how she knew I needed this right now, and she told me that when she connected with me, she realised that she'd been where I've been too; she could see that in me. She knew exactly what I needed, and passed it on. So it's that same thing of passing on the gift – if that just touches people, that's enough.

Now I'm reconnecting with movement, and just keeping it real in a way where I'm not being apologetic or overexplaining myself. I realised as well, that a lot of people had access to me before. Now, I'll get around eight phone calls a day, and I might pick up one. Maybe. Because I realised a lot of those calls were just people passing their own time, and I needed to give myself quality time. I like myself – am I making sense?

Kevin You are making sense. The lockdown did this for a lot of people, and forced them to stop in their tracks and ask themselves, 'What am I doing?' Most people – if not all of us – get into the routine of the thing, and maybe don't even realise it. They don't question that routine, or see if they should try things out another way.

One time, Tom and I went on this course for the learning provider Hyper Island. It was really amazing, and showed us how to approach creativity from a completely different angle than what we were used to. Basically, it helped us break down those old habits and routines in favour of something new. It taught us to look at the idea of leadership as being about providing people with what they need to stay in a space where they enjoy what they do – where they're not burned out or tired by it, where they're not overwhelmed. And once you've got people there, you have to know that you'll need to keep looking at new ways to bring them back to that happiness – because not only will new challenges come up, but what was a new way of doing things, again, just becomes routine. And what's more, they actually split Tom and I up, because they knew we spent all our time working together and they wanted to disrupt that.

It was an emotional week, because this course was really intense and I felt like I couldn't even talk to Tom about it – he was literally on the other side of the room all day. I was with people who I didn't know and, unlike Nana, I'm not good at small talk – I just want all the big talk. So towards the end, I'd really started to have enough – only for them to teach us some of the actions that bring people into that new, more productive state of happiness, by actually implementing them on us. We realised that while they'd been teaching us the course, they'd actually been putting us through that philosophy for ourselves so we could experience it. That was completely mind-blowing, and it made me completely rethink the idea of a comfort zone. It's actually something to be scared of. When you've got too comfortable, it's time to go. Otherwise, things start to wind down, and people box you in, and that's when they start taking the piss with your time. You have to keep your energy flowing forward. You can respect the history of the thing and how you got there; you can be nostalgic and all of those warm feelings. But all things come to an end – the energy has to be passed on. If you don't pass it on, you're dead in the water.

Recently, I spoke online about how I try to live one year on and one year off. Last year was off for me, and by that I mean that I wasn't trying to put out any content, make short films, or anything like that. I was just spending time with myself. I think that's another way of resetting that routine and taking a step back. I always learn something, and this time it was just how much I love being by the sea.

> **Selma** I see the sea a lot from you. I live in your Instagram and I'm telling you, it feeds my soul. The sea is so beautiful, and so simple. When I'm by the ocean, I can sleep – I feel free. But what you said about those two versions of you made me think about Impostor Syndrome. Someone asked me last year if I suffer from it in certain places, and I said I don't. But what I did think about is how people don't know me. I'm not saying that they need to, but they know me as Selma the founder, not as someone who's been living with post-traumatic stress disorder (PTSD) for twenty-one years, and having CBT for the same amount of time. Not literally for all twenty-one, but more that within that time period there have been at least seven occasions where I felt like, 'Okay, I just need someone who can listen, from a place of just reminding me how to manage my behaviour.'
>
> Because when things are stressful, I start to behave slightly differently. I just tell people about themselves and they can't handle it. It's like living two lives: there's the life of CBT, the spirit – all this stuff. And then there's Selma the founder, and what she's doing. So people think they know me, but they don't. They talk to me like they do but they have no idea. I don't feel that is Impostor Syndrome – I don't know what the name for it is – but it feels like having a double life.

I do get it, because if you notice, that's where my need to speak so candidly on the internet comes from. Because I'm, like, 'This split personality that's being forced upon me? I'm not doing it anymore.' So I want you to know there are good and bad bits. That's why I'm very like, 'I'm from Croydon, I am a Virgo – you lot stop playing with me. These are the things I love.' You know, I love rom-coms and all those things – I'm still the same big kid I was in the '90s – but at the same time, I am a road yout; I will switch.

Selma But you turn up and do the work as well. So I see you, through your work and your creativity. I see you and I see that it's complex – all different layers and colours – but I see it, and it's easily digestible. I think that's my issue; I don't necessarily see myself in what I'm putting out.

Kevin Do you have a plan for that, even if you don't have an answer? Because for me, yeah, that is that 'on/off' mentality for each year. What is the ling?

First of all, I feel like I've just woken up from a very long time spent sleepwalking. So for now, I've just been enjoying being, right? But what came into my head as you were talking is that, because you show up as yourself on Instagram and what have you, you create a safe space. And that's the same here; I know this conversation is going to end up in a book, but I feel safe sharing it with you. So for now, I just wanna show up.

For instance, it starts even with how I show myself on Insta. It's very rare to ever see a full-body shot of me; there's maybe three or four on my whole feed. I don't show myself. I watch Candice Brathwaite (see Chapter 16) – I love her! I get such life from seeing her showing up. Beautiful woman, just dressing up and being. Allowing herself to be seen in all her light and glory.

So what I've learned is that there is beauty and power in that idea of just showing up. Not in the sense of like, 'Hey, look at me,' but just allowing myself to step out and be seen as I am. Just facing that. All the small things that get me fearful, just stepping into them and allowing myself to be vulnerable in small, subtle ways. It's not some big monologue thing, but just like learning to like those things, such as taking photos of myself, and allowing people to realise that I'm not just strong and powerful. I'm vulnerable, nervous, anxious, and quiet. I'm all this other stuff, you know?

I don't know exactly how I'm going to share that. But I know it will be in its simplest form, so that it can just be genuine and honest.

It doesn't need to be any bigger than those small steps. It's like the idea of going to the cinema by yourself – growing up, it was like, yeah, no one does that. And then, I think it was in my early twenties, I finally just went on my own because I wanted to go and see a particular film. I just didn't care if everyone there thought I don't have any friends. It's okay. And that, in itself, is just a really small act – and to be honest, today, probably sounds a bit ridiculous. I don't think it's looked at in the same way now, but when we were growing up, going to the cinema on your own meant you were a weirdo. But there are loads of people that just go to cinema by themselves now, because we have the words and language for it: self-care.

Even you saying that brings me back to the cruise. Because that was gifted to me, right? I had that life-changing experience, and so they offered for me to come back again with a VIP experience. But I have to document it this time, so on the one hand I'm like, 'This is amazing,' but on the other, I'm like, 'Oh God, now I have to show myself.' I'm not trying to be an influencer, but if I can share something really beautiful – this place that let me find peace; that fuelled me and my soul – and let people see elements of that for themselves? That would be so good, to influence people to go and travel on their own, to explore life.

Trust me, I'm already thinking about this cruise. But I think it is just about doing these things, step-by-step, and always asking, 'What else can I do by myself?'

Recently, Tom and I went to LA for industry meetings and then, afterwards, his girlfriend came out and the two of them drove up the coast. Meanwhile, I've always wanted to go to Santa Monica and San Francisco, these two names you hear in film after film growing up. So I wanted to see them, just for the context. So I spent the next week going to them both, walking around like this rich old lady in Santa Monica before flying to San Francisco and just wandering around, seeing it all.

I also think it's really important when you do these things, that you just absorb, absorb, absorb. Just let it come to you slowly and take it all in, rather than watching for this epiphany to burst in your head. It might hit you six months later, and you find it's inspired you to go do this other thing. But I think what a lot of people wrongly do is put weight on it, you know? 'I went on a trip and I didn't get the answers.' You're not in charge of time; you don't know when you're gonna get those answers. You just have to have the experience and let it bake.

> I think, within the experience I had, what really helped me see and connect everything was just keeping my phone in my bag. I didn't take no pictures, I just enjoyed and was present. I think that ability to just tune into the thing and be accessible to life fuels you in a different way. And in doing that, I found my inner light. So I think how I'm gonna show up in practice is by just always looking at the situation at hand and thinking, 'How can I be me?' No frills, just simple – letting myself be vulnerable. And I'm not doing that for people; I'm doing it for me. Because I just found me.

Have you seen that already starting to have an effect?

> Yeah. People have been connecting with me, and it's a different energy. Some people have just seemed to pop up out of nowhere, and one person said that everything seemed to be going great for me based on my socials so would I be able to go and do this talk? I'm getting those kinds of emails. I'm being mindful, and I'm receiving the positive energy that I feel I'm putting out, and, in turn, I'm reciprocating that back tenfold. Now I'm having meetings with lots of people, and I feel lighter. Everything is flowing; I'm not forcing it.
>
> I can already see things manifesting. But I've also had to make sure that I've cut ties with those whose energy isn't clear, honest, and transparent. I think that when you love yourself, you realise that actually it's okay to call it a day with certain people. With love and respect, good night and God bless. You're not wishing them harm. I wish everyone well. But it's just accepting that this friendship or relationship is no longer working. It's not serving either of us.

Yeah. There doesn't have to be a wahala or an argument.

> This is it. And I don't need anyone to trigger me so they then have to have CBT, because I want to murder someone! Like, I need to be able to just move calmly. And that ties in to what was probably the biggest thing I learned last year – after I went on the cruise – that your thoughts are not fact.

Kevin I think Erykah Badu says it in a song: You don't have to believe everything you think.

> **Selma** That's really registered with me now. And I think, ultimately, the real difference you're seeing in me right now is I am here, present. Listening to you. I haven't got a million thoughts racing through my brain. I haven't. I'm just calm. And I think finding that inner peace ... I ain't letting it go. Because that's the most precious thing for me in life; peace of mind.

ARE YOU FIXING, OR ARE YOU HEALING?

Self-care before self-care

You can't heal what needs to be fixed.

A broken leg needs to be fixed, cast, and set so that the bones can mend. The healing process happens after – in the form of physio, massages, and rehabilitation. Before you can practise self-care, you need to be honest about the level of injury you're mending.

TODAY'S TAKEAWAY:

You need time to heal

Sounds obvious. But what I mean is, healing isn't always the first step – fixing the problem is.

Don't rush to just heal, take the time to understand what needs fixing first. And accept that that will take as long as it takes.

19

DISCIPLINE

There is a duality to most words. For me, the word 'protection' usually brings to mind the sense of a safe space. Those spaces vary – they're not always physical, sometimes existing in a mere moment – but are mostly warm, familiar, and where good memories have been made and are kept.

You can feel protected by the simple act of holding a loved one's hand, or from the sense of security created when, home alone, you double-lock the front doors. This sense of protection is individual and nuanced; the way society differentiates us all is a very real thing, requiring different levels of protection depending on privilege – and that's before you even add race to the equation.

But 'protection' can also be the word manipulative people use to justify control over others: 'It's for your own good . . . You need protection from yourself.'

And I think the same can be said for 'discipline'.

For children, it is a word to be feared; a consequence of not following rules, always resulting in something being taken away. As a child, if I were to imagine 'discipline' as a place, it would be small, dark, and claustrophobic.

A word that instantly makes me feel restricted.

But when I think about it now, there's a disconnect; adults never seemed to follow up and explain what discipline can actually get you. How it can aid you and, ironically, protect you.

Discipline seems to have only been spoken about when you're not doing as you're told, so it became a word that meant bad things were going to happen because you were already doing bad things. Even if that bad thing was simply thinking differently.

I remember a day at primary school when I refused to eat my lunch because I didn't like what was on the plate. When the dinner lady came over, I was told that I was 'letting down children in Africa'. A second dinner lady, hearing this, laughed and began singing the chorus to 'Do They Know It's Christmas?'.

I remember looking at them both and saying, 'I can't wait to tell my mum you said that.'

Fortunately for me – although I didn't know it at the time – I'd been taught actual discipline at home; mainly around race and identity. At eight years old I was adequately educated in not only the understanding of how my Blackness would be used against me in this country, but that my Blackness was beautiful; something to be proud of and protected.

In that instance, I knew that my refusal to eat that lunch had become a matter of principle. A Black one. The dinner ladies caught fright and got someone else to negotiate with me. Still, I refused. I sat there for the rest of the lunch period, starving but determined to stick to my goal. Disciplined in my disobedience.

As I sit and write this, I realise I've been a master of discipline this whole time, but it's often had another word ascribed to it: 'stubbornness'.

Sometimes the duality of words allows something less pleasant to be used in place of another. (I wanna caveat that statement by making it clear; at times I've definitely been a stubborn arse. I repeat, at times.) But there is a clear difference between 'discipline' and 'inflexibility', and I think many times society and our cultures distort (sometimes unintentionally) the two.

I could have started this chapter off with the dictionary definition of discipline, but that's not what I'm talking about here. I'm really asking you, the reader, to take a second and think about when and if ever you've separated the real art of discipline from actions that are just grabs for authority.

It wasn't until my mid-twenties that this idea of true discipline, as part of my creative practice, became a necessity. More so, that discipline became fun.

Being disciplined in practice is one of the most important parts of any creative journey; it enables focus and dedication. It allows you to enter a creative space that ensures your journey on any project has dignity and merit. The project is happening because of a need – because of a respect for you, and your art.

If I think of what 'discipline' means to me now, it's a word that makes me feel . . .

Capable.

"ORANGES."

MARAWA THE AMAZING

Guinness World Record-holding performer, athlete, and author

ON DISCIPLINE

Kevin I think a lot of people look at what you do – with the hoops and the roller skating, all of it – and think, 'Oh, it's fun, not that serious.' But actually, when you deep it, there is a lot of discipline. A lot of focus. There's been a lot of hard work for you to get to where you are: a lot of the things that you do business-wise, and the way that you exist in the spaces. And yes, it is fun. But I know from behind the scenes – as well as just from common sense, as far as I'm concerned – how hard the work is to get to where you are.

I don't think most people understand how much it takes to get to that place. Anyone working through their personal creative practice – regardless of their process – is really always working towards a space where they're able to look back at the work and say 'I've done everything that I could have possibly done. I gave it my best shot.'

When you hear those words come out of a creative's mouth, when they're like, 'Cool, well, it is what it is', when you see someone comfortable with that point of view on their work – despite it seeming to have a laissez-faire energy – it comes from doing a lot of hard work, learning, and sacrifice. I couldn't think of anyone better to have a conversation with about that point of the creative journey, and what level of focus and discipline it takes to get there, than with you. Visually, the things that you do are so fun. But the dedication to have, or rather create, such fun is on a whole other level.

> **Marawa** It's really funny. You said something earlier, that I think actually links to this, about going to the University of YouTube. I can't remember exactly how you said it earlier. But basically, you can't get around the work. This idea of like, 'Oh, you're a freelancer? You do arty things? Like hobbies?'
>
> But the thing I've come to learn and the thing I didn't understand, is that it's a way for people to write you off as uneducated. 'What a self-indulgent thing to be.' Yet we all know hundreds of people that went to university who are so dumb. They don't do anything. They don't learn anything. *[Both laugh]*
>
> You know my parents growing up were like, 'Education, education, education.' It was a big conflict, from an early age, drilling in this idea that education is the most important thing.
>
> My question though has always been, like, if I learned how to do this really complicated bit of algebra, when am I ever going to need that in my day-to-day life? If I were to learn physics or economics, or any of these institutionalised approaches to education, where you go and get a degree, only to then need the Masters, then the Doctorate . . . when was I ever going to use them?
>
> I knew clearly that I wasn't going down that path. So, I felt like I must be lazy, that I had nothing to contribute. But then I'm looking around at the ones who did do all that and I'm like, well, you got the degree, you work your nine-to-five, you've got the salary package, and your two weeks off. You're given projects to complete, and if it works, it works. If it doesn't, it doesn't. No big deal. You're not really invested either way, because it's not your company, and it's not your work.
>
> Here's me responsible for everything that happens in my business. The buck starts and stops with me. But my choice to forge a new path, to work for myself, is seen as less than, and I never questioned this until one day it clicked. I was like, 'Oh, wait. I am working. I'm doing a lot of work.' Actually, you could say more work – it's just that it's not tangible by traditional methods of how we measure success.

More broadly, this is what I think our view of education is going through right now – a democratisation; a real diversity in learning. All the geniuses we know, all the people did that crazy thing? They sucked at school. School was terrible. They couldn't concentrate, they were the class clowns. When actually, you were just teaching them the wrong way. You only had one way of teaching. It's like sport, right? If the only school were softball school, it would be the same. You'd get your few kids that were really good at it and then some kids that weren't because they'd be better at soccer – and they wouldn't even get to find that out.

Institutions haven't worked that out yet. But when I go beyond that limited, traditional view, I've actually experienced a lot of different types of education, a lot of different types of teachers. I used to be confused. I'd have a teacher that was so engaging, and so interesting that it could have been the most unlikely subject, but I was fully invested. And then the subject that I would have thought I'd be good at, and the teacher was terrible? Then it was a struggle.

The older I get, the more I'm able to reflect back and filter out the opinions of others and say, 'No, I actually am really disciplined; I do work really hard. It's just that you can't understand it because you have your worldview on how things should go, and that's fine, because mine is set like this.' And it's just different.

One-hundred per cent. But when that difference in approach is used as an excuse to ridicule or gatekeep you, it's no longer about recognising discipline, but about making you smaller because you don't fit with what makes them feel comfortable.

I think it'll be really interesting in the next twenty years. Because in one way, we definitely are improving and opening up ways of thinking, and kids are starting to get different options in how they can learn. Bachelor of Circus Arts definitely wasn't a degree until the year before I started doing it. It didn't exist. Even now, when I tell people that's what my degree was, they're like, 'Are you hanging upside down? You did forward rolls all day?' I did two years of social science and interactive multimedia. I did two years of full-time unit theatre. We might have had the odd lecture here or there, but we had the theory and the practical side, and sometimes it was exhausting.

I think being someone who was sort of in the first generation of circus arts as a recognised academic discipline, I was setting the tone for a lot of this stuff. Because there weren't other people that had done the degree. It wasn't even about breaking the world records. It was, like, creating new world records, new divisions – things like that. And by being that person, and by being around for MySpace, Facebook, and then all these things – the joy of hashtags – suddenly you can connect with all these other people who aren't necessarily hula hoopers, but that roller skate. Or they specialise in some type of specific head massage that involves braiding your hair and hanging upside down, all these different weird things, and that's the stuff my journey is made of.

That goes back to that idea of the University of YouTube, like how even with that formal education, a lot of your journey still came from exploration and self-discovery.

Marawa Yeah! It's not like, 'Oh, and then I connected with all the hula hoopers in the world and we started a hula hoop school.' No. It's the coming together of people that couldn't make it work in the nine-to-five, couldn't do this generic thing where you hit these marks at the university, and then you get the degree and then you get the job. It just doesn't work that way anymore. I turned forty this year. And I can list off people that have these very unique, specialised lives and careers that are not easy to explain to other people. A lot of people, as you said, will just write this off as being like, 'Oh, you're just having fun, or you're just doing that thing.' No.

The flip of it is that you don't finish a project that fails, and go, 'On to the next.' Because it was personal. Because it took years of your life, and then it failed. That's like losing an arm or a leg. The bounce-back isn't easy. You are more invested. The projects are your babies. It's not like you're babysitting someone else's child. It's different.

Kevin Yeah, it's really interesting.

I talk a lot about foundations, and how all of these spaces – education, whatever industry, the media, etc. – were built specifically with certain men in mind. They were built to service those men in a way that makes sense to their lives: their needs, their desires, their wants.

I don't look like any of those men. You don't look like any of those men. Therefore, we will never, ever, ever go and fit into that world. We had to find new ways, and new people.

Sounds about right.

I don't think I've ever said that out loud to you; how instrumental meeting you was to my life. Because at the time, I think you came to the night we used to run – Bounty – and you were there on your skates, hair flowing, and you just skated right up to the DJ booth and said 'hi'. You were, and still are, just full of life.

I remember I asked, 'Why the skates?' You were like, 'Oh, yeah, I'm part of the circus.' I remember thinking, 'That's your passion and you're fully following it. What am I doing?' And from that point on, I was like, nah, my mate is at the circus. I got to go find the thing that I love as well, of course. And that is why whenever I've been in your presence, or when we've seen each other, the smile is so big on my face. Because I'm like, 'Ah, inspiration.'

[Marawa gives the biggest grin] I think the thing that has made it work . . . you know, you see the little lady walking over the street, and she's got one of these little carts and the oranges fall out, and they start rolling down the street and you run, you pick them up? Because that's what you do. And then when you see there's a train and you could run and get the train, but there's another one in two minutes so it's fine, so, you don't run. But then also you're like, 'If I get that one, if I do run and get the earlier one, then it means I'm going to connect to the other train that I really need.' So, I really do need to go because I want to get to whatever I need to get to. You know that feeling? The 'yes' feeling? Like the lady who drops oranges, you pick them up? Standard. You just have to do the thing.

I often have the conversation with people, or get asked the classic question, 'How did you know what you wanted to be?'

I didn't. How could I?

Tiger Woods is a bad example, because you don't make decisions when you're six months old. But when you start playing golf at six months old with your dad, then you're going to be Tiger Woods. But you hear these stories, 'Oh, I knew from the age of five that I was going to . . .' – and I just didn't.

Everybody knows that you have to follow your dreams. If you're not passionate about it, then this can't be your life. I find it a very difficult question in conversations, especially when it's with someone young who looks like they have the world's hopes in their eyes. Because the underlying thing – the thing I often want to ask back – is, 'Do you think that this means that you don't have to work? Do you think that if you do what you love, you'll never work a day in your life?' Like all that shit – all those motivational coffee cups.

Because no, if you want it, you're probably going to have to work harder. I'm obsessed with Oliviero Toscani, the creative that did *Colors* magazine. He's the greatest. There are not many interviews of him, but I was listening to this podcast the other day. And the guy interviewing him was so rubbish, which just made it so much better. And the interviewing guy was like, 'Oliviero, your ads are so iconic. And everybody just thinks they're amazing. Like, where do you get your ideas from? How do you get your ideas?' And he's like, 'What do you mean ideas? If you have to look for ideas, then you don't have any.'

It should be there, you should feel the need to just do it, like picking up the oranges for the lady.

Even within that, I think there's still discipline. Getting to that level of confidence takes work. And I love that analogy of the lady with oranges, because I have a thing with oranges. I lost my grandmother a few years ago now. And every time you'd come to her and my grandfather's house, when you were leaving, she'd always pull an orange out of nowhere and be like, 'Take this with love.' That was her thing. I bring that up just to say that it's also about the connection of things and appreciating the slower things.

The fact that you've mentioned oranges, and the old lady – that's the sign, to me at least, that I'm on the right path. And it's working towards having that kind of openness and skillset to be at one, and quiet with your fucking phones off, eating your salad, and absorbing what's around you to be like, 'Okay, I need to be over here even though no one understands why I need to be over here.'

When we met, I was thinking about my purpose. At the time, there seemed to be nowhere where I fit in. And, as I said, you came in full of life. And you were like, 'Yeah, I do this.' You were so sure of it. You loved it. You loved what you do. And I was like 'Cool, follow the White Rabbit.'

Just trying to answer the question of what's my thing that I love that much. At the time, my main thing was photography. I hadn't moved into moving image as yet. So, I still have all of these beautiful images, me, you, and Marty in that flat on Soho Square. Those are some of my favourite images I've ever taken. I swear down, when I took them and got them back, I was like, 'I don't know if I'm done with photography. It doesn't need to be more than this.' It was a real moment. And it really meant something to me. And I've captured it. And that's that.

Marawa What was next?

Kevin Slowly but surely, that's when film and moving image came in. And I was like, 'Oh, okay, I love stories.' I love people, but I don't love people, you know – I just love their stories. And so at Bounty you would see me next to Marty while he DJ'ed, and I was just watching people dance, woo and break up, ignore each other, and also miss each other. I was collecting stories and learning.

You were percolating. You were watching it. It was like a film. You were taking it all in.

Exactly. So, I know the culture inside out now. And I know the way that people move. I've seen countless amounts of first interactions, people falling in love for the first time, the beginnings of one-night stands, the beginnings of breakups, watching memories dance across people's faces when certain sounds come on. I understand – I don't want to say better than anyone – but I'm excellent at understanding human emotion. Then when I apply that to storytelling, that's where that magic comes from. But it's always been about being in the moment, which takes extraordinary amounts of discipline and work because of the world that we live in.

We're both sitting here, talking about the amount of work that goes into our art to make it sustainable, to make sure we can care for our friends and family and all the things that we want to do. But it's only now that we're seeing the fruits of that labour, to be able to pass them on, to be like, 'Art is an option for Black and Brown kids. It's fine.'

Because it takes years to be able to say that, and having to trust in that for fifteen years is tough.

I can't tell you how many uncles I knew of growing up that could, like, really sing, how many aunties that were amazing choreographers. Even my mum, I've lost count of the number of stories I've been told by her friends who are now my unofficial aunts. They'll be like, 'Do you know how good your mum was at...'

What's the jumping one in sports where you jump over?

Hurdles.

Hurdles. They'd be like, 'Do you know your mum could have gone to the Olympics?' And they say it with such seriousness.

And Mum is like, 'Yeah, I didn't have time for that. There were bills and stuff. And then you came along. So, I just got on with it.' . . . She doesn't say it in a way like, 'You ruined my Olympics.' *[Both laugh]*

We are the first generation that is starting to prove the fruits of artistic labour exist. We're the proof in the pudding. Half of me is really proud, of course, but I also feel sad, because I think about who else should have been here before me doing this?

I think it's really ironic when you're first-gen, that our parents' desire was for us to just be safe, and do the normal things – get the degree, get the normal job and be the safe ones. It is actually because of that, plus the extra that they gave us, that has got us to being this version. Which is not what they wanted necessarily, or at least not what they thought could survive. But it was actually through that that we are here.

Going back to the oranges . . . I'm not taking away from the fact that I do what I love – I definitely do what I love. There's no question about it. This is what I love doing. But you need that unquestioned, unwavering love to be able to put in the amount of work needed to see it through.

Just enjoy it, whatever the thing is. And how do you tell it's the thing? When the oranges are rolling down the street, and you're just like, 'I have to pick them up.'

That's when you know it's more than that.

You're going to have to work for it.

Discipline.

YOU'RE GOING TO HAVE TO <u>WORK</u> FOR IT

So make it fun

It will never be easy, but definitely worth it. There is no such thing as microwaved success – that's to say, instant gratification. It's all hard work, it's all dedication, and the only thing that makes that journey a little bit easier is discipline.

TODAY'S TAKEAWAY:

Anchoring

I've found that anchoring your discipline to a separate rule, goal, or even person is a really easy way to get your discipline on lock.

In the same way that I treat mine and Tom's friendship as more important than just what it means for our careers, when it comes to getting stuff done, Tom is who I have anchored my discipline to. The worst thing for me isn't to fail at a project. It's the idea of letting him down in the work. Projects will change and evolve – not always for the best reasons – so if your discipline is rooted in something you believe in that's bigger than the project itself, then regardless of the bullshit that may arise, you'll see it through.

20

THE GAME

Staying late, just because the boss is? Downing another pint with colleagues who'll snipe you tomorrow, all the while knowing your partner will be vexed that you're coming home drunk again? Taking the blame for the decision a client forced on you, when you already said it was a bad idea? Swallowing the notion that the workplace can only function when following white Eurocentric dogma, no matter the pain it causes? Never congregating with other Black and Brown people in the building for longer than thirty seconds, for fear of being labelled a gang (true story)?

All of these – and more – are the rules of 'The Game'.

The Game is a method of control that actively wears down any aspects of our character that don't conform. Even those with privilege have to play it – they just have an advantage in certain areas that others don't. The Game exists in many an industry, whether that's commercial creative work, entertainment, or even party politics. Just think about how perfectly aligned the circumstances need to be in order for celebrities to begin talking up on important issues.

In the conversation below, I talk with my good Judy, Michaela, about navigating The Game when you're Black and queer. Ultimately, what I want to highlight, reflect upon, and loudly love is the state of Black. The magic of Black before any interruption.

It's the peace in Blackness that we experience even when other Black people aren't watching. Too often though, that peace is only ever discussed with regards to how hard we work to maintain it.

For me to only talk about the magic of a thing, person, or people from the very deliberate angle of their durability is simply to be using that subject as a stepping stone, a resting place for one to drop off their own guilt via the act of acknowledgement.

Is there ever a space for acknowledgement? Yes, of course. Respectfully, I direct you back to Chapter 2 of this book. But there's a difference between measuring your personal growth, and someone else using it as justification for repeated abuse.

Now that I have your full understanding, I want to say this:

Black is magical, not because of its durability but because of its innocence. And to be queer is one of the most natural things in the world. I can explain my love of another man from A to Z, from one to infinity – because it's true. The evidence for this builds up relentlessly, day by day, begging to be present and testify to the inevitable conclusion that my existence cannot and should not be questioned. To be both queer and Black is to sit at the centre of the human condition, to express only open welcoming, whilst nevertheless being attacked.

To be Black and queer is a flex.

The journey to create authentically while playing The Game as a queer Black person is a long one, and unfortunately it means that sometimes you'll have to visit regions of hell just to get the work done. These different states – or levels – of hell can reveal themselves in a ridiculous array of forms. I've remixed a few of Dante's circles of hell from *La Divina Commedia* below, to illustrate some of these realms:

PLAYING THE GAME IN GENERAL
Lust and Fraud:

Souls are blown about in a terrible storm without rest, forever chasing invoices while running back and forth under the whip of culture vampires (who fear washing their legs even more than the sun's warmth).

BLACK AND PLAYING THE GAME
Treason:

You're now working, but the foundations of that company you're in never actually had you in mind. Instead, it's full of old ghosts that were used and forgotten, dodging between men who never cared about the consequences of their actions.

Here you will meet Judas, Brutus, and Cassius at the coffee machine, looking out from inside this dire skyscraper to admire the view of a frozen lake.

QUEER AND PLAYING THE GAME
Avarice, Prodigality, and Treason:

Every day, this dire skyscraper collapses on you. You feel like you're trapped in the jaw of some great, evil thing. Meanwhile, the greedy and ungenerous smash their heads together over and over again – hoping that some new idea will stick.

BLACK, QUEER, AND PLAYING THE GAME
Avarice, Prodigality, Treason, Wrath, and Sullenness:

All of the above and more. It's gloomy here; eternal fights occur over who came up with what first. The old men that should have retired try their best to drain you of your life and ideas.

THE GAME

BLACK, QUEER, FEMALE, AND PLAYING THE GAME
Avarice, Prodigality, Treason and Limbo:

All the woes already visited in this hell, but with an
additional, overwhelming sense of uncertainty that just
won't leave you. You feel as if you're in a state of endless
sorrow, forever separated from your god – your own creative
work in its most authentic form.

BLACK, QUEER, TRANS, AND PLAYING THE GAME
Everything outlined above,
by the power of ten.

I won't then add the effects of having a disability to the mix,
just so you're able to sleep tonight. But know that when
mental and/or physical disabilities are also factored in,
you can find yourself in other, entirely different, realms of
hell. As Black, queer people, our position, standing at this
nexus point of culture, is that we're able to look at these
hellscapes and still make art or music, inspire trends – even
revolutions – and offer insightful social commentary that's
able to sit somewhere between stand-up comedy and
'Question Time' (when David Dimbleby hosted).

To be Black and queer is a flex – who else can handle
such hells, whilst still protecting and evolving the culture
like we can?

"HE CAN MAKE FURNITURE AND SHE'S JUST THERE LIKE, 'OH, MY SHOES.'"

MICHAELA YEARWOOD-DAN

Multidisciplinary fine artist

ON PLAYING THE GAME

Kevin I wonder if the reason I have such an affinity for James Bond, and spy movies in general, is because I feel like I could do that. It relates to the many different guises that I think, as a Black creative, you kind of have to put on.

> **Michaela** Yeah, and I pride myself on being genuine and honest, truthful and authentic in myself. I take pride in how I carry myself and interact with people in that way. But if I have to play a role to get to where I need to get, then I will play that role to get to where I need to get.

Like, blame the system. I don't know what you want me to do, I don't know what you expect of me? Just fix the system.

> Even being successful as an artist, I was like, 'Oh wait, capitalism is the game. Oh, okay, fine.' I like winning games, so I'm gonna try and play this game then. I know it's nothing compared to whether the work is genuine and from the heart . . . but if little Becky Smith is getting paid X amount – with her blonde hair and her private education – and I'm getting paid B amount? Then I'm like, 'No, no, no. We're all playing the same game. I wanna be paid X amount, please.'

I really like the idea of the two of us talking about playing the game, because I think – given that we're both Black, queer, and from South London – playing the game really is a full-time job. And we do play it, but I think we do it differently to the way other people do, because others will fully go and sell their souls. I've never, ever been about that life. I aim to fully play the game, but somehow still remain fully authentic in myself too, so that by the time I'm out, you have absolutely no idea who the real me is.

> Yeah.

I don't know how I do that though.

> I get people constantly telling me how confident I am, saying how great I am in group settings or whatever. And I'm just like, 'I go back home afterwards and have to be quiet for, like, a full twenty-four hours after.' Because that is what's required of me in that space, if I'm to be consistent within the role. And yes, there's authenticity within it. But at the same time, the people who I'm being truly authentic with don't need me to fill space like this, and I'm not gonna have to do that for them. And I'm happy to do that in these moments because I know it helps me stay authentic in the other, most important, areas of my life. So, I do it.

It's about – in that moment – sacrificing the thing or doing the thing that I normally wouldn't really do, because while I'm at work, I am protecting and fighting and working for the things that I love the absolute most. So yeah, I'm the same. When me and my other half first got together, I think he thought there was something seriously wrong. And then slowly but surely he was like, 'Ah, right.' So now, when I'm back from work, I will just walk in, take off my coat, la la la-la-la, and then just sit on—you know, that meme of 'New York' from Flavor Flav's 'Flavor of Love'?

Yeah, on the bed.

Yeah, and just sit there in the dark. Very much 'New York'. I just need a moment to remember what I need to be doing.

I had a very similar thing with my partner. You know that scene in 'Sex and the City' – I don't know if you've watched the show – where Carrie says to Aidan that he can't talk to her for, like, fifteen minutes when she gets in. That was me. And we have stairs as you walk up into the maisonette, and we're in the upstairs flat. And Elle would be like, 'Hi, hi' as I got in. And I would literally close the door behind me and just stand there for a while, not replying to her. So she'd then have to question whether I was in or not. But I just need a moment. Like, I've also just done the Seven Sisters Road, and that road is a nightmare. It's been a day, I need a moment to flex myself, hang up my coat, so I can think about what my day has been, and what my evening is going to be. I just need to pause.

When you explain that to people sometimes they'll just think you're in a mood, but it's not that; I just need to decompress. And sometimes you do wanna come in and just be about it, like chat, chat, chat. But other times you've got to re-engage with your authentic self and just let the day kind of drop off you for a second.

I do watch 'Sex and the City', and I was saying from early on that she should've chosen Aidan. I dunno what the hell she was thinking.

I don't, I don't, I don't.

You know when I fell in love with Aidan? When he ate too much chicken and asked her to rub his belly. I was like, 'You know what? I love you, I really love you.'

I think Aidan is brilliant. He deserved better than Carrie, so I'm glad she didn't end up with him. Because it would have been a Steve/Miranda situation in the new ones, and you're just like 'Steve, you deserve better. Miranda, you also deserve better, but you just needed to realise you were queer a lot earlier on in life, and everyone would have been happy.' But Aidan was just ready. His light was on, he was able to commit. He was able to give her all those things and that was scary for her and it was just like, 'Great, go to therapy. Figure it out, it's not anyone's business.'

The man said they should build a life together.

Kevin, what do you mean a life? It was, 'I bought the apartment next door and I have a house upstate.'
He can make furniture and she's just there like, 'Oh, my shoes.'
[Both scream and laugh]

Okay . . . let's talk about being Black queer artists, and Black creativity, because I really do think our peers – specifically the breeders—

Oh gosh.

Kevin —specifically our straight peers – do not comprehend the levels that are involved in what we do. And I'm specifically talking about Black artists. We really exist in the middle of intersectionality like no other. bell hooks wouldn't agree maybe, but that's what I think. We are constantly trying to represent our Blackness in a way that communicates our authenticity to the rest of the diaspora. At the same time, that diaspora should be our home, yet we're made to feel that our Blackness has been watered down by our queerness. Not to mention all the other ways that Black queerness is simultaneously being put under scrutiny, like how some white queer people will treat us in a very particular way because we are both Black and queer. The gymnastics that we have to do, just to get to a single, clear, creative thought and execution? At points, that can't even be fully quantified. Yet every day, day in and day out, we seem able to move and make magic.

So how do you do that? What are the methods you use to try and get those spaces to make sense at all?

Michaela Yeah. I mean, firstly, whether it's in professional or social settings, I rarely tend to navigate around people who are not othered in some way. I don't have a lot of time for white straight men; my tolerance level for them is minimal. I feel similarly towards straight, cis white women who don't surround themselves with diverse groups. It's interesting though, in the art world, because at a certain level everyone's a fucking white cis man owning these successful galleries, so I've always chosen to build relationships with women, and so far I've only had white female gallerists. It's been a process, but in some respects, those who feel like a minority within a space will tend to have a minority-focused agenda. My American gallerist is a Jewish woman – with a diverse roster and team – and I've heard some of the discrimination she's had to face for being a woman clearly rooted in her heritage and just, like, brush off. I think when there's that cloak of whiteness attached to you, sometimes you forget how discriminated against you are too, because of other traits you hold that would be considered in the minority.

So I don't surround myself with people I need to explain myself to. It was a conscious decision I made round about when I left university, because I'd had to deal with a lot of those people there. And I realised that, actually, I don't have to deal with this in real life, so I'm not going to. There are enough people who will get me on some level in every context, so I don't need to invite in those who don't.

I also stopped trying to feel responsible for my Black or queer communities, in terms of, like, telling a wider collective story. Instead I realised that my story – what I found interesting – was simply enough. Because it will naturally feed and relate to others. I'm not special or unique. My thoughts are shared by many people, and I don't have to feel the burden of telling this wider macro story about Black existence, queer existence, or Black queer existence. By just engaging with my authentic self, I already am telling those stories.

And I think in recent years, I've witnessed that a lot from Black creatives across the board. Whether in music or cinema, they just do what they like to do. And people will connect with that. And it will broaden the nuances within Blackness and Black creativity. So I just want to feed into that instead of fear.

I used to feel responsible if I came out of, like, arts education thinking, 'Okay, I'm a Black, queer woman with Caribbean ancestry, and I need to make sure everyone feels like they're relatable to me.' And I was like, that's a lot of people. That's a lot of people who might not even appreciate it. So, let me just do what I need to do or, rather, what I want to do, and those who will connect with it will connect to it. And they don't have to be Black, queer, West Indian, from South London, or a woman, to do that. It can be anyone, because if they're choosing to engage in it, they're really choosing to engage in the context of the artist as a person – not just the visuals – and if that engagement is a follow on Instagram, or buying an actual piece of art, it's still an act of coming into the circle or community that I'm building around myself.

I agree. I got to a place a couple of years ago where I realised that whatever I do, it's inherently going to be Black and queer – it's as simple as that. But I did also feel that stress for a minute of like, how do I make this South London? How do I make this Jamaican? How do I make this Blackity Black, Black, Black? All these things – and I was just like, anything I do has all of those things.

It's interesting because, on this note, I've been having a thought that I almost saved especially for our chat, because I feel like you'll have an opinion on it. The conversation around artificial intelligence – AI – in art is really funny to me. Whilst I get the concern about the ethics around it, at the same time, a lot of the conversations are actually just describing what humans already do on a day-to-day basis. Because you were just touching on how you, as a person, bring all of your references with you – like literally, in this conversation we've gone from race and queerness to why Carrie's a dickhead. We are already a combination of all of these things. Even in my most personal shorts, the editing and visual references come from all over the place. It's not me trying to be edgy or anything like that, it's just that I'm naturally drawn to these juxtapositions. Bitch, I didn't even notice I was doing it.

I'm just absorbing, you're just absorbing everything around you. And it would be stupid if you weren't. You're trying to be there inherently within yourself, you are a relatable person. There is a warmth in wanting people to understand where you're coming from. If I can absorb something that I've seen on TV, or an advert that I heard on the radio, and then apply that to my sense of the world – intellectualise it – then I'm sorry, I'm actually just a genius. I'm sorry, pop culture is like this. I'm also not trying to be highbrow to a point that it feels inauthentic when I do that. If you wanted to only use philosophical chat, or highly regarded literary references, then I'm sure you could. That is still pop culture.

That is the space that, basically, we all dip into as a collective, then come out being like, 'Oh, okay,' before then going off and starting new conversations. And then, oddly enough, these new conversations somehow end up back in the popular culture. We're just coming back to look at ourselves, again and again and again. It's a really simple cycle that doesn't actually need to be complicated in the way some spaces try. I do believe they're trying to add a level of complexity as a way to create barriers; in terms of class, race, gender, sexuality, etc. But the fact that I can sit here and talk to you about film theory in detail, then throw in a 'Drag Race' reference, has them shook. Not to mention the fact that popular culture calls Black social spaces 'mother', anyway.

Michaela 'Toxic' is the best pop song that's ever been written – and I will fight anyone on that fact. Because, like, those little drum cadences, and the little breaks . . . I will give a real TED Talk about this song, then switch into talking about some article I read the other day, and how that actually relates back to the song. And I'm like, 'What have I consumed?' *[Both laugh]*

Like, I don't even know – what am I visually and mentally eating? I'm connecting XYZ to this and that, and I have to pause and be like, am I a genius? Or do I just need to shut up?

And sometimes it's a bit of both.

Kevin Yes, I find that. Sometimes I say the wildest things and I'm like, you can't say that out loud because you will get sectioned. Then the next thing I know, it's the biggest trend. I always have to double check the things I'm thinking, because I don't put a cap on my imagination. I really don't, I let it go wherever it needs to go.

Let it go. Let it go. You can rein it in later if you want to. Let it go where you need to let it go.

This conversation about pop culture is really interesting, though. It really is just this big mirror that we look into to constantly revise ourselves, before taking another look. I wanted to hear your thoughts though, because for me, the root of pop culture is Black culture.

When I first got into advertising, I made that connection, and it felt like a real breakthrough. If you're not in the world of commercial creative – whether that's advertising, art as a commodity, or whatever – where ideas have to be sellable, I don't think you understand how much stuff is sold on the back of mood boards full of Black culture. Like, they just go shopping to find the most obscure, interesting young Black and Brown kids on the internet and say, 'Thank you, thank you, thank you.' To themselves, mind. Then they come back to work and are like, 'Here's the campaign.'

There was a time where I was really annoying, just constantly pointing out trends on Vine when that was a thing. I miss Vine. It was so good, and it really rubbished a lot of people, because it was like, if you can't tell your story in six seconds, you're no good. Whereas there were lots of really interesting Black kids that gave you a six-second story that felt like you'd watched a whole movie with all of the cast. You were like, 'What, that's six seconds?'

Literally, like the original culture of old-school YouTube, where the BuzzFeed crew were really impressive, or Vine, early Black Twitter. They were the best. I came off Twitter in 2016 because the world was falling apart and I just didn't want to read it every morning. But I still get people to send me the tweets, I still know the jokes. I still will watch something and see a white girl doing something on TikTok and be like, 'Let me wait like a week and I'll see the original Black person doing this, 'cause I know you did not invent this.'

You know what, you saying that made me realise that I will just automatically look through the description of a TikTok I enjoyed, to find where they say, 'Thanks to so-and-so.' So yeah, it's not your content, is it? And then I go find that originator.

It's so wild, because people will just do the same thing over and over again. Copy other people's things and get more tweets, or more followers. Because you're what, more conventionally attractive?

I think the language of advertising has seeped into it all in one way or another. So now people are like, 'Oh, I didn't steal that idea. I'm just using the format.' Do you ever look around at some of the work that is coming out, specifically in the art world, and think, 'Oh, I'm a mum'?

So for me it's very interesting, because there are so many different categories within the art world. Predominantly within painting, everything falls between abstract or figurative. The figurative girlies (that's non-gender specific) – I just let them do what they want to do. I didn't study art, I studied painting, so when I see a really good painting, that invigorates me, I'm like, 'Yes, go off.' I look at what other people are doing but I try to not let it pull focus in my work. I'll probably take things and see things and be like, 'Oh, yeah, I used to do that. I've done that before. Let me bring that back. That was a nice technique. Oh, I love those materials.' And then you start using those materials again, because they are interesting and you've missed using them. If my work starts looking like someone else's, it won't be seen. I won't put it out, because I don't want that connection to be drawn. I get a bit irritated when younger artists will adopt my style, especially if they know me or have met me.

The truth is though, no one is original. No one is solely original; the only originality we can have at this point, as creatives and people living on this planet, is the combination of techniques we've pulled together. That's the most original thing we can do. Everything is pulled from something or other. We've been on this planet too long for it to not be that way. How you bring those together, and how you then represent them? That's the original thing. It's the people who don't like to own up to having inspirations that annoy me. I'll be in conversations where someone's work will look like a dead copy of someone else's. So I'm like, 'Oh yeah, so you know XY?' And they'll be like 'No, I've never heard of them.' Don't lie to yourself. That's not cute. it doesn't make you seem more intelligent. Just be a fan. I think people feel it's uncool to be a fan.

Because they have an inferiority that is based on trying to get their own ticket; their own foot in the door. True creators, true artists, don't worry. That only happens when you really get into your own groove and you're very honest. I'm the same. Do you know how many things of mine people have never, ever seen? As you said, nothing is new under the sun. So, really and truly, all we are ever doing is reinventing things with our own personal spin.

You know, I had this recent thing where people kept on taking my work to auction and they were making hundreds of thousands off work that they bought for like £10,000. It made me feel irritated and annoyed that they were profiting from it in a way where I wasn't able to profit. But now those people are on my list. They're never going to work with me again. I've lost friends, or else had massive shifts in friendships, from being successful. If they can't understand that everyone should be eating, that's not on me. It's going to be so lonely; surely, you would want everyone in your circle to be able to achieve their dreams and see their successes become manifest in the way they want? I don't understand why that wouldn't be your goal.

I was just in Paris the other week, for an exhibition at the Louis Vuitton Foundation. When I was walking around the show, I literally turned to Elle and said, 'Thank God they're dead.' Because if they were alive, I'd be jealous. Thank God, no one can get any more work from them. We should only be comparing ourselves to ourselves; comparing what I did last to what I have the ability to do.

In the lockdown, I really taught myself how to make ceramics. Like, I'd aired dry clay, I'd been to two classes, then the lockdown happened and I was just like, 'Cool. Okay, let me not go insane. I live on my own.' (At that point I was living on my own.) I decided to learn how to do this skill and be so, so good at it that people will be shocked. But actually, it was about shocking myself: seeing how I could better myself every time.

I FEEL PRETTY,

OH SO PRETTY,

To the baby queers out there

You shouldn't have to convince anyone you're worthy of love.
They don't see your talent, leave that to them and Specsavers.

TODAY'S TAKEAWAY: Black and queer

Create the spaces you need; they do not exist otherwise.
Specifically on playing the game:

More time people don't even know the game they are playing
with you, so I have always found that remembering what you
are there to do and why – and then manipulating the game to
where you need it to be – has always worked.

You can also just let them think nothing of you or your
trajectory. Let's say you meet your new boss, and it's clear
they do not rate you. You don't need to convince them
otherwise. They will block doors you're not even trying to
walk through, so let them think they've won.

Some of my fave moments in life are seeing old gatekeepers
realise I was never trying to get through the gate they once
protected so much.

I FEEL PRETTY AND

WITTY AND GAY

21

INTEGRITY

We have a few dictums in Jamaica that are immovable. Combinations of words that, when spoken, become unbreakable spells. When we use these sayings, we are almost calling forth every ounce of rectitude we carry. Proud like peacocks, but rather than puffing out feathers on their train, we show off our various examples of integrity. Some of these spells – protective audible trinkets – come in short form. For instance, 'I don't business' is a spell, a warning, and a war-cry that translates to: Everything can burn if it needs to.

Another example? Let's say my friend started dating a person. They ask for my approval and, on meeting them, I can instantly tell that the potential love interest is on some fuckeries. I don't approve. Rather than beat around the bush, all I really need to say is, 'My spirit didn't tek.' That will be the end of the conversation, and probably their last interaction. Their last date. 'Don't it?' is another one, and probably my favourite. My grandmother would use it at the end of a sentence to reassure me, or whoever else was listening, that what she was saying was above the laws of any man or god, old or new. It's always delivered as a question, but a rhetorical one.

There is a seriousness in everything we do as Jamaicans, whether it's how we love or hate. You'll never meet a Jamaican without some form of conviction. If nothing else, we will be believed when we speak.

For every elder I have met from back home who knew my grandfather, they only ever spoke of him in one way: 'Ya see ya grandfather, we looked pon him like a god, may God fi giv mi, but God wouldn't want mi to lie. Don't it?' Blasphemy be damned; in their eyes he was a god. In mine too. He was kind, wise, giving, and for his community. It's here you will find the birthplace of my morals and integrity – my love for everything that is Jamaican. That is my grandparents.

You may be reading this and not share my heritage or culture, and that's fine. The point of this next conversation is to draw on whatever is personal to you. My work is based on the idea that anything I leave behind should inspire good in this world. That's a big job, and it means my morals should inherently be based within something robust enough to support the task at hand. We are most robust when dealing with love; specifically defending it and, in this case, remembering love.

Fighting for your work, day in and day out, is a tiring thing. But if the work's foundations were built in dedication to something or someone that you revere more than your own self, it becomes child's play. The barbed words of pushback from uninformed clients will feel like tickles.

Your work should be founded on integrity, and your integrity should be connected to something – or someone – so personal to you, that the emotional bond becomes your driving force.

"WHAT ABOUT WHO I AM?"

A CONVERSATION WITH

JAMELIA

Artist and presenter

ON INTEGRITY

Kevin There is a thing within advertising, where it's like, how do you get to the essence of the problem – the authenticity of the thing? How do you tap into the insight of what it is that makes people fall in love with the thing that you're trying to sell them, or introduce them to? In short, what is the essence that will grab you and speak to you on an honest level of connection?

Now, you, Jamelia, to me, are the master of that. In 2003, I was working as a supervisor at the Levi's Covent Garden store. And I had a really great team there. It was the first time I'd worked in a place where absolutely everybody was cool and individual, but I also had to really become aware of the politics of the situation. You know, to realise that everybody was so different, that the balance of the thing was always gonna change if you didn't keep the vibe. And it was a good, calm space to learn that lesson in.

Your album 'Thank You' came out at that time, and I remember there was another Black gay boy where I worked, who really wasn't out of the closet, but was like super feminine. I just assumed he was comfortable, and asked him who his boyfriend was. He almost wanted to fight me in the store, so I had to very quickly apologise and reel it back in.

Up until that point. I'd really thought I was a don at just cutting to the quick of what needed to be said, but I learned that – outside of spaces where sometimes it was armshouse on sight – I needed to change how I related to and empathised with others.

For the first time, I really had to flex my emotional intelligence, you know? And for me, you're just part and parcel of that moment in my life, because I had your album on repeat in the store. And everyone had their favourite song in the store – everyone loved the album. But for me, I was obsessed with this one song – 'Antidote' – to the point where everyone was like, 'What is it about this song that you will not let go?'

And I was like, 'I do not know; this song is talking to my soul in a way and I don't understand it.' And then obviously, all these years later, we had a conversation in the DMs and you broke it down. And let me say, I was sat there in silence when I read your message like, 'I'm sorry, what?'

As soon as you said what it was about I was like, 'Of course, all the things that I love.' Like, I love nothing more in the world than I love being Black, and nothing more in the world than I love being a Virgo, and nothing more in the world than I love being a Jamaican. I cannot explain to you how much I love being a Yardie.

Jamelia Yeah, same.

Sorry, that's a big introduction. But I just really needed to let you know the impact you had in that way, and how you sit within my life.

Bless you. Bless you. Thank you.
I mean, none of my songs are ever just songs, do you know what I mean? I really think very deeply about them, and I can always tell you the inspiration – where it came from or what I was trying to do. I never want my songs just to be songs. Each one is a piece of art, you know? There's levels to it; there's layers to it.

But I also know that to millions of people, it is just a song. So to hear that someone has kind of, I don't know, held on to one of my pieces of art is like, dunno man, it's a bit much! It's beautiful to hear. So yes, thank you.

Kevin Are we able to talk about the song and where it came from?

Because I think it's such a beautiful segue into, like, essence and integrity. And I guess, on one level, the song most obviously speaks to me as a Virgo because sometimes it's almost like I'm fighting to be broken hearted, so I can then complain about being broken hearted. That's where my art comes from.

But then also wanting to be that antidote, that superhero, to somebody else as well. So, there's all of that, but there has always been this bass line in the DNA of the song that I didn't quite understand just why I was drawn to it.

Jamelia So first I think I should tell you a little of the environment in which I wrote the song.

I grew up in inner-city Birmingham, Jamaican family, single parent home. The whole spiel. Then I get signed to a major record label and have to move to London, totally out of my comfort zone. But I'm very happy because I'm doing something I could never have imagined.

I always say that me signing my record deal was like the girl who dreamed of becoming a princess actually becoming the princess. That's what it felt like to me. So it was all so surreal.

But, I quickly got wind of the fact that, as a songwriter, I was trusted to write my songs – which was fantastic for me. But I also started to become aware of what they wanted me to put out, and what they wanted me to essentially sell to my people. And I was kind of like, 'Yeah, but what about me? You know, what about who I am?' If I had my way, I probably would have done a dancehall album. Which was not what, you know, I signed the deal for. [Both laugh]

I signed as an R&B artist. But I want people to know I'm Jamaican; that's part of my DNA. And I wanted that to be a factor in my music. Within that, I slowly but surely realised that it also had to be palatable to the British ear. And so it was kind of like, well, how can I do that? So I took inspiration from one particular song, one of my favourite songs ever, by Sanchez: 'Lonely Won't Leave Me Alone'. And if you're Jamaican, and your mum's ever cooked rice and peas, you know the song.

So I snuck it in, kind of like mashing vegetables up into a mince or something for your children. That's kind of what I was doing with my music.

I've had so many people love so many of my different songs, but it's always Jamaicans that pick up on Antidote. It's one of their favourites. And that's great, because it makes me be like, 'Yeah, I did it.' The song I did with Beanie Man was a little bit more obvious, but obviously, he was a feature. I wanted to get that Jamaican heritage into my song.

It floored me when I found how you'd brought that heritage in. Because as you said, if you are Jamaican, that song was playing on Sunday, while meat was being seasoned. It was also, maybe, there when you got up to do your chores this Sunday. That song is just dripping in the vibe of it.

We couldn't have like a dancehall beat, but if you listen to that song carefully, you'll hear that the instrumentation is doing that, you know, if you alone, da da da da—

This is what I'm saying! I was just sat there like, you're a genius. You're actually a don. Because – and this is what I'm talking about – this is the essence of, like, advertising to a certain extent, because it's like, yes, you can do advertising that's overt, right? You should have this car because it will sort out your midlife crisis, whatever.

The advertising that I'm interested in, which I feel is a lot more holistic and a lot better for my soul, is like the ones where I attract people to products they actually have a connection with. As opposed to pushing trainers that look shiny on kids that can't afford them yet do a madness to get them.

Unfortunately, we live in a capitalist world; we live in Babylon. As a real, true Jamaican, I really just want to live good. I don't want to see anybody go without, and that is the essence of me. So for me, it was sometimes difficult being in advertising, and I can relate to what you're saying, because you're in an industry that is also like, 'No, we have to be palatable, this, that, that, and the other.' They are asking you to bring all of your sauce in with you . . . but then, oddly and within the same breath, showing that they don't actually want the sauce. That Sanchez thing is just so good. With the flute in the background, too.

For me, this conversation is one of the most important ones in the book. Because it shows how, yes, you might end up in situations where the powers that be are asking you to go against yourself, to forget yourself or move yourself to the side. Sometimes you just have to manoeuvre in a way where it's like, I'm finning to get this message out to my people in some form of Morse Code. They're gonna get it. You've got what you want, but they're gonna get this message, and feel seen and heard. I love the action of people picking up things, finding their own thing in the thing, and then they go off and create their own thing. That is, in a sense, creatively opening a door, and then keeping the door open.

As your career unfolded, did you find it got easier for you to bring more of yourself into those spaces? Or was it the reverse?

It was definitely the reverse. I think the more popularity I gained, the more difficult it was to be authentic – to the point where it became actually unbearable, and I literally couldn't continue.

I wouldn't change my experience because I know that that was the only route to achieve the thing. But that being said, I definitely feel like I walked away. I walked away. And the thing is, I was raised as a Rastafarian. And so we are very, very spiritual; we're obsessed with being clean-hearted, kind, and good to people.

If you look at my career, you can see that I was wearing less and less clothes. And I know that might not seem like a major thing. But for me, I was becoming so offended because I was like, 'Why do you want me to sell this to people's children, to little girls that look like me?' And it was something that came up again, and again, and again – until, as I said, it just became unbearable. And the thing is, I was making so much money. And when you take someone from the hood, and give them loads of money, you know, you will dance. You know what I mean? [Both laugh]

Yeah.

Jamelia Trust me. They say money doesn't bring happiness, and it's true. Money couldn't erase the fact that I was not living authentically. At least, not the public version of me. I just felt like I was getting paid to lie, and it didn't sit well with my spirit. I only did three albums and by the end of the third one – when I was in Japan on tour – I just thought, 'You know what? I can't go another day doing this thing. I can't go another day selling myself inauthentically.'

So then the next ten years have been about me actually trying to find who I am, and then being that person authentically. There are certain things I owe to my Jamaican heritage, like the fact that I've never been afraid to be without money or status. Those things are just not important to me, you know? But I do love having a public platform because I see it as something I can use positively. To change the game in a way that sits right with my soul. Even if that means losing opportunities, or not being in certain spaces and places. Like again, being Jamaican, I can't tell you the amount of times I've said to my manager, 'I don't business.' *[Both laugh]*

Kevin I'm laughing because you know how many times I say to Tom, 'I don't business'?

I don't fear not having the trappings of money and fame, and I feel like that makes me fearless, scary even, to some people. I got offered silly money to do very silly things. And I'm just like, 'Yeah, I'm not doing that.' And now, I do live a very different lifestyle, coming to the end of being a musical artist. I had to learn to do things, like walk through a crowd. I've never been in a crowd before. I've never – apart from Carnival as a child. So I would walk places and bump into people because I was so used to having, like, bodyguards and stuff like that. I got on a plane with my daughter, you know, and she was like, 'Oh, Mummy, the seats don't lie down.' So, as a family, we had to make a whole adjustment because we're not doing that anymore. But I am so much happier now. I'm so glad that I made that decision. And if I was to put out music now, I would be able to have that authenticity, which is much more important to me than anything else. I don't know if that answered your question, sorry!

No, it did! It did. I feel you and I hear you. I co-founded a thing called Pocc, which started out as a WhatsApp group of Black and Brown, and global majority creatives in different forms – whether writers, editors, creatives, producers, whatever. It was just a WhatsApp group. And now, today, there are more than a thousand people in that group in the UK, plus others in the US and Netherlands. Not to mention Pocc Studios, Productions, 2Pocc, etc. When you create a safe space like that, brands are like, 'How do we get involved?' And like, I don't know – we created a safe space because you wasn't.

So then out of that grew a mini agency, studio, production house, and a jobs board where we consider these opportunities coming in and control them to be like, 'Well, no, this is how much people actually need to get paid. This is how you consider childcare within the make-up of this thing that you wanna make. This is how you do this, that, that, that.' I realised I'd built up these skills in advertising and I know I've got to use that skillset to help my community.

So yeah, everything you're saying connects with me. The more I started to read into Rastafarianism the more I'm like, 'I'm naturally within that space.' It's very interesting. It's like we are all here to add our particular piece of spice. And I think more time, people believe they are here to add not just something, but the whole thing. And they have no way of sitting back and thinking something like, 'No, those three albums were the thing that I was meant to do, to then move on to the next thing.' Does that make sense?

Absolutely. And I think, especially when you come from a particular background, it's very easy to kind of get caught up and to tell yourself, 'This is okay, this works. I'm gonna keep doing this for the rest of my life.'

No, sometimes things are a stepping stone – sometimes huge, incredible things can just be a stepping stone. I've experienced ridiculous fame. I wasn't Beyoncé, but in my head I achieved Beyoncé status, because my ambition until then was to go work in a corner shop. Literally to go work in a corner shop. So for me to achieve international stardom – that was incredible.

But if my spirit is not feeling what I'm doing on a daily basis, I can't stay there. And so what else is there to do? I have actively pursued different avenues, and still continue to do that to this day.

I feel like, as you were saying, the culture changes. Within that, I think we change as well. We evolve on a daily basis. And one of the things that I teach my daughters to do is really tap into those feelings and messages that you're getting – your intuition. My whole thing is, I lead with my gut.

I've gone down the road with contracts before, I wrote a book with a publishing house. Massive deal. I've got the book in my hands, and I was like, 'Nah, I'm not doing this.' And my management was like, 'What? You're gonna have to give all that money back. This is so embarrassing.'

I was like, 'It's not. I'm not supposed to.' Because when I read the book, all I saw was the stories you see in *The Sun*, and I don't want this to be my story. I know what they're going to pick up on, and what they're going to focus on. And you can't take an excerpt of my life like that. If I'm not in control of my own narrative, then you're not hearing it. And it was similar with the music.

I don't want to live a lie. I'm not here to portray an image of myself that people feel they can't afford. That's me down to the ground.

Like, I have a swimming pool in my back garden. That's not something that I will promote. I can't promote it to you, because I don't have the cheat code. Unless I can tell you exactly how to do this, then it doesn't make sense to me telling you, 'Oh, look at this. Look at the car I drive.' I don't wear designer clothes, because I understand that me wearing designer clothes is me promoting items to people they can't afford. So what am I doing to my own people? I can't contribute to that part of the culture.

There's so many people living in the background that I grew up in, who are coveting these things, and if they ever get a one-to-one with me, I will tell them straight to their face, 'That's not something to aspire to. That's not something to want, you know? It's not worth it.' What I value is being able to feed my children. I value being able to – I was just about to say keep them warm, but our boiler's broken, we're freezing. *[Both laugh]*

I guess I just want to have a positive impact on people. My legacy, and what I leave people with, is just as important to me as any music I may have made. If you've met me, I hope that my impact was a positive one. I'm very consciously curating that on a daily basis.

Kevin I think individually, we all have an essence, right? And some of those essences we share. Clearly you and I love, love, love being Yardies. But if I was to guess what the essence of you is, after everything you just said – it's just really beautiful – I think it's integrity, the essence that is integrity.

I know that mine is loyalty. It's really funny, Tom and I were literally talking about this the other day, because we have only ever had one argument. And it was because he worded something in a particular way while he was telling me how he felt about something. But the way he worded it made it sound as if he was questioning my loyalty … And when I say I switched in that moment!

Because my thing is, I'm ride or die. If you do a madness, I will be there doing the madness. Now, when we get behind closed doors I'm gonna be like, 'Are you all right? Why would you?' But I'm gonna ride with you. I don't spill people's secrets, even when I've fallen out with them. You can say I was brash, facety, or renk. Cool, you can have all of that. But what you can never say is that I stole from people or lied to people, or did people dirty like that.

So I think the essence of me is loyalty. And I would humbly guess that the essence of you is integrity.

Jamelia You won't believe how weird it is to hear you say that. I had a conversation with my brother today – he's my best friend, we're so similar – and I said that when we break everything down, the thing that's most important to us is that we have integrity. It is my core value. I want people to say that I'm honest, to know that I would never lie. I'll never do them wrong, even if you've done me wrong. I'd rather just lock you off.

And I think in order to have integrity, you have to know yourself. You have to know who you are, and be committed to that. And a lot of people don't, especially in this day and age of social media and, you know, the performance that we're constantly putting on online. When I do post something, I want you to know that I'm a person you can trust; that I'm honestly recommending the thing to hand. Even the other day, I got paid to do this toy ad. But one of my prerequisites is, I'm not doing it if I don't believe in it.

I feel like that's what's really important for us to know: when you get into positions of power, please use them wisely. Like when I did the music video for 'Money', they asked me what I'd like the concept to be. And I love period dramas, but before 'Bridgerton', I'd never seen myself in those shows. So I was at this boardroom table of sixteen or so people, and I just said, I wanna do that. I want everyone to be Black or Brown in high society. Because we never got to see ourselves in those environments. But I want us to dream and believe that we can. And I know that the success of 'Money' wasn't just the fact that I did a song with Beanie Man; it was also because I was doing something that people tell you shouldn't be done. 'You're not white, so you're not supposed to be there.' Listen, me and Beanie Man? We're gonna show you that we can.

It's always been about that. Especially as my songs, and my kind of look, became more pop, it was like, 'Well, how can I still do a little nod to let people know I'm still one of you lot? That I'm still … not gang … but, you know, gang.' Not because I want people to think I'm cool. But because I want people to know that, you know, you can do it.

When you get into a position of power, have some sort of intention behind the things that you're doing. Don't just do it. It's the same when posting on social media. Don't just post a post; it's an opportunity. I don't care if you've got three followers – it's an opportunity to educate and say something that needs to be said.

You do have to be careful even within that though, because it will be twisted if you let it. I was on TV all the time, talking about racism, Meghan Markle, all of that. And again, it got to a point where I was like, 'No, I'm not doing this anymore. It's serving no one, and you guys are using my tears – my anger, my PTSD – as entertainment.' And so I had to stop. I don't talk about those things online anymore.

When you go on these shows and you have these conversations, they don't care. They just move on to the next news segment. But this is my life; this is literally life. Not just for me, but for people I love, you know? My community. And for them, it's just a little short. It's just thirty seconds of air time to fill.

Now if someone wants to give me a two-hour programme or a series to explain it and break it all down, let's do that. But if we can't, I'm not involved – call somebody else. Even then, when I see my Black sisters on the TV, I feel the pain. Like I actually feel it. Literally, pain being inflicted on us. We have to work out ways of doing this better. Look at the documentaries and the programmes that we have on TV at the moment; they cover a plethora of subjects and topics. Don't just call us on for, you know, six minutes and give us a couple hundred quid. Give us the grands, give us the budget to speak properly.

It's true. I found this when I did my series of Black History Month films. I did them first in 2020, and another set in 2021.

Yes. I loved them.

Thank you. Thank you so much. And so you know, you also get credit for that, because the way that I write my things, 'Antidote' is in there. You taught me how to express that side of the thing. The way that I write my stories, or the way I present my ideas, is based on the way that you wrote it, you know? So, you're in there.

Oh my God. Yeah.

So I did that first series in 2020, and I didn't like 2020. I didn't take anyone's money in 2020, because I was like, 'You lot are playing dress up for a year. Come 2021, you're gonna leave these people, and all of a sudden all of these opportunities are gonna be gone.'

I also felt weird about it because people who had been silent for the longest of times started speaking up. On the one hand, I got it, because it was all of a sudden safe to be . . . I don't even want to say political because it's, as you said, our lives. It's not a joke. It's not a political ploy. My people are dying and you lot, in one way or another, are contributing to that. That's the conversation that we should be having.

But with that being said, sometimes people who are more . . . palatable, shall we say . . . were getting through to certain people and I'm like, 'You know what? You know that thing, "every mickle makes a muckle"? Or whatever it is? That saying.' *[Both laugh]*

Jamelia You know what, I say that all the time. My daughters hate it.

Kevin It's hilarious, I think that philosophy lives across. But in that time, in 2020, I was like, I can see how this is helping here or there, but overall, I'm not really with it. I would have been making these films anyway. That's what you lot don't understand. I was trying to start new conversations because I'm tired. I'm not telling white people anymore that it's racist to touch my hair. I'm not doing any of that; it's ridiculous to still be there.

That's the thing, if you don't know that by now, I'll just box you.

One-hundred-and-ten per cent. If you don't hear, you must feel you've been told. In 2021, I did my next series. And I could've done another five in that style in 2022. But I feel like I've very much evolved out of it to avoid becoming another inadvertent method of hand-holding white people through their role in oppression. This is why the way I fund my work has to remain independent. I sell art to make art. The only problem with that is, I've always found that six months down the line, others have now slightly tweaked my words, and presented them as if they were their own.

I don't want to be part of that cycle, just endlessly repeating the same conversation points and feeling constantly robbed. So I pop up with art when I need to. When they start to fund me correctly, with all the right creative freedoms and ownership, that's when we can talk about all that.

I want to make anthologies about Black joy, not whatever conversations you lot want me to be added to. And that's what's really maddening about being Black at times, because we possess so much joy, and you lot just want to stifle that with your nonsense. I want to get to that; I want us to enjoy and witness that. Because you all know what racism is. You all know how the system works. But we are somehow still having the same conversations we were having years ago.

I was having a conversation with my daughter yesterday and she was like, 'Mummy, why are they cancelling [rich white TV personality] again? Haven't they done already? Is he cancelled or not?' And I was just like, 'What you need to understand is that there's a message in this. Doesn't matter what you say about this man, he's gonna go and thrive.'

We have to make sure we're in the same position. Even if it's not thriving in the way that they thrive. Because this is another thing you have to remember, capitalism has conditioned us to want to be rich and famous like the white people on TV. When really, Black people are already joy experts, joy connoisseurs. Like the joy that we experience – despite the shit that is going on – as a people, as a community. I think we are our own safe space. But we keep trying to enter into these spaces that are unsafe. Moments like that, with that man in particular, they're letting you know, in black and white, that we are not safe.

So we need to take a step back and take a hold of our real, true joy. That's what we need to be putting out – especially in public forums. Privately, it's another thing. I'm not saying bad things don't happen. But that's not the conversation I wanna be telling. One of my biggest regrets is me slating Javine on 'Never Mind the Buzzcocks'. I feel like my career on television took off after that point, and I believe it was because it was a Black woman slandering another Black woman. And it's embarrassing for it to be built upon that. And so, since that point, it's been very important for me not to contribute to a negative perception of us. I just want people to see the good part.

One of those stories that I did during 2020 was called 'Laundry', and I was basically telling white people that slavery was their history, not ours. I make a point of definitely not arguing with Black and Brown women online. I tried to do it with Black men, but Black men are wild towards Black women. My priority is Black women. So therefore, those Black men have to get smoke sometimes, unfortunately. I try the whole, 'Yo, let me just talk to you one-on-one. No? Okay, cool.' And unfortunately for you, I'm me – a whole Yardie and a whole gay. The sass of that altogether? I'm gonna read you for real. It's your fault. Because I don't understand how some of you move in a way that you move towards women who look exactly like your mother.

There is some sort of epidemic going on right now when it comes to men. There are these influencers online turning them feral. What Black women endure and have to deal with, it doesn't make sense, especially from, you know, our own. I don't feel particularly protected by Black men. But I do also believe that it's because they haven't done – or had the opportunity to do – the work that Black women have had to do. They haven't had to carry what we've had to carry, what we've had to bear. We will burn down Rome for Black men. But to see that energy not reciprocated by them ...
   I think we're seen as superhuman by Black men because that's what we've been in their lives. You know, we've got it, we've got our capability and resilience. And that's why I love the whole soft life era. I love this for us. And I feel like that is where we need to focus. I am letting go of every single thing that doesn't serve me, every single thing that doesn't feel good. And I don't care how shallow it makes me.

You're preaching to the choir. Why should I not be able to enjoy myself? Because within my bones and within my DNA, I carry the trauma of all of my ancestors.

And that's the thing. The intergenerational trauma is what gives you the licence to be able to live soft now. You started this conversation by telling me that you have identified the things that you need, and identified the things that you love. And to me that's half of the work done. Because when you know what will return you to centre, you're basically invincible. Because life may throw something at you, but you know how to realign your soul. You know what I'm saying? And when you have that kind of power, it makes you a very scary person to others who don't know themselves.

YESTERDAY
MIKEY CALL ME
'PON MI PHONE

Everything matters

Finding it hard to love what you do?

Tie it back to a person or place that you wanna make proud. The brief doesn't have to change; just your perspective.

TODAY'S TAKEAWAY:

Here's the thing. Whether you operate from a space of openness or not, people will do the wildest of things to throw you off track, or else to get their own foot in the door. Playing as dirty as they are, or just going with the flow of the crowd can often feel like the best way to trudge through the work.

Just beat them,

It's certainly the easiest, but it's in no way the best. In the long run, disregarding your own integrity will leave you feeling mediocre and unfulfilled. And we both know these aren't traits you're hoping to achieve and, in turn, leave behind as your legacy.

don't join them

22

MONEY

MONEY

When I was about six, and my brother four, we sat with our uncle in his pride and joy – his white Lotus Esprit. Everyone on our block loved that car – was impressed by that car – more so because everyone knew it had been purchased legally.

My uncle, like my grandfather, is a hardworking man. Disciplined, and clear on what needs to be done before any fun.

We would sit in this car just to sit in the car, and marvel at its interior. A compact amusement park. Although it was his pride and joy, nothing gave him more pleasure than us rummaging through the crevices of the car, asking which button did what, and finding new cars, machines, and superheroes to race against in our imaginations.

On this particular visit, my brother and I found some coins in the dashboard. My brother, who had always been something of a magpie, swooped in and grabbed what he could, picking up all the gold and bronze coins while ignoring anything silver, which ended up being my cut. At this point, we still didn't really know what money was, the rules of money, or how it worked. Yes, I could count. I knew if Peter had six balls and Mary had three, that meant she had less.

What I didn't know at that point in time was the science of valuation. I looked at my coins and saw that Byron had a lot more than me. I must have made a face because my uncle felt the need to let me in on a secret. He leaned in and said, 'You've got more, don't worry about it.'
He put a finger to his lips, instructing me to keep this secret.

Later on, he showed me that the coins I had were worth more than the coins my brother had. Byron had scooped up a ridiculous amount of pennies that barely equated to £2.50.

What I had was eight 50p pieces, or £4.
I think that was my first encounter with worth.

In my teens, proving your worth meant showing off whatever patterned Moschino you could get your hands on. The louder the brand, the better. When I got that first job at a prominent fast-food restaurant, I was on £3.20 per hour. Their meal deals back then were £2.88, and we had a till target of £150 per hour in sales.

Sometimes I would sit on break and realise that my shifts were eight hours long, so on an average day, I'd make £25 or so. I then worked out that selling at least nine of those meals in one shift paid for an entire day's salary, and normally I'd hit that till target of £150 an hour with no problem. To do that, I had to have sold at least fifty-three of those meal deals.

I was only doing two shifts a week. Meaning I only had to sell around seventy meals in a four-week period to cover my salary for the month. So, within that first shift of that first week – in the first two hours alone – I'd already, just in the process of chasing that sales target, made more than they would need to pay me for that month.

I still thought that £3.20 was a flex.

I've made a lot of money in a lot of ways since those days, some of which I can't put in this book.

Where I sit with money now is that I don't care for it. I don't chase it or worship it. I prioritise my comfort, and I make sure I am paid what my experience is worth. Most of all, I am not scared of money.

What I will say, though, is that in an educational system that teaches you maths but not finance – despite living in a world that is in fact ruled by finance – it's no wonder that people run around allowing money to determine what they're worth.

Personally, I'd rather the level of my integrity that I have been able to maintain provide the barometer of my worth.

When you know your worth, you know how much you need. And if you know how much you need, you'll be surprised at the ways in which everything will fall into place, ensuring you get what you need.

"NO ONE TALKS ABOUT WHAT 'ENOUGH' LOOKS LIKE."

A CONVERSATION WITH

AJA BARBER

Writer, stylist, and consultant whose work deals with the intersections of sustainability and the fashion landscape

ON MONEY

Kevin Lockdown 2020? I have … they're not even mixed feelings. I just hated that year.

Aja Oh my God, I hated June 2020 so much. But at the same time, it's a double-edged sword, right? Because I finally felt like my work was being recognised, but it was being recognised for the wrong reasons. I don't want my work to be recognised because four Black people died in a short amount of time. That is not what I want. I want my work recognised because it's important. And because we're in a climate crisis, a cost of living crisis, and people still feel like they have to spend $300 at Shein for clothing they're gonna wear once. Like, what are we doing? I want my work recognised for its own merit.

And unfortunately, in June 2020, it sort of just became, 'Follow this Black person and do it quick.' And, yes, I actually felt really overwhelmed, because I opened my Instagram and I was like, 'Wait, what is happening?' And each time I opened it, the number would jump by one thousand followers. And I finally had to put my phone away because it was making me really anxious.

I had a similar experience with that sudden influx of new followers – I'd always been talking honestly and with intent only, same as you. I'd made my little films, and it was actually therapeutic for me. It was getting stuff off my chest, but it was also just trying to find other Black and Brown people with a shared lived experience to be like, 'Hey, you're not mad. I feel this too.' At that time anything I posted went viral. I remember thinking, 'I don't really like this,' because before, I was specifically talking to my community and hitting my goal of reaching the community.

I got so many people being like, 'Okay, I'm here, what do I do?' And I'm like, 'I don't know.' Like, I don't know what you're supposed to do. If you're here because you're looking for firm directions from me about how to end racism in five easy steps – that's not what I do. Like, I can talk to you about the ways in which the systems that you buy into perpetuate racism – that I could do. But there was this feeling of, like, impulsive impatience and looking for absolution through buying all the books, or signing up to this person's page, doing this or that. And I just … I hated it. I hated every minute of it. There were also some people who got platforms where I was just like, why?

Yeah, why?

Why? This person does not have anything to say; they're not shaking up the status quo. They just fit the part. And that was also extremely problematic.

Yeah, I call them baby gatekeepers-in-waiting, because not all the gatekeepers are white middle-class men or women. Right? *[Both laugh]*

Exactly, exactly. Sometimes it be your own.

Not all skinfolk are—

—kinfolk, exactly.

283

Aja One of the things that I struggle with is that my work is being attributed to people who aren't doing any of what I'm doing. It makes me really mad, because these people that are being credited or turning up in the same spaces as me aren't doing the heavy lifting. They don't want to join in the conversations I'm having, because they're hard, right? They don't have a moral compass when it comes to who pays their dollars. Ultimately it comes down to colourism and thin privilege, because that's what the fashion industry loves. You see it in instances where it's like, 'Oh, this person is biracial, so let's just put them in the Black slot, even if they have fuck-all to do with what we're talking about.'

Kevin Because then that goes into a conversation about palatability.

I've actually tried to raise this with people, and they don't want to talk about it. You can't be out here talking about racism if you're not willing to see the ways in which you're playing into something that's causing me harm. So I don't fuck with every person who got a platform during that time period.

I'm one-hundred per cent the same. And the thing I wanted to talk to you about was actually money, and the way in which we talk about money. I think we're the same in terms of how I don't really care how much the amount is if it goes against our morals. I'm really invested in dismantling this thing we're talking about; I want the world to be a better place. I want equality.

That isn't a one-time 'we'll bring you in and do this'. That is consistent work.

I do make a point of, within my heart at least, holding space for the wayward ones in my community. Because I'm like, 'You know what, do what you gotta do.'

We all exist in capitalism. I hear that, but I think it's deceitful to basically take anything, any message, and be a part of it. Just to slot a Black person into any space because it looks good.

So there was this article about how Black women have largely been carrying this conversation, and they named myself and others. And a few of the others definitely did carry this conversation alongside me. But they also named a few folks that have been nowhere to be seen. Some who even work with brands that oppress garment workers. I had to message the journalist and say, 'Look, put the correct people into the conversation. It's not about glory or the credit, it's about the things we've had to go through to keep this conversation going.'

Basically, we just get people flinging poo at us constantly, because the pull of consumerism is so hardwired into us that the response is to get defensive when you learn that, like, maybe you shouldn't be buying clothing from Shein. Especially if you don't have to. It's just people getting angry at me repeatedly, until they stop and do some critical thinking – a little soul-searching – and then they come back and go, 'You know, when I first found your platform, I actually started a fight with you in the comments. But you know what? You're right about everything.'

These are hard conversations where I have to have a really thick skin. And I get that not everyone is cut out for it. But what I don't appreciate is someone who just sits back and takes the glory when given.

One time, someone listed me as one of the 'Ten Black British people you need to follow'. And I had to email them and be like, 'Hey, guys, thanks so much for putting me on the listicle. Except I'm not British. I don't want to take that space away from a Black British person who should be there. I'm American, I'm happy to be here. But that doesn't fit me.' And they were really nice ... but then they said, 'You know, maybe we should just expand the definition.' And I said you can't do that, but if there's another Black person who is not getting put on this list just go ahead and put them in instead; there's more than enough.

And I feel like because the currency of online culture is all about greed and getting what you can, there are not enough people doing that for others. There are not enough people saying, 'This is not my lane, put this person in instead.' And I will happily do that. Because I know that I don't need all the things. Every year, I turn down at least $100,000 worth of work. Because every brand wants you to tell the world that they are really great and they are, you know, the most sustainable brand in the world. And when they fart, it smells like roses. And that's just not true. It isn't true at all for the majority of brands. So I have to bite my fist and tell a brand why I can't do it. Even if they do want to throw $30,000 at me, I can't do it and I won't do it.

Where does that moral compass – specifically around money – come from for you?

I grew up without generational wealth. I don't have parents that can bail me out. In my twenties, I was mostly broke. If you looked at my tax returns then, I was making poverty wages and I had insufficient work. I was working in TV and film production, and just wasn't getting by at all. I was in and out of my parents' basement a lot. It was hard. I felt like I was never going to be in a position where I would ever be able to buy a property, or not live with roommates. And that was a sucky feeling.

I remember one such day when I was just lamenting about not thriving in capitalist systems. And I had this moment where I was just like, 'How much money would I need to be technically happy?' And I started thinking about what that looks like. There was a report where they studied people at different income levels. And they did this measure of happiness, basically. So we have a person over here on 50k, then another over here making 70k, someone making 500k, and this other person making two million. And what they found – and this was in 2010, so it's probably gone up – but $90,000 was where everyone's happiness plateaued. $90,000 was what you needed at that time to be able to pay for health insurance, to be able to have a home and a car, and to feel like you were secure enough to start a family, take a vacation, or maybe treat a loved one to something nice.

That was the type of money that you needed to do those things. And so, reading that article really blew my mind. I was like, 'Okay, so if I can make like six figures one day, that's all I need.' Everything else is extra. I can pay for my bills, do some nice trips with my partner, take care of loved ones, and be generous with friends – because that's really important to me, generosity with people you love. I took my sisters, my niece, and my nephew to France for a little mini-break when they came to visit me in the spring. I paid for all of that, and it felt really good. I've never been in a position to do that. I don't need to be a millionaire or a billionaire to do those things.

I think I've kind of always known that it was a bit of a scam – even when I was a kid. I remember in the '80s, Donald Trump was like, on top of the world. Everyone thought that he was amazing. And I always thought he was a clown. Like, why would I want to be like him?

Kevin Why would you want that?

Aja Look at this asshole, he is clearly a miserable person. He has a gold toilet. Like, who needs that? I remember as a kid not aspiring to wealth at all. And then there was this thing where I felt, particularly in the case of the little white boys that I went to school with, there were other kids clearly obsessed with wealth.

It just became a thing where I began to realise that, in order to be socially accepted, you were supposed to care about these things. That wasn't a natural inclination of mine. They'd be like, 'Ooh, how much money does this person that I admire make?' I just didn't care.

I realised that that sort of obsession with endless wealth is something that's taught to us. But that was never what I aspired to, and it is still not what I aspire to. If what I have now is my lot in life, I will have done really well. Really, really well.

Maybe I'm able to say that because I come from like, a long line of broke people. I feel like I am literally on top of the world with what I have. There are places I want to see, things I want to do, but so much of my message, and unpacking the obsession with fast fashion, really ties into this idea that in our society, no one talks about what 'enough' looks like. We don't talk about it. Because if we actually have an idea of what 'enough' looks like, capitalism cannot exploit us in the same way.

Because capitalism introduces the competition element of it.

Yes. Once I had an idea in my head of what sort of money I personally would like to make to do the things I wanted to do, it meant I could step away from that trap. So when a big greenwashing brand is waving a cheque in my face, I can go 'No, thank you.' In the weirdest way, the more exposed you are, the less capitalism wants you. The more I keep my integrity high, the higher those cheques are that are being waved in my face. I always try to tell content creators not to sell out for a corporation, because the truth is, they're offering someone else twenty times the money that they're offering you. You're setting your own rate pretty low, and you can't buy your integrity back. Once it's gone, it's gone.

I think white women have the privilege of like, flitting between things. I've seen so many white ladies who one day say they're selling fast fashion, but the next day, they're all about the planet. A lot of them do not have that moment where they're like, 'I was part of the problem.' Because that's the privilege of whiteness; you can just sort of skate between being the problem, and then joining the solution – without ever acknowledging that you were the problem.

From an advertising perspective, I always try to recommend talent from a space of like, who authentically fits that brand. Ensuring there's a thread all the way through. So, although I have to be involved in capitalism at that level, I try to do it from a very holistic place of, like, 'You know what, these people do this thing in real life.'

> Right, they actually care about it. The problem is only certain people have the privilege of doing that. I don't, can't, and wouldn't. Like if I took a cheque from H&M, it'd be over for me, that'd be the last cheque. It'd be, 'She's a sellout, blah, blah, blah.' So I have to keep my integrity high. Only certain people have that privilege.

Yeah, I think I grew up in kind of the same way. I was going to the worst school in England. My mum then sent me and my brother to this school that was way out in the middle of nowhere. As we'd say in London, it was mookooland, and it was very middle class. The kids there had swimming pools and ponies.

> What was your commute?

Norwood Junction into deep Purley.

> Oh yeah.

My mum never thought about the distance. She was just more excited about the fact that she was gonna get these boys out of this school. I think that school was my first introduction to that level of wealth. Those kids did not stress about a real thing. Their parents had no financial worries, so they didn't have any. My mum had to hustle every single day to make sure we had our new school uniforms. I was aware of that, you know. I knew every year how much money we kinda needed to get together to get those new uniforms. I had like one pair of trousers that God forbid I ripped in any kind of way; it'd be a wrap. Because we could only afford those ones.

> And this is part of the sustainability conversation as well, right? Because, honestly, we should be at a place in our society where everyone has second-hand school uniforms. And when you graduate from your school uniform, you turn it back in to the school, and there's a system where it goes to another kid. And the expectation should not be that parents have to buy new school uniforms every year. It shouldn't be. And this is something that we as a society can do. Because there's enough stress on parents. Obviously, there's a lot of stress on some parents and some parents don't worry about that, right? We're not all in the same place within the cost of living crisis. But there is room for all of this in the sustainability conversation. How much better would it have been if your mum didn't feel like she had to hustle to get you school uniforms?

When I heard what people worried about at that school, I just thought that if being rich gave you these kinds of problems – which aren't real problems – then I don't want to be rich. I don't know what your existence is. I don't get it. You've got everything that you'll possibly need, and yet you seem to be even more unhappy than me. I'm talking about some of these kids that had, like, a nanny who was gonna cook for the whole family. I knew that I was going home to have corned beef and rice, but I was happy with that. I was never shitting on that. I was just like, it is what it is, but I always knew that our small flat was a home. Most of these kids had the big houses and only the big houses; they didn't have homes.

But this was ironically also a time where I really discovered what the need for money was for me. Regardless of whether I preferred the simple things, I needed to get a job because now I'm arguing with my mum about money, and I'm not gonna sit here and pretend that I was an understanding teenager who just got how all of that worked. But I did understand that money, as much as I hated it, had a use. I had to learn that at a much younger age than some. And so my aunt was like, 'Cool, got you.' So me and my aunt forged my birth certificate. [Both laugh]

And I got this job at this fast food restaurant where I was paid £3.20 an hour. Almost everyone that worked there was a student. So because you got paid every two weeks it was flexible in terms of time off, right? So everybody I worked with was either in uni or college. You could turn around at any time and be like, 'I've got to finish my dissertation. I need three weeks off.'

'Okay, we'll cover you with so and so.'

Aja That was the Whole Foods Market where I worked as a teenager.

Kevin Right, right. So it was really convenient, but people would come and order their food, and then talk to me as if I'd failed at life. Just because I worked in this place. It never really made sense to me. I was like, well, if this is such a bad place, why are you eating here?

> You can always tell what's in a person's heart by how they treat people in the service industry. That is the most revealing thing ever.

Very much so. I didn't get why people were trying to shame us for earning money. For me, it's always been about looking at the different examples of how money works, how it doesn't work, the freedom it does and doesn't give to people. Examples of how money could be accumulated continued to show up throughout my life, up close and personal. Legal and illegal. Large amounts of money because of acting or singing friends in the public eye. I noticed how rich people would tell you nothing about their money while poor people would explain their last pennies. I watched the relationships both the rich and the poor had with money change. I saw how some people worked a few hours a night and earned what it took me a month to earn, getting it in four hours by shaking hands at Blue Orchid. I'm not religious, but money being the root of all evil is probably one of the truest things that ever came out of that book.

> I think if you are not strong in your convictions and yourself, it will change you for sure. I think my relationship with money has changed since I started getting paid for my writing. I was thinking about this, actually, on my wait to get a train for work. I've never missed a train yet, knock on wood, but I'm sure my day is coming.
>
> Anyway, I suddenly had this thought that if I missed the train, I could just get another one. I had never had that feeling before in my life.

That must be what it feels like to be a rich person. I wasn't rich. This was 2019; I was just starting to earn money. I moved to this country and I couldn't work until I got my settlement visa. So there was a time period where I really wasn't making any money. But I had that moment where I realised that if I didn't get to my station on time, I could just buy another ticket. And that was a real 'whoa' moment for me. And that's what money can give you, too. It can give you a little bit of comfort.

There is a thing in Jamaica that we say – I don't know if it even is Jamaican, it's just because it's from my household, which is Jamaican – and that thing is 'vex money'. I always have a pot of vex money for if a situation gets me vexed and I just don't need to be there. I think people call it 'fuck-you money' as well. But it's that pot of money that allows me to just be like, 'Is it? Here's your money back.'

Even with this book and the deal, there's just a pot of money if I need to be like, 'Oh, I don't like where this is going so here is your advance back, here are all the costs back. I'll just self-publish.' In short, I've had that moment too, that 'I'll just buy a new one' moment.

It's a real weird moment, isn't it?

Yeah. I've got to a point with money where, though I do not like it and I do believe it is the root of all evil, I will still be paid correctly for my time. Because I've put in the effort, the hours, and the years, to learn the things that I have learned. So when it comes to that exchange of money, I have no qualms with asking what I am worth. And even with friends—
[Kevin's phone rings]
No, no. Decline, sorry. See? Speak of the devil. What I was about to say, is that me and Kelechi, for instance – and you can ask her this – every time we go out for a meal, she has never paid. And she will never pay. That's the same with most of the friends in my life.

I love being that person. I want to be generous with people I know, with everything I have. Whether it's being able to treat people to lunch or coffee, or being able to say, 'Of course, you can come and stay with us, don't even think about it.' So for me, the pursuit of money and the things that I want is, on the one hand, about doing better than the previous generation (and I think everybody who is ethnic knows what that's about). And on the other, it's about paying that back.

Because I think you're one of two people: you are either a person that can ask your elders for money constantly and be fine with it. Or you are the person that knows that you want to give back to your elders. Maybe there's an expectation in your culture that you give back to elders, or maybe your parents don't have a retirement fund, so you might need to have some money in the future to help them out. I feel like the side that doesn't know what that feels like has no idea, basically. That's part of why I strive. I strive to make money only so that I can be generous, so that I can take care of the people I love and give generously to everyone. Down to the person on the street who asks me if I have money, and all I got is a fiver, but I'll give it to them. I like being able to be that person.

GIVE ME THAT CASH, GIVE ME THAT WONG

It's up to you

I know I'm talking from a place of privilege, so me talking about money from my perspective could be helpful, or just annoying. I get it. What I will say is that understanding your worth is paramount.

Once you've figured out what you're worth, the rest is easy.

TODAY'S TAKEAWAY:

The amount of money you command is determined by your worth. It's up to you what your worth is measured in. Personally, I want to be worth my weight in integrity (see Chapter 21). Work on your worth – however you define it – and watch how quickly the money comes.

Worthy

23

FUN

We carry so much guilt. Heavy and sodden, like wet, woolly hats caught in the rain. Over time it will leave us shapeless, agreeable in the most self-destructive sense of the word.

Look at us, gulping down sparks – fragments of potential – until our bellies are full with tart shards of regret.

We worry about the things our parents didn't get to do, while also worrying about the things we don't have to do. Crippled with it, we hobble away from everything that could be.

Always looking back and never being present to look to the future.

Guilt sits heavy on our chests, and makes an afflatus of excitement feel like panic and last breaths.

It will sit on your shoulder feeding you laboured whispers of wet lies. Falsities that convince you that opportunity is dangerous, that letting go is cowardice – it will even make you believe you are ugly.

The opposite of guilt is fun.

The worldbuilding, life-changing, mile-wide-smile kind of fun. The skipping home or to the function, bumping into the love of your life, first-of-its-kind, creative fun.

Generational guilt killed the radio star ... and the video, internet, and OnlyFans stars.

The enormity of it will have us believing that we can never make a mistake, try new things, or – most dangerously – find out who we are.

To be creative is to make mistakes, and then try and try again. If your work is an extension of you, if your work is truly a space where you express your essence and the makings of you, what quality of creativity will you produce when your core is gunked up with guilt?

There is a place for guilt, though. I think guilt should only come knocking when you have done ill-intentioned things. It should sit with you long enough for you to own and learn from your behaviour.

The goal is always to evolve and get to your higher self as soon as you can. Take the L, learn, and move on.

Sometimes your work will be so honest, it will upset people, but our experiences are big enough pieces of reality to facilitate two things being true at the same time. In short: you are your work, and your work is you (see Chapter 5). When you have fun, your work does, and inevitably the people consuming it will, too.

"EVENTUALLY."

A CONVERSATION WITH

TOLLY T

Writer, podcaster, and one third of The Receipts

ON FUN

Kevin So, I spent several years in advertising while still working on my film stuff, mostly from a space of learning more about the commercial side of creativity. Basically stealing those ideas to then go away and do my own thing. Never had any formal education. So in order to navigate those spaces, I had to, you know ... well, I'm from South, I'm a road yout, so—

> **Tolly** Everyone who's from South takes like two minutes before they start telling you they're from South. It's not a personality trait, guys! Relax everyone, we heard. *[Kevin laughs]*

But alongside that, in a more positive space, I guess I've always tried to match the energy of the Black women that surround me and inspire me. And because of that, if you ever need me to back you in any way – other than just being a bad breed – if you ever need any creative support, I always want to be able to say, 'I've got the skillset.' Because that's me paying it back, and I suppose in some ways those are the two sides of what I've moved through in my creative journey.

And I wanted to talk to you about that lighter side, and specifically within that, the idea of fun. Being fearless in the pursuit of fun. Because if you're a minority – but particularly if you're a Black woman – it's a luxury expense. You're not 'meant' to be having fun; you're supposed to be strong yet depressed, and all of those things. So yeah, I wondered where that fun comes from for you.

> Do you know, for the longest time I tried to avoid being the fun girl? I was a beauty writer across many publications, before I landed my job at BuzzFeed, and all that time I thought if I was fun then no one's gonna take me seriously. They're gonna think I'm an idiot. There was something about being fun that felt audacious. I like to be outside and around people, but I just thought no one would buy that.
>
> And then I realised that I enjoy play. And this is no woe-is-me story, but I think that stems from my background. My mum was a single mum who worked whilst supporting three girls, and I got my first job when I was fourteen. I was an empathetic kid; I thought that if I started working early, I'd be able to stop asking my mum for money. What that meant was we didn't get to play. We always had to be good kids. 'Sit down, stop running around, stop shouting, eat your food, and watch telly.' No playing and not being naughty meant that my mum's life was easier. And I wanted to make my mum's life easier, because then my life was easier. She wouldn't be shouting and so things would be fine. We just didn't play, yet I'd get so much joy in being playful.
>
> When people ask when I feel genuine happiness, it's honestly when I'm with my niece and nephews and I can rugby tackle them to the floor. And so I thought, I've spent so much time working, why can't it be fun too? I've been working since I was fourteen, and I've always been asking, 'Where is the play here? Where is the version of joy?' Even in spaces that don't necessarily seek to provide it. That's why I now just want to add play to everything I do. There's something about tapping into joy, even when things are really shit. For a while, when things have been bad in the past, it felt like I was collecting joy. It was like, 'Yo, this thing is about to happen, so go out and collect all the joy now, because you're gonna feel so shit afterwards.' So I think that's what

it is, I just enjoy collecting it, in whatever space I can. We could be walking down the road and I'd be like, 'Let's race.'

I also think some of it is reacting to how I had to treat my body shape growing up. I was a little girl who got thighs early; I just had a bit of a body, and so I had to shrink. Because, obviously you don't wan mandem to be looking at that – it just wasn't safe. And all my mum wanted for us was to be safe, so when I got thighs at ten years old, people started to notice it. And that meant that, again, I couldn't just go and do that thing of like, just jumping up and down; I had to start learning 'conceal, conceal, conceal'. Now, I free up my body, because my body was previously so linked to me being a decent girl. I just decided, 'Nah, screw you lot, man. I'm a decent girl. And if I'm not, who's gonna beat me?'

I think all of the fun and the joy that I missed out on, I try to seek it out now. I'm making a decent amount of money now, and I'd rather spend more on things that will bring me joy. You know, I'm the sort of person that would rather pay a lot of money to hire out some bouncy castle, than get a designer item or something like that, because I just want to have a good time. And it doesn't mean I don't realise that things should be serious. But I've got a philosophy; everything is funny eventually.

Whoa, where's the lie?

Eventually. Like, right now it can be the worst thing. And that was so apparent to me when I lost my dad in 2020. He lived in Nigeria so I didn't see him that often. He wasn't around that much when I was growing up. But I always knew who my dad was; I lived with him for about seven years before I came back to England, and we spoke regularly.

And then when he died, I remember we got the call and we had to go and tell my mum. So me, my sister, and her husband got together and went over to my mum's house to deliver the news. So we're all in her house waiting – she wasn't there for some reason – and she walks in and clearly knows what's wrong right away. And then we start seeing her list off everyone that's important to her. 'Where's your other sister?' We are like she's fine. 'Where are the grandkids?' They're all fine. And you can see she's like, 'Well, who else could it be, then?' And then we tell her that my dad has died, and I remember at the time she had a wig on and a turban – all so well done – and she just took it all off in one sweep and dropped to the floor.

I was like, 'You have not been with this man for thirty years.' Like, hun. She was like, 'But I just spoke to him this morning, he'd sent me some WhatsApp chain.' And so all three of us are just in this space watching my mum, and we're all thinking different things. My brother-in-law decided that this was the right moment to go and change the batteries in my mum's living room clock. I was looking at my mum's feet and thinking that she's never had a pedicure; we'd been in this country all this time, and I genuinely don't think she's ever had a pedicure in her life. And, don't get me wrong, I was distraught – we all were. But I knew, even then, that eventually, things are going to be funny. You see that when family gather after someone dies, eventually people laugh. They'll just remember something about them, and I think that just shows there's fun and laughter in everything. It's like that meme, with the basketball player crying?

Kevin Oh, Michael Jordan. Yeah.

Tolly And then at Kobe's funeral, Michael Jordan did a speech and he was crying. And he was like, 'They're going to meme me again.' It's in that particularly sad moment that he's like, 'Oh, God, I'm going to be another meme.' Yeah, I just live for things like that. That's important to me in work now, too. I wouldn't do anything if I didn't find it fun.

I think I often say it's not that deep. And that will just come from a place of knowing I've been through worse and survived worse. This isn't drama, like, trust me, this is fine. We can make it. And I think the thing you said about funny moments is really interesting because when I'm writing scripts, the type of film or story that I love the most is comedy. I've always used comedy, because real comedy is really smart. You were saying you were worried about people thinking you were just being silly when you were having fun, but actually – look at how many comedians are ridiculously smart. There's a real awareness there, and that's what people miss about having fun in the moment, because nothing is promised. But you've just blown my mind with that philosophy – you're absolutely right. Everything is funny eventually. When I look back at some of the maddest stuff, it's just funny now.

Funnily enough, I recently met up with my good friend Bushira (see Chapter 15). And when we were growing up, she was like my Cody – in South. *[Tolly laughs]* We were – and actually, we still are – the best of friends. We would dress in the same tracksuits. It wasn't just that we were kiki best friends. I'd been in some serious fights, and she'd fully drop in with the man and was just in there.

Anyway, we were reminiscing about this fight that ended up going to court, and it was really funny because the prosecutor tried to blame the whole thing on me by labelling me as the head of the Black Gay Mafia in London. It was a wild, wild case. We were talking about that, and she was like, '…and then he tried to barge you, so I just boxed them.' And we remembered how another girl took her heels off to fight the guy, and thinking back on it, we were just screaming and laughing about this situation that I guess was now eighteen years ago. But at the time, it was stressful; we had to go to court all because of this guy going left.

And you're right, everything is funny in the end. But I guess, as Black and Brown people across the diaspora, we're not afforded the space to even realise that. And that's why I'm such a big fan of yours. I recognise that in you – that you're really focused on going for the fun. My time is hot right now, and I'm going to take everything, expand it, and have fun while doing it. And I wonder if you realise the impact that you have in that way, how inspiring you are. If there was ever a picture in the dictionary for 'live your best life', it's you.

Do you know, I have this thing when people talk to me about me, where I'm like, 'Who the fuck are you lot talking about? I would love to meet that person, she sounds great.' Genuinely, it makes me so happy to hear you say that.

Because of the internet, a lot of people will never meet me, so the experience they have with me is purely what's online, right? And, good or bad, they'll take it how it is. And the internet has a lot of shit; there are fake psychologists every day, fake therapists every day. Just all this stuff. And I don't want to add to the noise of 'bad'. I get that, for some people, it's really important to show all aspects of their world online. But I open my vagina every Wednesday to listeners of the podcasts, so I want to keep certain things to myself.

I only post things that I want to. I've been asked before if I can post a make-up tutorial, and I won't do it, because if I'm doing it out of being asked, it's not going to be good. I'm not doing it out of joy, so it's going to come off as an obligation. And I think that's what we're seeing when people feel like they've been inspired – it's that they're reacting to someone doing something that they actually want to. That was a huge lesson for me, because doing something from a place of wanting to was rarely a reason for anything I did before. It's funny, I think I wrote a newsletter about it not too long ago. I was listening to Billy Piper's song 'Because We Want To' for some reason, and I was like, 'Rah, you don't do anything because you want to.' But that's a good enough reason.

Yet for years, things had to have more of a reason for me; it had to be because it wasn't going to be for the good of this thing over here, or it was going to help my career over there – I barely did things because I wanted to. That's why I'm much more audacious now in doing what I want. Obviously, there are still obligations that need to be met, but what I put up on the internet in my own time are things that I want to. There are people who have the range for content that can be sad – you know? – and talk about certain things. But that's not me, I just don't want to do that on the internet.

Yeah, there's enough of it. I completely get it. I've got to a space as well where if something completely enrages me, or I feel fully compelled to speak up about it, then I will. But recently, for the most part, I just don't have the capacity for it anymore.

Yeah! And there's this weird thing where, actually, a lot of people don't care, right? And they're using that anger for entertainment. And that's the last thing I'm gonna let you use for entertainment, because this feels very real to me. My upset is very real to me, and you lot are just…

You end up becoming their resident Black woman, like 'Hey, have you seen this? Haha. What do you think of this?' I don't think. I don't. No thoughts about anything. *[Tolly laughs]* Because what do you think, sis? I'm not your resident hire-for-help Black woman here to get angry about things.

Yeah. I'm good. Kelechi has that problem as well. But even within that space, she is actually only talking about the things that she wants to – regardless of whether that covers a wider range than mine or yours – but then people get that confused. They'll send her stuff hoping she'll post about it, and she has to say 'No, you're confused. This is my space, and I will use it how I want to.' And I think you're right; we don't talk about the fact that society has been programmed to think that Black women are not here to have joy, and that's what then leads to this confusion.

We've been conditioned in a certain way, and I think – for me – that's probably my biggest battle, and the thing that I want to, and need to, concentrate on. There are all these other things going on in regard to race, sexuality, etc. And yes, I will back them, in situations where it's right for me to back them. But when it comes to Black women enjoying themselves, and having fun, that's where I'm at. That's probably a response to some of the things that I saw my mum go through, so now I think, 'Not on my watch.' I'm gonna take off heads to ensure that Black women have space to do exactly what they want to do, because that's the minimum I can do with all the privileges that I have in terms of how that hierarchy currently works.

Because when you guys are having fun and enjoying your lives – just exploring – the world changes, we evolve, and we find new answers to problems ... You can't quantify it. It's just when you're in your element, and flowers are growing, then everyone's growing. It fucking infuriates me that people cannot see the correlation between that magic and your progress. When Black women are in their element, it just vibrates across everything.

> **Tolly** But that's even down to what we eat. These people who talk the most about weight or whatever, they don't care about your health. They don't give a shit; they say that's their angle but it's not. And every day there's something new that we're not supposed to eat. All these things that Black women love and we can't have them. So it's like, okay, well what then? What shall we have? Mac and cheese – we can't enjoy it. Shit, give me something. Mac and cheese and chicken wings.

Kevin You're right. It's a constant attack. And it's weird, because the same amount of energy that is used to try and confine that fun, would serve people so much more easily if they just decided to join in and have fun. No one said that you can't join in. You realise how many people have issues, and how they're projecting those out. Because that's all it is; why else wouldn't you join in when you see that energy? The more the merrier.

But I'm interested in whether there was a particular moment when you stepped into that philosophy of seeking fun, and it having an immediate effect. Because for me, I'm in the process of shedding my trauma, and probably always will be. And I've talked about this elsewhere, but this year for me was really discovering how important it is to have water around me, being in the middle of the countryside. I've learned that trauma informed certain behaviours that I don't want to do anymore. I previously felt I had to reside in London, energising all of my actions via the adrenaline and the trauma of it all. But now I try and get near the seaside as much as possible because I've discovered that, not only can I still create in those spaces, but what I'm doing there is ten, even a hundred, times better. Because I'm at peace. But I've only just come to that conclusion.

I think the turning point was actually my grandmother passing away. If I had the option to burn down the world to bring her back, I would. When she went, I spent a lot of time thinking about the things that we spoke about growing up, and all of them revolved around her time in Jamaica, surrounded by nature. So I tried to follow that, and in doing so found that those spaces are where I naturally thrive. And actually, I can still have my very strong Black opinions on things even when I'm not in the middle of it all.

But did you have that one moment that you can look back on and say, yes, that was the perfect catalyst for me to head towards everything I dream and desire?

> Yeah, definitely. The age of twenty-seven knocked me for six; there was something about it that made me just inhale sharply. I'd quit working at BuzzFeed so that I could work on The Receipts podcast full time, because

I wanted to see what would happen if I gave all my time to that. So I was a freelancer who didn't fully understand how that world worked, and then on top of that, the age of twenty-seven meant something within my family. I'm Nigerian, and my mum has a lot of expectations for her lastborn. So that was the age where the conversation of marriage and being committed to someone was really turned up. You know, it started coming out from every speaker in the house. I love my mum to bits, but it got to a point where I just thought, 'I can't do this.' Within ten minutes of being around her, it would get brought up.

It was really affecting me. I know a lot of people say they just want to make their mum proud, but that's not a desire of mine. It's just not, because I realised that what makes my mum proud is the version of my life my mum wants for me – being married and having kids. I'm not saying I don't want those things, but it was at that age I realised that I have to stop thinking about what would make my mum proud. What I want is to earn enough, and do enough, for my mum to be able to enjoy that. That's such a big thing for me. There was a video years ago of Stormzy's mum; she wants to go to Ghana and she says, 'Make sure you book me first class.' That's exactly what I want for my mum, that she knows she deserves to be in first class and, more importantly, can be. So at twenty-seven, I realised that I have to drop my search for this woman's pride, because it's not going to happen until I'm married. That's when I thought, 'That's not your guiding factor, sis. Go inside of you, what are you doing all this for?'

And it's not just so I can be proud of myself in the future, though I do think ahead to how things will affect me in say, ten years' time. I will long it out on the spot, before I've even done the thing, and see. But the thought that came to mind when I looked inwards was that I want to be audaciously myself, and being that means existing outside of anybody else's expectations. That means accepting that some people aren't going to fuck with you anymore; you might have to leave people behind. Not in a sense of thinking you're better than them, but just accepting that they're not going to see this for you because that's not the version of you they know. You're the first in your family to do this. And now, you know, I see my niece and she thinks I'm the biggest 'it girl' in the world. I went to her house yesterday and she was FaceTiming her friends and I heard her say, 'Yeah, it's actually Tolly T – I told you guys. I told you.' I want her to see that there's more to it than just having to get married, having to be this or that.

I say all of this to say that the specific catalyst for me, looking back, was this one conversation with my mum. She was sat at the edge of my bed, listening while I talked. In that moment I realised that I had achieved so much. Like, we'd literally just been on the front page of a magazine. I told my mum this and she just said 'Oh, by the grace of God, you will have your husband.' I looked at her and knew that there was nothing I could say that would make a difference. I could tell her I'd cured cancer and it wouldn't matter. I rid myself of the need to make my mum proud there. Like fuck that shit. What do you need to make yourself proud?

That is a real conversation that I've had with other people recently, too, about what we experienced growing up, and what that means for the happiness we find now. And it's not the same thing at all in terms of like, marriage, but I remember the conversations I had with my mum when I first started being a photographer back in the day. It's that thing of like, Black parents and creativity, right? 'That's not a living. What do you mean you're creative? You're just taking pictures.'

Tolly So you're a joker, yeah?

Kevin Literally. So I'd show her the magazines and she'd be like, 'Yeah?' And I'd say, 'I shot that. I also came up with the concept behind it.'

'Oh, that's nice.' Then when I got into advertising, I'd show adverts on TV and say how I wrote them, and again it'd be that thing of, 'Oh, that's cool,' but not actually getting it. So then we had to have a different conversation about me forgiving her for certain things – not just me accepting that she was never going to get it, like you said. But also just things that were said as jokes growing up that nevertheless stayed with me. 'Why are you crying? Boys don't cry.' Whereas my grandma was always saying that if you feel browned off, let it out. Because otherwise, the next thing you know you're pent up, and it still comes out anyway as a much bigger thing.

So we were talking about all this and she was in tears, because she genuinely was only joking, and only ever wanted me to be who I wanted to be. She didn't realise it had affected me. So within that space, I was able to forgive her and move on. That didn't change the whole thing of me showing her what I'd done and her not getting it, though. It's just that we're living in different worlds. But this is why this book is so important for me, because I want people who've come from similar backgrounds as us to see that they already have all the skillsets they need. There's nothing you can't do when you hold culture in the palm of your hands. You can go into any space, apply your personal brand of magic – your essence – and find fortune, good favour, and happiness. So long as you're allowed to be who you are.

I do think that's a big thing for kids of immigrant parents, this idea that they've done this, this, this, and this for you. So that's why the burden of making them proud is so heavy, because you want to make their journey here worth it. Whatever experiences they had to endure, you want to make it worth it for them. I'm the first person from our family to be born in the UK, and even then I've lived in Nigeria for some time. But because of it, there was this weight. I remember that my mum was always very careful with her words; she never cussed us out. She wasn't that kind of parent. But what she would say was, 'You're not one of those white kids.' You had to behave in a certain way to make it all worth it.

And it's so funny now because whilst my mum doesn't have a clue about what I do or whatever, I'm, like, an immigrant's mother's dream! I'm able to take her to Soho House, and I remember people were saying hello to her and she was like, 'Oh God, they know me.' That was such an excitement for her, and I was able to provide it. But if I hadn't dropped the burden of that being my main aim, I would have never done it. It doesn't mean you don't love your mum or that you don't rate your parents; it just means that you're giving yourself the freedom to do what it is you want. I'm sure many a doctor would've been something else if they were allowed that freedom. Your pride doesn't have to align with your mum's, and that's okay.

WHAT ARE YOU LISTENING TO?

Some thoughts can be ignored

Don't have, entertain, or look for regrets.
I advise you to get good at trying that out,
even if it feels difficult at first. Practice will
make it real.

TODAY'S TAKEAWAY:

Just one rule

If it's not fun, walk away.

You are a living, breathing, ever-evolving
piece of the universe. Everything – especially
the work you produce – should be fun. If it's
not fun, walk away.

24

A SAFE
SPACE

What is a safe space?

A good place to start answering that question is by looking at what safe space you can offer others, and how often you remember to be open and welcoming. The more you practise that quality towards others, the more you seem to invite it into your own life.

What I'd also like you to take away from this conversation is that I didn't always understand the politics involved inside the workplace. Moreso, I just concentrated on the best ways to be kind and supportive of others, as my conversation with Nana will show.

Look for the safe spaces wherever you can find them. The spaces that feel easy to breathe in, the spaces that operate on reciprocity. I promise, staying in places that are determined to misunderstand you makes no sense.

In certain circumstances, look out for your own version of Nana, or at least a work colleague you can find some respite with. They don't need to advocate for you, they don't need to campaign for you – they're simply able to provide space in the day for you to talk to someone who sees you for who you really are.

In providing that, they'll help you remember that the job at hand is nothing more than a stepping stone to the next, bigger, and better place.

"I COULD DEAL WITH IT BUT I DIDN'T WANT IT TO BE YOUR FIGHT."

A CONVERSATION WITH

NANA BEMPAH

Co-founder and CEO of Pocc

ON SAFE SPACES

Kevin What are you talking about?

Nana This is just being recorded for the audio and not the image, right?

Yeah, I'm not making a film. It's a book. Do you know how books work?

[Nana laughs for a long time]

All right, so I spend most of my time trying to get away—

You do?

—from talking to you, because you don't know how to stop talking.

I don't. I don't. I think that's the narrative being peddled, anyway. It's actually a smear campaign.

All right, sure, Jan. Let's start this conversation shall we, because ... I would love for you to give me your version of the events behind how we met.

Yeah, I would love that. Firstly though, I just want to say that I really love being part of this book. And that I'm part of its journey. *[Nana goes from thought to thought for several minutes]*
And I love talking as well, so ...

Yes, you do.

That's a good thing. *[Nana starts laughing]*

Look at us. Twelve minutes in, and we haven't even started the actual conversation. Nana, tell me how we met. Then I'll share my memories.

So I was at ... let's call it 'the agency' ...
And I'd been there for some time, working externally before joining permanently. It was definitely a big position to be taking on for my age at that time. It wasn't something I'd gone for from a space of ego, just that I was always following my drive. I just kept pushing forward, and then I found myself in that position. It was definitely a huge moment.
Looking back, I can say it was a lot to bite off at that time. I remember first going into the agency, and it was just full of men. There were probably two other women there, and they were like, the PA and the receptionist.
At the same time, the agency was turning into this different thing. Their main client, let's call them 'Big Blue', was becoming the sole focus. The agency was changing into Big Blue's marketing arm.

I thought you was gonna say Big Blue's tax haven. Sorry, go on.

[Both laugh] It was just so male-dominant. Not like I was unfamiliar with that, but there was ... it was very 'ripe'. I don't know how else to describe it. You could just feel it. Toxic.

Kevin It's weird going back and dissecting this, as you forget we didn't have the vocabulary we do now. And we're probably still searching for that vocabulary, by we definitely weren't talking about misogyny or misogynoir like we do now. It hadn't kicked off yet.

Nana No, no at all. And even recognising the things to define like that can only come with hindsight. In the moment, you're still stepping in and figuring out this new environment.

And you go in looking for the positives, or why else would you be there? So I saw this space that was growing into this new role purely servicing a client with a very, very big wallet, and a lot of faith in what they could make happen. So I thought this was somewhere I could create impact and change in a very particular way.

And I could see a route for that, as they'd specifically tasked me to grow content creation. Remember, this was a while back, so that was a very different world to the one we're in now. People were still trying to figure out what content even was, and it was all about commercials at that time.

I was tasked to work closely with the creative department to help modernise the Production department's approach, and that's how we met because one of the creatives was someone you'd worked with at the place you like to call 'Coronation Street'.

My nickname for a prominent designer clothing store that was just full of drama...

This specific creative was always introducing me to interesting people, from places outside of the industry. He was making very different sorts of connections. When he told me about you, he mentioned the work you'd already done together, and how creative you are. But I feel like he potentially made a reference to race in there, too. I'm just pausing because I'm trying to think of the reason that's coming to mind, exactly.

Oh, you think this is a therapy session? *[Nana laughs hysterically]*

Anyway, I remember you coming in to have a chat, and you being very different to the other people I'd met. Before, it was either people I'd already known in my own network, or those that just epitomised the standard kind of advertising world. And you were different. *[Nana laughs uncontrollably for several minutes]*

So I'm a West girl, and you'd go out and see all these different types of guys at places like Garage Nation, places where the MC would shout out West London, and then just – *[Nana does an impression of a record stopping]*

'Right, right, right. Where is everyone? Where is West London?' And there'd be a moderate level of noise. Then they'd call out North and East and it would be louder. And then South? 'RAAAAH RAAAAH!' People would just go mad. And you were so of that era.

Oh my God.

South London mandem. Anyway, we don't need to go down that particular avenue of how I know the South London vibe. *[Both laugh]*

But yeah, people like you didn't step into those creative agencies. At the time there wasn't really anything going on to involve you in, but I knew I wanted to keep the conversation going. I wanted to find you a role, because you'd said you wanted to get into advertising and I really wanted to help with that. Because there just weren't people like you in those spaces.

But I also found your creativity really interesting, as well. I knew it would be so good for the department having your voice in there. Because it wasn't just about content, it was about being able to make that content in-house. And you had all this experience in photography, editing – so many talents. I thought having you on the team would really be amazing. And, as you know, eventually a role became available. And we can leave that there. *[Both laugh]*

In short, I came in and was covering someone for a week. But that wasn't cover, was it? It was a trial period. And then you gave me a role in your team.

Your arrival was a godsend, really. The way you approach things lives within a space that I see a lot within the Black community. You just came in and got stuff done. You have initiative, you do things. You actually overdo things because you know that you don't have the option to fail. Like, it's just not an option for you not to be good, because as soon as you drop the ball for any reason – then the ramifications, or rather, the penalties of that?

And I think that's something in life generally, but those agency environments are very severe in how they judge what they deem as inadequate. Even when I was really on top of my shit, people were just waiting to blame me – in particular – for things. For whatever reason.

So you came in and saw how messily organised the office was, both physically and digitally. And I dunno if it was 'cause of something I'd mentioned, but by, like, the second day you'd just organised absolutely everything.

No, you never asked me. I did that on my own. *[Both laugh]*
You had every kind of wire under the sun just in one box, so I separated everything into labelled boxes, cleaned up the spaces, and filed the hard drives by year and project. You'd gone for lunch – which for Nana, was never an hour.

It was never the hour. Sometimes the day. *[Nana laughs]*

Yeah. And I remember, when you came back, not really knowing what to think. But I looked at others working in the team there at the time, and they were just giving you this smile. In hindsight, I know they were trying to tell you telepathically to get rid of the other guy. *[Both laugh]*

To be honest, I was also sad about bringing you into that environment because there was behaviour that I'd maybe ignored for the greater good before, or else I could deal with it but I didn't want it to be your fight.

And then you remembered I was from South London and was like, 'Oh no, that's a problem for them.' *[Both laugh]*

Nana I don't know. It's fine for you to have your way of coping with the thing. But for me, I had different, strategic friendships in that building.

Kevin It's survival because, as you said before, the ramifications for a Black woman running a whole department in charge of, like, millions of pounds? It would be peak. Meanwhile, there were other people who were really bad at their jobs, and every other week they'd be like, 'Oh we've lost the account... hahahaha!' *[Both laugh]*
We knew if that was ever us? Peak.

Yeah, a hundred per cent I remember thinking, why is everyone looking for someone to blame? I remember knowing that I have to be on my shit because even when there isn't blame, I'm being blamed. So if there was ever something justified, that was gonna be it for me. I remember trying to get one of the creative directors to look through your book in the hopes you could get other projects within the agency. Anyway, it took ages but he eventually looked through your book, and he flipped through it with such disrespect. There wasn't anyone like you who was working within the team.
And there were definitely things going on from a gender perspective with the women in my team. You know, how people treated some of them because they looked young, or because they fancied them. But with you particularly, I guess there was this...

... This shared lived experience.
But first, with that creative director. I knew about all of that, but don't forget he later lost his job and came and worked at an agency where Tom and I were already working. And then, it was me signing off his work and him having to deal with us as peers.
And with regards to that shared lived experience? Do you know how I knew you felt like that? When you ordered us twin sets of silk pillows.

[Nana screams and laughs] Oh my gosh, I forgot about that.

You were gassed. And I was like, 'Wow, she has been starved of Blackness in this building.' Like, you were so gassed. I think that happened after somebody tried to make a comment about your hair and I switched in the room. I was like, 'If you're gonna fire me, cool. But I'm always going to defend a Black woman.' I just knew it was the right thing to do. I understood my position of privilege.
Then those people would see me pop up in certain places via my proximity to certain celebrities, or else my name being on different things outside of that building. So they were like, 'Hold on a minute, who is this guy?' And it's like, 'Nana was telling you from early but none of you actually listened. And now we're out the door.'
But I remember you really ordered the pillowcases from Amazon. Actually, one was silk and one was satin. And we were meant to come back with the results of which we thought was better. Because I had just started my locs.

See me with the weave.

No. I'd seen pictures, but you just had your braids. You'd taken your hair out and you started growing it. You were trying things, like you bought a bike that you never fucking rode.

You bought these expensive hats that somebody had made down on market and you were like, 'Yeah, I think hats are gonna be my thing.' Never saw the hats again.

You were on adventures that year. It was just a time when you were trying different things.

I think it was our friendship that helped that, because I looked at you, and knew you weren't allowed to be who you really were there. Even when you laugh at the volume at which you laugh, you were using it to punctuate situations, and no one even clocked the rhythm of when you would launch those laughs.

So you would do the laugh and it would throw everyone off. They'd be like 'Nana, you're so funny,' and you'd be like 'Yeah, cool, but about that money though.' And I deeped very quickly in that place that everything was always a negotiation. You were always trying to get to the thing that needed to be done, so nobody could say that you were shit at your job.

But have you finished your story time yet because it's nearly been an hour? *[Both laugh]*

> Just one thing. Looking back at that time and feeling . . . I don't want to get, like, emotional about it. *[Nana proceeds to get emotional]*
>
> . . . I guess I just wanted to help with the things that you said you needed help with, and to protect you and to help you to thrive in that environment. But I never thought it was gonna be a thing where, actually, you were protecting me. No one was really ever protecting me in those environments, you know? *[Nana starts to cry]*
>
> I just never expected that. So silly things like those pillowcases, or the jokes I'd make, were just my own armour and way of dealing with the situation. But you were really there for me. Sorry, it's so silly, just give me a minute. *[Nana starts to cry emotionally]*

That's fine. I'm just gonna put brackets in the book saying 'Nana starts to cry emotionally.' It's a real conversation.

> *[Nana laughs and cries at the same time]*

But I can always tell when you're going through it. And for some reason, you get really tickled by disrespect from me. Like, you just don't take it seriously.

But we're also able to do very different things very well. So when we are working together, there's not much we can't do, I think. That's something I don't think we've ever said out loud to each other. I've told you before, as well, that your skin is the same tone as my grandfather's. So even before knowing you, you already looked like family to me. Which meant I instantly felt so protective of you.

I remember a creative coming into our office, and you'd just been gassed about your new expensive hat from wherever you bloody got it. He comes in and says 'Oh, what have you done to your hair?' I don't think you even finished the sentence and I was on him. I read him for filth. The creative left looking hot and embarrassed and I thought, 'Oh, she's gonna tell me off.

And I think you just said thank you. I also knew from that moment on I could ask for like two months of holiday and you'd be like, 'Yeah, do what you want.' *[Both laugh]*

I could see what a relief it was because you couldn't take on that stuff directly or there'd be repercussions. But if I did, you could just be like, 'Oh, I'll have a word with him.' But you never did. *[Both laugh]*

> **Nana** I think it's because whilst there have obviously been Black men in my life, none of them – apart from my brother and dad – defended me like that. It was a lot.

Kevin And then you left me in that hellhole and never looked back. *[Both laugh]*

> Oh, wait. My laptop's crashing and I don't know why.

Maybe because you've got ten million tabs open and your battery's on eight per cent.

> How do you know?

Because it's always on eight per cent and you always have all the things open.

> That is exactly what it's on. *[Kevin does his impression of the 'Oprah-knowing-she-was-right' meme]*

I had been in the internet streets, *[whispers]* and the real ones, for a while.

And I've done many things, creatively – I'd always done photography, and then I was styling (only for a little bit), I had worked at different magazines, even the first couple of issues of *Love* magazine. Things like that.

Then I was concentrating on photography, all the while having that job at the place we'll continue to call 'Coronation Street'. But I met really interesting people there that were doing really interesting things with their lives, and it was the best time.

There would be no other period in time that beats when I worked in that store – on floor three, we had two sets of twins that dressed the same every day – it was just, like, a really incredible place to work. Different people would come in, celebrities would come in.

But there was one person that everybody was scared of. And that was that particular creative that we've been talking about, the one who introduced us at the agency later on. Everybody was scared to ask him about anything to do with his displays in the window. If something happened within the display, nobody would touch it, because they were so scared of what the repercussions would be.

And I was like, 'He sounds cool. I wanna be his friend because he's gossiped about as much as I am.' And also I was interested in how he got to the ideas behind these iconic displays. People came to this store just to photograph the displays. Selfridges and Harrods wished they could do what was going on in these windows.

So I would just leave my post, which was either in the suit room or the shoe shop, and just go and follow him around. I would just follow him around and he'd be like, 'Who are you?' But I'm from South London. You can't intimidate me. And he just thought it was funny, so we very quickly became friends. Met his kids, they all call me Morosky, met his wife and she is a very close friend now. They were and are both very creative, but also very 'Fuck the system. Like, this is bullshit. This is The Matrix.' And so any creative ideas I had, I finally had someone I could show them to and ask for advice.

In time, he left that job. He left that job and went to an advertising agency, and then when he got there he worked on MINI's 'It's a Mini Adventure' campaign.

I was still shooting for different magazines between all the goings-on at Coronation Street, where nevertheless I was still around this real mix of different people. Like one person, who I was really close with at that time, realised in the middle of working there that she was actually a lesbian. She got a whole girlfriend, then got lost in the vajayjay. *[Nana laughs]*

And I haven't seen her since. But you know what I mean, it was just this moment where I felt like I was surrounded by people realising what they wanted to do, or who they were. I had one friend called Michael Browne there, who's now one of the few Black tailors on Savile Row. We had so much talent in that shop.

So I think that helped spur me on. I knew I had my own skillsets, I knew I'd always shot on film. I knew I'd always told stories and written poetry – so I needed to start seeing how that would work with moving image. And this mentor we've been talking about had worked on loads of music videos – so we discussed that, too.

Anyway, he was working on this MINI campaign now, and he wanted someone to come and document. That was in Brighton, where I first met Perri Shakes-Drayton (see Chapter 8). I didn't really know what advertising was then, but I knew I liked certain ads. The more I spoke to him, the more I learned that there were a multitude of disciplines within advertising that I could use to bolster my own skills.

Was he with his creative partner at the time?

Yeah. I can't remember what agency they worked at, but they left not long after. He said, 'I'm going to go and work with this old friend at this lovely little place. It's meant to be this new thing where we're going to be able to create some interesting stuff.' So we would meet up every so often or just text each other, to the point where we didn't even refer to each other by name. We just called one another 'Brother Face'. And that came from how he always used to say – and you'll probably hear this in his voice – 'Everybody is just a cunt, aren't they?'

[*Nana chuckles*] Yes, I heard his voice.

And he'd say, 'But not you, I'm always happy to see your face because you're always happy to see me. It's such a brother face.' That's always been the thing; how we related to each other.

Anyway, I'd been working really hard as a photographer by then, appearing in almost every single publication around. And I didn't have the words for it then, but in hindsight, I was really outgrowing the vibe at Coronation Street. When I feel that now, I know it's time to respectfully move on to the next thing.

Don't get me wrong, I'd had all these great interactions happen in that place – that's where I met one of the people I started Bounty with. That led to me being part of the music world, understanding that world – being spoiled with (and Tom will hate this) free Glastonbury tickets and guestlist spots that I could just turn down if I wanted.

That was when I started to really learn what a network was. I was also in one of the biggest relationships of my life at that time; the one I wrote my book *Notes* about. I'd be thinking up these poems while hemming Jonathan Ross's trousers.

All of these things were happening in that space, but I knew it was time to move on. I needed to evolve. Brother Face really didn't want me to go into advertising; he told me it was disgusting and would drain everything out of me. 'You'll hate it, and it will either break you so that you lose all of your magic or, knowing you, you'll go to jail because people pushed you too far.'

That's genuinely what he said, and that conversation went on for about three years. He refused to introduce me to people, so me being me, I'd gone off and had conversations at Wieden+Kennedy, Mother, all of these places. And then finally, it was his fortieth birthday at Ace Hotel. You were there as well, and he said he really wanted me to meet you. But I think we missed each other that day.

If I didn't call him Brother Face, it was Master Splinter.

> **Nana** *[Nana laughs]* Obviously, I now know the depth of your relationship. Like, if you're going on holiday with the guy, and then there was that birthday party at your house and he was there. But for all the time we were working in that agency, I never knew the extent of your history. At all.

Kevin I did that on purpose. It was another form of protection. For me, and for you, because it couldn't be used against us if nobody knew. But like I said, it took a while to even get to that point, and that MINI job was part of it, like him letting me in a little bit. He put me to work as a photographer, hired me freelance so I was still external to the agency world in a lot of ways.

Then, after that, there was another MINI job where the art buyer was trying to bad me with the prices. And Master Splinter talked me through how much things were going to cost – how much the media buys would be that featured my imagery. He said, 'They owe you at least £15k for usage.' Imagine this art buyer wanted to use nine of my images for nationwide out-of-home advertising and print ... at £900. I was just ready to take the money, because in my head they'd already paid me a day-rate. Master Splinter really taught me all about that, so when you hear me say 'I didn't understand the price of things,' this is what I meant.

So I saw that advertising would teach me how creative would be commercially valued, and it was just becoming more and more clear that advertising was where I'd find all my answers. Even the concept of partners I learned from Master Splinter and his partner, and I just thought, 'I hope I find a partner too, and you know, we're actually friends.'

> That's a really cute thought.

Tom also had that thought. Tom went on dating sites for creative partners. I think one was called 'Single Creatives'. Seriously. *[Nana laughs]*

Anyway, he finally gets you and me to meet. And, as I said, I'd already met lots of middle-class white men in these agencies – without Brother Face's help. These men who knew nothing about culture, but didn't want to admit or even begin to comprehend that fact. They just wanted the ability to say I'd been in the building to see them, which is why they'd taken the meeting. But once I started asking certain questions, and it dawned on them how much power I actually have and could bring into those spaces, they started to feel very uncomfortable. I worked that out very quickly – and bear in mind I never had any formal education. I really am just a road yout.

But we finally meet, and I remember thinking that we really got each other. Regardless of the differences in culture – even though you pronounce 'plantain' wrong – we completely understood one another.

So yeah, I came in to cover for that week and just deep cleaned the whole place. I didn't want to fail, I wanted to show I could do the job, yes, but there was also just a feeling of common-sense in that. Like, this place is so messy, how am I gonna efficiently run this stuff if it's not organised? And I'm gonna be real, that's a lesson I learned from that first job in fast food. The thing that was repeatedly and violently shouted at us was 'Clean as you go. There is no time to stand around. Find something to do.'

And I did. If I was waiting for a file to be sent through, I'd just think, 'Cool. I'm gonna clean as I go.' So I'd look for what I could be getting on with while I waited for the other thing to start. And it's interesting, because that's kind of the opposite to what Tom and I now do. We're very diligent now in knowing when to take in the information and then let the idea bake in the back of our heads, to just go off and do something else – or even nothing – while our subconscious does the work. But that was a real thing I had to learn, because I'm just used to always being on the go.

Anyway, I was there for that week and, I'll be honest, I felt like I'd done a really good job. Not in an ego way, just that I'd felt this weight on my shoulders that I'd managed to meet. You'd invited me in, and I wasn't finning to embarrass you in front of your peers. That's not something you pushed on to me, obviously, but it's just how I felt. I wanted it to be that, even if I never, ever step foot in this building again, you will all know that Nana made the right choice asking me to cover for that week. That was my goal. Next thing I know, you're telling me the guy I was covering had to go.

Come to find out, months later, you'd fired him. Rah. *[Nana laughs]* Then within that first week, I met Tom. And it all started to make sense. When you'd come in, I knew you were performing for those others. And I don't think it's a dirty word, and I don't think it's something for you to feel embarrassed or stressed about, because it really was a case of survival. That place was really wild.

I think the biggest game you gave me going in was that you were very, very particular in terms of laying out the groundwork on how to get stuff done, and who holds the money. You also taught me to use jealousy as a way to get people to move. *[Nana laughs]* You'd be like, 'These two here hate those two over there. If they find out you're working with them on that thing, they will make this thing happen for you.' Ask Tom, that's a lesson that's really stayed with me. In all of the agencies we've been in, I've continued playing that game to get us exactly where we need to be – I've never fucked anyone over or, like, stolen anything out of anyone else's mouth – but when things start to slow down I'll drop a little gem of information in the right place, and all of a sudden that's being passed on and it's led to Tom and I getting an interesting project sent our way. But I also saw very quickly what Brother Face meant when he spoke about the ugliness in that industry, and how he tried to combat that for me. He would do wild things like turn to the other creatives and say, 'You should all pay attention to Morosky.' I don't think I even told you about that, or if you knew about it.

Nana I think I do remember this happening.

Kevin I had to let him know that he might not always be there for me, so I had to make my own space. I think it also made me recognise how I could manoeuvre to protect you in the relationship we had; how I could present my defence as simply and clearly being my actions. So if anyone's gonna answer for them . . . *[Kevin sings 'It's gonna be maaaaay' in his best Justin Timberlake voice; Nana laughs]*

I let him know that I'd got it under control, and I was gonna do it my way. I preferred them thinking I wasn't a threat, that I had no future in this business. Because that meant they weren't paying attention to me, and so they didn't think to block the doors that I'd need to go and open. I came with that knowledge of how to scan a room, but you taught me how to apply that to the structure of the business, walking me through what everyone did.

You gave me options too, because there was no way I was gonna be about that mad agency pub life. So you showed me other ways I could get the results people got by drinking with their colleagues. 'You've got charm, so use your charm.' I think you were one of the first people to tell me that. And again, all this is going on while I'm just looking around thinking, 'What the fuck is this place?' *[Nana laughs]*

Tom asked me if I'd watched 'Mad Men', and when I said no, he told me that we could talk about what this place is once I had. So I burned through that show very quickly, and I understood that 'Mad Men' was a documentary. All these people are mad; all these people are chasing something very odd.

When I think of that against what me and you were growing through, I knew that even as a gay Black man, I still had more privileges in that space than you – and you were one of the most powerful people in that building, with the department you ran and the budgets you held. And I understand what a good job you did of masking the pain you felt in that environment, because it didn't dawn on me just how much hurt you'd been through until you left and you were like, 'Bye bye, see ya,' and you didn't even look back. Because they really tried to take the piss with you in those last days, but they didn't know your brother's a lawyer. So very quickly the bullshit stopped, you got a big severance package, and that was that.

Just to conclude this story because obviously, you didn't vanish from my life then, Tom and I went on to work at our next agency with your old boss. And I knew how much he loved you, and I knew I was gonna get you back there. So I just didn't stop talking about you. For a good six months, I kept bringing you up whenever I could. Until one day, he really thought he'd decided for himself to get back in touch with you. So you came and we worked there together again, but now we'd evolved and progressed – yet we were still saying, 'What the fuck is this place?'

Look back. How many Black and Brown people did you actually see in those buildings? That first agency had hundreds of staff, and I can count the number of Black and Brown people on my two hands. Two of them didn't even work in our agency; they just worked in the same building.

Oh, gosh.

Yeah, and then that second place. Let's call it 'the kebab shop that no longer is'. There were even less. There was Ebele, the freelancer, and we'd just look up and catch eyes with her, laughing. It was just another mad place, yet somehow not quite as mad as 'the agency'.

But I think it was the perfect storm for us; we looked around and really asked, 'But where are all the normal Black and Brown people that do creativity?' Because we knew they were out there – everybody else was ripping them off.

Then we went to watch 'Black Panther', which got us really hyped. And we realised we needed to make our own Wakanda, and that's when we started the WhatsApp group. Ten people to start, then within a couple of days it's up to two hundred. Then we hit the group limit, and had to start another one.

That's how Pocc – People of Culture Collective – was born. Shortly after, we had our first IRL (in real life) meet-up and about a hundred people showed up. I think your auntie even made bare bowls of jollof for everyone.

Yeah.

Now it's five years later and we have a whole business with employees, a community interest arm, and relationships with household brands.

If that doesn't justify the concept of this book – that the support offered by Black women can move the earth – then I don't know what does. It's not just impacting individuals; it's helping the world. This whole journey of mine has always been ushered on by the Black women around me – in ways big and small.

I think the worst thing I could do is have my life end without saying out loud all of the ways that Black women have saved me, loved me, rated me, defended me, remembered me, read me, forgiven me, and protected me. It's really important for me to recognise all the women who go above and beyond, often without asking for thanks or recognition. But they should get all the gratitude, and all the recognition.

Quite often they actually get disrespect in return, so it's a really good thing just to be able to say that out loud. It's important, and it has an effect. I know people reading this will be able to look back on similar times in their lives, and see that they can open doors. Just take the gentle way for one another, and show appreciation and respect.

Because sometimes you walk into spaces and you meet other Black and Brown creatives – sometimes younger, though often older – and they are just at that level of survival. They will be the only Black person in the company, and then you come along and it's almost like they're saying, 'Shush, stop. Before they realise we're both Black.' I hate that.

I would much prefer to just enjoy being Black and creative, without any of the need for survival.

ACKNOWLEDGEMENTS

Contributors
Julie Adenuga, Marawa the Amazing, Dame Elizabeth Nneka Anionwu, Bushira Attah, Aja Barber, Nana Bempah, Candice Brathwaite, Africa Daley-Clarke, Audrey Indome, Jamelia, Kuchenga, Gynelle Leon, Ashley Madekwe, Mpho McKenzie, Mum, Selma Nicholls, Kelechi Okafor, Lady Phyll Opoku-Gyimah, Rivah, Remi Sadé, Bianca Saunders, Perri Shakes-Drayton, Shygirl, Paula Sutton, Tayla Morosky, Tolly T, Terri Walker, Michaela Yearwood-Dan

Pavilion Team
Kiron Gill, Stephanie Milner, Laura Russell

Editors
Rachel Ayeh-Datey, Tom Dunn, Shari Last

Design
Abi Wright

Art Direction
Kevin Morosky, Abi Wright

Support Crew aka Dons
Leeanne Adu, Ayo Sule, Chinazo Ufodiama, Bukola Bakinson, Krystal Jumbo

MVPs
Shakira Stewart – Although not mentioned in this book or, come to think of it, in detail to you, I've been chronically ill, with my energy levels sitting near zero almost all of the time. Not to mention, waiting to find out if I did or did not have a tumour (I don't). I felt like you sensed I was pushing through something, and not once did you pry or gossip. Instead, you blindly supported me, arranging all business and hospital appointments without missing a trick. I truly appreciate what you have done for me. There is no better assistant in these streets.

Papa B – When I wasn't sure who I should work with on this book, you handed over names and contacts without blinking. You understood how tricky it can be finding the correct people who will move and act honourably. More time, people hold their recommendations hostage as a way to amass and retain power. You are always ready and willing to share. Thank you.

Thanks to Rissas Locs, Nerissa and Kermichelle: it's not just haircare but therapy. I have done some of my greatest problem solving while in your chairs.

Tom Dunn – The norm. Kev.

Kelechi – Point them out. Kev.

Grandma – I miss you most. To the person reading this book, I'll say the same thing my Grandmother would say as you left her house, while giving you an orange: "take it with love".

KEVIN MOROSKY, IN THE WORDS OF REMI SADÉ

He truly is a wizard in a tracksuit.

I'm sure you're wondering what that means and who he is.

He's Kevin. He's a genius. He is so much of the essence! He could've been a regular man but that was nearly impossible; he's known too many lifetimes.

Without thinking, Kevin can give references to some of the most niche corners of pop culture. In his mind, he's kept a twenty-plus-year archive of many trends. Not just the fashion trends – the culture trends, the people trends, the advertising trends, the emotional trends. Our trends. Formerly Black, currently global. Oh, and he communicates them so beautifully.

One of the many things I've always admired about Kevin is his knowledge. He understands and recognises where there is something missing. Knowing him is akin to a taste test, when you feel there's one last ingredient to be added for things to be complete.

He has a constant appetite to be among his people and tell incredible stories with them. Or should I say, make magic. Either way, much love to one of South London's finest. Thank you for sharing all the wisdoms in your wizardry.

Kevin Morosky *is a multidisciplinary creative and film auteur. In 2018, he co-founded Pocc (People of Culture Collective) with Nana Bempah, where he acts as Chief Creative Officer. His award-winning short 'Bruce' aired on Channel 4 in 2021 and was part of the Edinburgh Film Festival in 2022. In the same year Morosky's other short 'Spun' won Best Short at Bolton Film Festival. His next film 'Gently' (co-written with his creative partner, Tom, and made as part of the Disney Imagine 2023 Programme) is due to release in 2024. He is currently working on three feature films and a TV show.*

First Published in the United Kingdom in 2024 by
Pavilion
An imprint of HarperCollinsPublishers Ltd
1 London Bridge Street
London SE1 9GF

www.harpercollins.co.uk

HarperCollinsPublishers
Macken House
39/40 Mayor Street Upper
Dublin 1
D01 C9W8
Ireland

10 9 8 7 6 5 4 3 2 1

First published in Great Britain by Pavilion
An imprint of HarperCollinsPublishers 2024

ISBN 978-0-00-860362-5

Credit
Page 176: Stormzy's lines from 'My Hood'
by RAY BLK ft. Stormzy – produced by
Courage, written by RAY BLK,
release date May 27 2016.

MIX
Paper | Supporting
responsible forestry
FSC™ C007454
FSC
www.fsc.org

This book is produced from independently certified FSC™ paper to ensure responsible forest management.
For more information visit: www.harpercollins.co.uk/green

Publishing Director: Stephanie Milner
Commissioning Editor: Kiron Gill
Editors: Tom Dunn, Shari Last, Rachel Ayeh-Datey
Editorial Assistant: Shamar Gunning
Design Director: Laura Russell
Designer: Abi Wright
Production Controller: Grace O'Byrne
Proofreader: John Friend

Printed in Latvia by PNB Print